LOST LOOT

Cursed Treasures and Blood Money

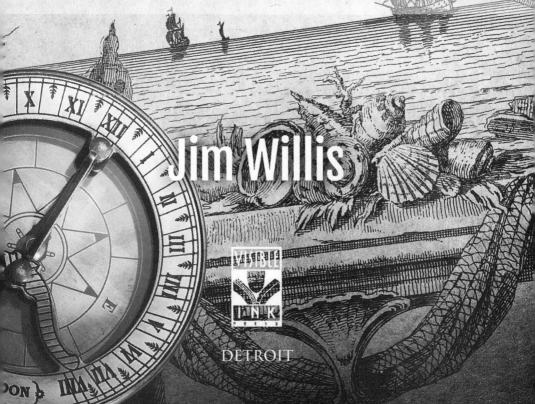

Jim Willis

VISIBLE INK PRESS

DETROIT

About the Author

Having earned his master's degree in theology from Andover Newton Theological School, **Jim Willis** was an ordained minister for over 40 years. He also taught college courses in comparative religion and cross-cultural studies. In addition, Willis was a professional musician, high school orchestra and band teacher, arts council director, and even a drive-time radio show host. His background in theology and education led to his writings on religion, the apocalypse, cross-cultural spirituality, and the mysteries of the unknown, including Visible Ink Press' *Lost Civilizations: The Secret Histories and Suppressed Technologies of the Ancients* and *Hidden History: Ancient Aliens and the Suppressed Origins of Civilization*. Willis passed away in 2024.

Visible Ink Press Books by Jim Willis

American Cults: Cabals, Corruption, and Charismatic Leaders
  ISBN: 978-1-57859-800-7
Ancient Gods: Lost Histories, Hidden Truths, and the Conspiracy of Silence
  ISBN: 978-1-57859-614-0
Armageddon Now: The End of the World A to Z
  with Barbara Willis
  ISBN: 978-1-57859-168-8
Censoring God: The History of the Lost Books (and other Excluded Scriptures)
  ISBN: 978-1-57859-732-1
Hidden History: Ancient Aliens and the Suppressed Origins of Civilization
  ISBN: 978-1-57859-710-9
Lost Civilizations: The Secret Histories and Suppressed Technologies of the Ancients
  ISBN: 978-1-57859-706-2
Near-Death Experiences: Afterlife Journeys and Revelations
  ISBN: 978-1-57859-846-5
The Religion Book: Places, Prophets, Saints, and Seers
  ISBN: 978-1-57859-151-0
Supernatural Gods: Spiritual Mysteries, Psychic Experiences, and Scientific Truths
  ISBN: 978-1-57859-660-7

Other Visible Ink Press Books

Please visit us at www.visibleinkpress.com.

Visible Ink Press®
43311 Joy Rd., #414
Canton, MI 48187-2075

Visible Ink Press is a registered trademark of Visible Ink Press LLC.

Most Visible Ink Press books are available at special quantity discounts when purchased in bulk by corporations, organizations, or groups. Customized printings, special imprints, messages, and excerpts can be produced to meet your needs. For more information, contact Special Markets Director, Visible Ink Press, www.visibleink.com, or 734-667-3211.

Managing Editor: Kevin S. Hile
Cover Design: Graphikitchen
Page Design and typesetting: Kevin S. Hile
Proofreaders: Christa Brelin and Shoshanna Hurwitz
Indexer: Shoshanna Hurwitz

Cover images: Shutterstock.

ISBNs:
Paperback: 978-1-57859-855-7
Ebook: 978-1-57859-868-7
Hardbound: 978-1-57859-867-0

Cataloging-in-Publication data is on file at the Library of Congress.

Printed in the United States of America.

10 9 8 7 6 5 4 3 2 1

Contents

Photo Sources

Airlinefan.com: p. 229.
Biblioteca Europea di Informazione e Cultura (BEIC) digital library: p. 12.
Bibliothèque Municipale, Besançon, France: p. 264.
Bibliothèque Nationale de France: p. 263.
Catskill Archive: p. 150.
Cavecouple (Wikicommons): pp. 82, 84.
Federal Bureau of Investigation: pp. 190, 191, 228, 232.
Foundation for the Advancement of Mesoamerican Studies: p. 104.
Franklin D. Roosevelt Presidential Library and Museum: pp. 225, 249.
Augi Garcia: p. 58.
Harvard Fine Arts Library Special Collections: p. 167.
Healinglaw (Wikicommons): p. 187.
Historicair (Wikicommons): pp. 203, 205.
History Channel: pp. 146, 155, 247, 252.
History.howstuffworks.com: p. 173.
Infrogmation of New Orleans (Wikicommons): p. 28.
Iolani Palace collection: p. 133.
Dennis Jarvis: p. 267.
JoJan (Wikicommons): p. 259.
Library Company of Philadelphia: p. 72.
Library of Congress: pp. 21, 45, 73, 88, 140, 143, 186.
Lobberich (Wikicommons): p. 27.
Ken Lund: p. 134.
Sky Marthalar: p. 199.
Larry D. Moore: p. 180.
Museo del Prado, Madrid: p. 56.
Museo Nacional de Arte, Mexico City: p. 89.
Museu Nacional de Historia, Mexico City: pp. 109, 114.
NASA: p. 54.
National Maritime Museum, London: pp. 8, 49.
National Museum of Anthropology, Mexico City: p. 99.
National Park Service: p. 66.
National Portrait Gallery: pp. 15, 37, 67.
New York Public Library: pp. 9, 142.
Pi3.214 (Wikicommons): p. 87.
Plains to Peaks Collective: p. 159.
Portland State University: p. 200.
Pyle, Howard; Johnson, Merle De Vore (ed) (1921) "With the Buccaneers"
    in *Howard Pyle's Book of Pirates: Fiction, Fact & Fancy Concerning the Buccaneers
    & Marooners of the Spanish Main, New York, United States, and London, United
    Kingdom: Harper and Brothers,* pp. Plate facing p. 76.
Qualiesin (Wikicommons): p. 19.
Rosenberg Library, Galveston, Texas: p. 25.
Royal Museums Greenwich: p. 55.
Runningbear0627 (Wikicommons): p. 61.

Saturday Evening Post: p. 94.

Shutterstock: pp. 1, 4, 31, 40, 43, 50, 63, 75, 78, 79 (top), 97, 100, 101, 106, 108 (top and bottom), 112, 125, 127, 137, 144, 184, 185, 189, 193, 196, 213, 219, 220, 223, 240, 243, 245, 253, 255, 256, 260, 262, 266, 272, 276, 280, 283.

Smithsonian Institution: p. 130.

Spesh531 (Wikicommons): p. 166.

TexasRanger.org/History/: p. 177.

Texas State Capitol collection: p. 90.

Tony the Marine (Wikicommons): p. 79 (bottom).

University Library Washington: p. 215.

U.S. Army Corps of Engineers: p. 170.

Don Wells: p. 68.

Berthold Werner: p. 261.

Public domain: pp. 7, 10, 20, 22, 35, 48, 92, 103, 110, 120, 122, 148, 152, 161, 168, 171, 198, 208, 210, 218, 224.

Introduction

During the summer of 1956, I had finished fifth grade and was gearing up for sixth, but September was still a long way off and I had the good fortune of spending two weeks on a Michigan lake, where my family had rented a cottage. It was a time of swimming, fishing, reading, and, best of all, exploring the creeks and rivers that flowed to the lake.

One of the books I read that summer was *Treasure Island* by Robert Louis Stevenson. Jim Hawkins, Long John Silver, Ben Gunn, and the crew of the Hispaniola were my constant companions during days that stretched out in a seemingly endless string before me. An old rowboat, outfitted with a five-horsepower Evinrude motor, was at my disposal, and I took complete advantage of it.

One glorious day that remains forever enshrined in my imagination probably changed my life. It was a day of mystery, imagination, creativity, and wonder that began when I nosed the boat into a shrouded creek, overhung with branches and vines, much too shallow for the motor. Cutting the power made me aware of a silence broken only by the cry of birds, the harumph of bullfrogs, and mysterious splashings of unknown origin. Turning a bend in the river, I caught sight of a boat that had obviously been stuck in the mud for many years. It was rotting away but still sported a metal box wedged in under the stern seat.

With Treasure Island fresh in my mind, my 10-year-old imagination turned immediately to thoughts of a lost Spanish galleon (although given the perspective of my adult memory, it was probably closer to half a galleon at best).

The next three or four days were spent trying to devise a way to get across the mud and rotting tree trunks so as to navigate my way to the metal box that I was by then sure contained untold treasure.

After a few days I finally made it and confiscated the contents, which turned out to be nothing more than a few broken fishing lures and an old injured-minnow bass plug, which, more than 60 years later, I still have. Maybe it's even worth a few bucks on the antiques market.

Little did I know, however, the nature of the real treasure I found that summer. It lay not in artifacts or the contents of an old fishing tackle box but the sense of mystery and wonder that stayed with me and grew through the ensuing decades. If a sense of childhood fascination and magic can be found in the juxtaposition of the right book at the right time, coupled with opportunity and means, and the resulting package stays with you throughout your life, that is treasure indeed!

Since then, I have hiked in the Superstition Mountains and wondered if the Lost Dutchman Mine was around the next bend. I've fished off islands in Lake Michigan, hoping my anchor line might snag sunken ships laden with contraband smuggled down from Canada. I've walked the beaches of Florida, thinking that maybe, just maybe, last night's storm had washed Spanish treasure ashore.

I haven't been rewarded with the motherlode yet. Oh, sure, a few artifacts and small prizes have come my way, but the real treasure is in the hunt itself and the experience of magic it holds. The elusive holy grail that still sustains my life is out there, though, providing motivation and wonder. Even at my advanced age, when I can no longer hike up into a mountain range or handle a pick and shovel, it's renewed every time I watch *The Curse of Oak Island* on television. Anyone who keeps hold of such magic throughout their life has found treasure indeed.

Maybe that's the real allure. Far bigger fortunes have been spent *searching* for buried treasure than have ever been acquired *finding* it, and even if a treasure is discovered, local laws often require at least a sizable portion be turned over to the government. Taxes usually apply to the rest, so in one sense the story itself is the real treasure. How was it accumulated and by whom? Why was it hidden? Can we decipher clues along the way? Does a real map exist to point the way?

The truth of the matter is that most pirates didn't bury their gold. When they managed to be successful in their endeavors, they worked for monetary shares that were spent on wine, women, and song within days of finding a friendly port. But, as we shall soon see, there were some exceptions to the rule. Two of those exceptions were named Jean Lafitte and William Kidd. Their stories are fascinating, and even a few such legendary pirate stories offer enough intrigue to fuel a legendary firestorm.

Far more realistic are the stories surrounding historical shipwrecks. Nowadays, the transfer of money from place to place is done at a computer keyboard with the push of a button. But for most of recorded history, the only way to complete such a transfer was to physically load money or precious metals in one place and manually carry them to their destination. Oceans were highways of transportation. The wealth of Central America had to be shipped back to Spain, France, Holland, or England. Any number of situations—from pirates and privateers to dishonest sea captains and hurricanes—could interfere, often sending ships to the bottom of the ocean. The wreck of the famous Plate Fleet off Florida's East Coast in 1715, and the sinking of the SS *Central America* off South Carolina, are examples of just two such catastrophes.

There are also tales of wealthy British landowners hiding their wealth, hoping to recover it when things got back to normal following the withdrawal of Roman troops south of Hadrian's Wall. These stories are based on truth. More than 40 such caches have been discovered.

In 1992, for instance, a farmer in Suffolk, England, was searching for a misplaced hammer. What he found far exceeded the price of a favorite tool. He put his hometown of Hoxne Village on the map when he unearthed a hoard of more than 15,000 Roman coins, dozens of silver spoons, and 200 gold objects that are now displayed in the British Museum. Its estimated wealth far exceeds $2 million.

The same experience was faced earlier by Celtic tribes fleeing the approach of Roman armies. In 2012, Reg Mead and Richard Miles were using metal detectors to scan a newly plowed field in Grouville Parish in the Channel Islands. They found a cash of coins minted between 60 and 50 BCE. The treasure is now on display at the museum at La Hougue Bie in Jersey and is estimated to be worth between $25 and $30 million.

Sometimes treasure is discovered that defies any logical explanation concerning its origin. There is simply no record of how it got there, who buried it, or why. The Saddle Ridge Hoard, consisting of some 1,500 gold coins in eight rusty metal cans, is one example. It was discovered by a couple out for an evening walk with their dog on their property in the Sierra Nevada mountains. The coins were minted between 1847 and 1894, but to this day no one knows who buried them or why. It remains the single most valuable buried treasure ever discovered in the United States.

Also important are the curses that almost always protect a hoard from unworthy seekers. Elaborate booby traps are found in Utah. In Nova Scotia, "seven must die" before a treasure is recovered on Oak Island. No one really believes King Tut can reach out from the grave to ensnare unworthy usurpers, but dozens of people associated with him died mysterious deaths in the hundred years since Howard Carter found his burial tomb.

Ethiopian monks who supposedly guard the Ark of the Covenant have a notoriously short life span.

Cursed or not, fictional folks such as archeologist Indiana Jones and librarian Flynn Carsen sometimes prove smart or lucky enough to navigate the pitfalls and reach the end of their quest unscathed, but even real-life searchers such as the Lagina brothers of Oak Island emphasize safety first, constantly remembering those of their predecessors who died on the job.

In the following chapters we're going to investigate tales of lost treasure and the curses that haunt them. We can't cover all of them, of course. There are over three million shipwrecks in the world's oceans, for example. Their estimated worth is about $60 billion. There are more than 400 treasure stories connected to the Great Lakes region alone, and even more in the western United States.

To go after hoards such as these requires resources average folks simply don't have, as well as specific knowledge that goes way beyond an internet search, so we will set our sights on a more reasonable goal. We'll stick to North and South America, selecting tales that deal either with great wealth or great intrigue, usually both. Some of them are beyond the reach of most of us, but others might be more accessible. In other words, for readers who live in the Americas, we will concentrate on what might be hiding in your back yard. But these are entertaining stories, wherever you might be.

Whether or not you decide to grab a shovel or stay on your couch, remember that the real treasure lies in the story, not the hidden wealth. Of course, if you find something valuable, that will be nice, too!

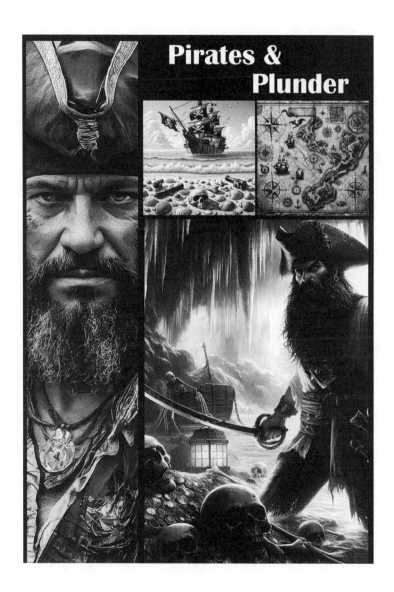

Pirates &
Plunder

The Curses of Charles Island

If you are interested in curses that are attached to treasure hoards, you almost have to begin with a small island off the coast of Milford, Connecticut. It is known as Thrice Cursed Island because it's been cursed by an Indian chief, Captain Kidd the pirate, and a group of sailors who supposedly hid some treasure on the island in 1721 after reportedly stealing it from a Mexican ruler.

Even without the curses, however, it's an interesting place to visit. Geologically, its technical description is that of a coastal moraine segment in Long Island Sound. What that means is that it was formed when the last glacier that covered New York melted and dropped a mix of rocks and sediments, called terminal moraine, in its wake. It is also called a "tied island" because at low tide, it is connected to the mainland by a causeway of cobble, rocks, and pebbles, most of which have eroded away over the centuries. Still, it is accessible on foot from the shore during low tide by a type of sandbar known as a "tombolo," a rocky mound washed by the tides twice a day. Visitors who attempt to traverse it during low tide are warned to be careful, but when people unfamiliar with the speed of the tides have been caught unaware, a few have died trying to get back to the mainland.

Over the years, after being obtained by various owners, it has served as a tobacco plantation, a fertilizer plant, a hotel, and a retreat center for Catholic monks, but none of those endeavors were successful. For a while, it was designated the site of a future yacht club and, later, an amusement park. The military considered it for various installations and, for a brief time, thought about building a nuclear power plant there.

The state of Connecticut bought it in 1999 and designated it through its Natural Area Preserve System. It's now a nesting place for a large population of herons and egrets because it is heavily wooded and an essential habitat for water birds of all kinds. The National Audubon Society designated it as an Important Bird Area because it provides a perfect habitat for endangered species such as Roseate Terns, Great Egrets, Snowy Egrets, Glossy Ibises, Long-eared Owls, and Least Terns.

A tiny, 14-acre island about a half mile off the coast of Milford, Connecticut, Charles Island might have been where Captain Kidd stashed some of his treasure.

Over the years, though, this has created a problem. Being an official natural preserve, people consider it public land, but because of its storied buried treasure, many people want to go there to hunt for gold and silver. This creates a conflict between crowds of people who flock to its shores for different reasons. Still, the state owns the land and closes the causeway between Memorial Day and Labor Day to protect the nesting endangered bird populations from excessive foot traffic.

The whole situation is further complicated because of a fungus that has attacked the trees and an invasive vine aptly called "mile-a-minute" that is overtaking the whole island. The state is working to eradicate the threats and plant native species such as sassafras and cottonwood, which serve as nesting structures for herons and egrets. But the future is very much in doubt because of environmental changes over the last few decades.

As far as curses go, the first one had nothing to do with buried treasure. Legend has it that in 1639, a chief of the Paugussett Indians named Sachem Ansantawae lost the island, which they called Poquehaug, to European settlers. His people had long considered the island to be home to sacred spirits upon whom the tribe depended, and Ansantawae summered there. According to the stories, before his final evacuation, he was said to have faced inland and declared that "any shelter (built here) will crumble to the Earth, and (the builders) shall be cursed."

Over the years since, the curse has proved to be a very effective one. The English renamed it Milford Island, and since that time, no buildings have ever stood there for any significant period of time. All have either crumbled away, were victims to natural causes, or were destroyed in the 1938 hurricane.

A man by the name of Charles Deal bought the island in 1657, and it has been christened Charles Island ever since.

The second curse is connected to a specific treasure. In the next chapter, we'll go into detail about Captain William Kidd, who was allegedly lured into a trap on this island, after which he was brought to trial in Boston, found guilty of piracy, transported to England, and executed. First, though, he supposedly buried his treasure, possibly beneath a huge boulder known as Hog Rock, so that it wouldn't be confiscated. In 1699, he supposedly cursed the island, which led to his doom.

Some of this story might be true. Kidd is said to have visited Milford on at least one occasion, spending an entire night carousing in a local tavern, so he might have been familiar with the area. Citizens still remember him in their annual pirate festival, where people dress up in pirate regalia.

Other locations claim the honor of Kidd's treasure, however, and we will shortly have much more to say about the captain.

The third curse took place in 1721. This one was pronounced either by Emperor Guatmozin of Mexico after he discovered the theft of his treasury or by the thieves who stole it. Legend has it that much of the emperor's wealth was acquired by sailors, whose names are lost to history, and buried on the island, presumably to be dug up and recovered later. Before they died a horrible death, however, the sailors were supposed to have cursed the island and anyone who discovered their ill-gotten gain.

No one seems to know exactly who placed the curse, but the idea might have some value. Two treasure hunters claimed to

William Kidd has been depicted with rather fanciful illustrations in the past, such as this 1921 illustration from a book about buried treasures.

have discovered the chest in 1850, but when they opened it, the curse kicked in big-time. All they discovered was a flaming skull.

Two versions of what happened next have come down through history. In one, the treasure hunters were both killed by ghosts. In the other, they spent the rest of their lives in an insane asylum. Neither version sounds particularly inviting.

Almost everyone who grew up in Milford has a story to tell about the island: either they explored it in their youth, looking for Kidd's treasure, or they walked over the causeway in the evening to share a romantic time with their sweetheart, sometimes missing the tide, perhaps on purpose, so as to be "forced" to spend the night there. As is the case with all mysterious islands in sight of the mainland, mysterious lights and sounds are regularly reported.

Are any of these stories about the presence of treasure true? No one knows, but most everyone who visits hopes so. After all, that's what keeps such mysteries alive. Perhaps it lies buried to this day, still awaiting discovery.

Captain Kidd's Buried Treasure

Captain William Kidd was probably the unluckiest pirate ever to sail the seven seas, if he even was a pirate. Popular mythology remembers him as a fierce, take-no-prisoners terrorist on the level of Blackbeard or Black Bart. Those who study pirate lore know better, but perhaps because of the legends surrounding his buried treasure, he is certainly one of the most famous of his infamous colleagues.

The truth is that he never considered himself a pirate at all. He was a privateer. Not a lot of *practical* difference exists between the two, but a *political* difference exists, and that made *all* the difference.

In the 16th and 17th centuries, privately owned and sponsored warships under the command of experienced sea captains were granted permission by the government to prey on ships flying foreign flags. Because of the private ownership of their vessels, they were called privateers and were backed by wealthy investors who, in effect, bought shares in the ventures. A consortium from France, for instance, might hire and outfit a vessel to seek out and capture Spanish ships sailing north from the rich areas surrounding the Caribbean Sea, intent on delivering Aztec treasure captured in Mexico to the Spanish government.

A portrait of Kidd by artist Sir James Thornhill has the pirate looking downright respectable.

Was it piracy? Of course it was! But the difference is that the French government got a share of the loot, along with those who financed the venture. What was left, after expenses were paid, was divided between the captain and the crew. When you consider the amount of money pouring out of Mexico and Central America, even the lowliest crew member could hope to receive a substantial payback for his time and effort. Outright pirates could claim the entire prize, but they risked capture and execution. Privateers had the backing of a government, should they be captured or brought to trial.

This was the situation when William Kidd was born in Dundee, Scotland, in 1654. His father, John Kidd, was a seaman, married to Bessie Butchart. Growing up in a seafaring home, Kidd gravitated toward that life. After putting in his apprenticeship, he eventually captained his first ship, the *Antigua*.

In the 1680s, he immigrated to New York, where he met and then married Sarah Bradley Cox Oort, who was a wealthy widow. Ten years later, he became a successful American privateer, the captain of a ship named the *Blessed William*, in which he roamed American and English trade routes in the West Indies, looking for French vessels, with whom America was at war. The English government put him in charge of "ridding the Indian Ocean of pirates," but his backers undoubtedly knew that he was really there to capture any ships that were carrying valuable cargo.

In September 1696, Kidd was in New York, readying a 32-gun vessel named the *Adventure Galley* and a motley crew of 150 men. His orders were to sail to the Indian Ocean, where he was to seek out a pirate by the name of Robert Culliford, who sailed with a surgeon named Jon Death. The pair was notorious for loading their cannons with china dishes. When fired, the porcelain shards would shred the sails of the ships under attack.

The *Adventure Galley* was a galley frigate similar to the one in this painting, which carried 32 guns and was deemed well suited for battling with Barbary pirates.

Little did Kidd know that this voyage would alter the destiny of his life and, perhaps, even that of world history. The rules governing the difference between privateer and pirate were about to change, and Kidd didn't know it. He would sail forth a legal privateer and return a criminal pirate.

The voyage was a failure in many ways. Kidd failed to find any pirates, and his crew reacted to their plight by threatening mutiny. By January 1698, when a ship named the *Quedah Merchant* was rounding the southern tip of India, Kidd attacked and captured a cargo of silk, muslin, calico, sugar, opium, iron, and saltpeter. The value was estimated at about $90,000. Because his own ship was severely damaged in the encounter, Kidd took over the captured vessel and renamed it the *Adventure Prize*.

During his two years at sea, politics in England and America had changed attitudes toward privateering. Pirates and privateers were now seen as equals. In other words, Kidd, although he didn't know it, was now legally viewed as a pirate.

Historical records indicate that he had been issued letters of marque, which sanctioned him to rob enemy ships, but he did not have them with him at the time of his capture.

Timing didn't help his cause, either. The notorious pirate Henry Avery disappeared with great wealth in a scandal involving Britain's East India Company. He had pillaged rich Indian moguls, who threatened to cut off all trade with the company unless the British government did something about the situation.

This was why Kidd's main investor, Richard Coote, 1st Earl of Bellomont, figured that Kidd would make a good example of so-called justice, thus freeing his investors from political fallout.

Richard Coote, 1st Earl Bellomont, once Kidd's financial backer, turned on the captain when he became fearful that Kidd's actions would harm his reputation.

The British Admiralty provided scant defense for Kidd, and he was found guilty of one count of murder and four counts of piracy. Centuries later, documents surfaced that supported Kidd's innocence.

Kidd was, after all, active in that area of the world. So, in 1699, when Kidd finally put ashore in the West Indies, he learned that he was now being hunted as a criminal.

The political pendulum had swung the other way. Pirate fever now gripped the civilized world. Kidd managed to negotiate a pardon from the English authorities by claiming that his crew had forced him into piracy, but he felt that the only way to salvage his reputation was to offer his plea in person to the American authorities, so he set sail for his Boston home.

So far, his story can be confirmed in the historical record. But it is at this point that legends begin to shroud his story. Yes, he did wind up in Boston, where Lord Bellomont, his previous investor and now New England's "respectable" governor, had him arrested on July 7, 1699. He was held in solitary confinement in Boston for an entire year before being shipped to England aboard the frigate *Advice* in February 1700.

His Boston trial was a rigged affair if ever there was one. He wasn't even tried for piracy, which might have led to an acquittal due to his negotiated pardon with England. Instead, he was tried for murder.

During the 1698 threatened mutiny of his crew in the Indian Ocean, Kidd had, according to some witnesses, defended himself by striking an attacking crew member over the head with a bucket. The man died from a concussion the next day. This was the "crime" for which Kidd was tried and convicted.

The real reason for his trial is somewhat different. Besides Lord Bellomont, many of Kidd's other wealthy backers were now leaders of status in New York and Boston. It would have hurt their reputations if it became known that they were connected with acts that were now considered piracy.

To protect themselves, they decided that it would be best if Kidd were silenced. Hence, he spent a year in solitary confinement in Boston, followed by a shameful trial on trumped-up charges, followed by another year of solitary confinement in England, after which he was hanged three times.

The Calendar of State Papers claimed that Kidd's ship carried 60 pounds of solid gold and silver ingots, but when he reached Boston, only a small amount was confiscated.

That's right, three times. When he was taken to the gallows, where a noose was placed around his neck, the rope broke when the lever controlling a trapdoor beneath his feet was tripped. He was dutifully returned to the scaffold, much to the approval of the thousands of people who had gathered to watch the spectacle.

When asked if he had any final words before his death, Kidd was reported to have said: "I have nothing to say except that I have been sworn against by perjured and wicked people." According to some people, this marked the beginning of the curse surrounding his treasure.

He was then hung by the neck until he was dead, fulfilling the sentence the judge had pronounced.

By this time, Kidd was considered to be a famous pirate. It was decided that his execution should serve as a warning to other potential pirates, so his body was tarred to protect it from the elements and hung on a gibbet at the mouth of the Thames River. There it swung for more than three years: the "thrice-hanged" pirate, Captain William Kidd.

Both his American and English backers, although somewhat tainted by the piracy scandal, managed to keep their estates and power.

After his death, the legends began in earnest. Kidd was known to have succeeded in accumulating a lot of plunder in the Indian Ocean. The *Calendar of State Papers* claimed that Kidd's ship carried 60 pounds of solid gold and silver ingots, but when he reached Boston, only a small amount was confiscated. Obviously, he had hidden the treasure somewhere before reaching Boston Harbor. But where? Newspapers began to print stories about Captain Kidd's lost treasure.

This is where the legends take over. They are legion!

One of the most colorful stemmed from the method of his execution. In some quarters, it seems, Kidd had become a bit of a martyr.

The *Weekly Journal* of 1720 published an account of Captain Thomas Roberts, a pirate who supposedly captured a rich prize, robbing everyone aboard of their money and personal effects. They even stole the ship's artillery and gunpowder, all the while "cursing, swearing, damning, and blaspheming, to the greatest degree imaginable."

The pirates, when told what the consequences of their actions would be, declared that they would "not be strung up in the gibbets like Kidd." If they were caught, they said, "they would immediately put Fire with one of their Pistols to their Powder, and all go merrily to Hell together."

Meanwhile, Kidd's buried treasure was still a mystery. Where could it be?

The first and most probable explanation is that he stopped at Gardiners Point Island in Block Island Sound, New York. This was the location of Gardiners Island Lighthouse, which, during Kidd's time, was connected to the 14-acre Gardiners Island. The lighthouse point was separated from the larger island during a rough storm in 1888.

Some of Kidd's treasure was later discovered here in an area known as Cherry Tree Field. Lord Bellomont, the governor, reportedly located it and had it sent to England to be used as evidence against Kidd in his trial. Whether or not he sent everything he found is disputed, but the very fact of buried treasure submitted as evidence in a popular trial fueled the fascination of

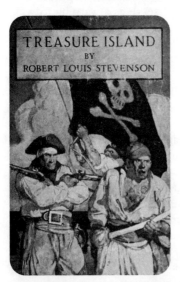

Kidd's story is said to have inspired author Robert Louis Stevenson to write his classic *Treasure Island.*

the public and helped inspire Robert Louis Stevenson's *Treasure Island* and Edgar Allan Poe's *The Gold Bug*.

Sometimes, Kidd's ship is confused with that of the famous Flying Dutchman, a captain who struggled to reach Amsterdam via the Cape of Good Hope. Confronting a fierce storm, he defied God, vowing to sail until doomsday, if necessary, if that's what it took to reach land.

Richard Wagner's famous opera *Der fliegende Holländer* (*The Flying Dutchman*) tells the story in great detail. According to legend, the ship is still out there somewhere, cursed by God to roam the sea forever until the final judgment. The mysterious ship has become a part of the mythology of the sea, showing up in various places during tempestuous times, sailing out of the mists of a storm. The Dutchman's only hope for redemption lies in finding a wife who will be true to him.

> *No treasure has been found there yet, but that might be because it is supposedly guarded by a demon who attacks intruders unless they recite Scripture while digging for the money.*

This might be why Kidd's story and the Dutchman's are linked in popular mythology. As we will see shortly, Kidd's wife apparently stayed true to him, even visiting him in his solitary confinement.

The Gardiners Point Island legend apparently has some factual basis. After all, some treasure was found on the island. But a variation of this story, with less historical evidence, replaces Gardiners Point Island with Lion's Rock, near Old Lyme, Connecticut. No treasure has been found there yet, but that might be because it is supposedly guarded by a demon who attacks intruders unless they recite Scripture while digging for the money. The demon's purpose is not to protect the treasure as much as to warn those who seek riches in order to indulge in earthly pleasure rather than public good.

Before you run off to Connecticut, however, remember that more variations on this theme place the story in Dunderberg, New York; a mountain range called the Crow's Nest, located along the west bank of the Hudson River in the town of Highlands on the northern edge of the U.S. Military Academy; New York City; Coney Island; Ipswich, Massachusetts; what used to be marshes outside of Boston; Cape Cod; Nantucket; the Isles of Shoals, a group of small islands and tidal ledges situated approximately 6 miles (10 kilometers) off the east coast of the United States on the border of Maine and New Hampshire; and Money Island, in Branford, Connecticut.

You might want to search other potential sites, such as the Bahamas and the Florida Keys; these are also mentioned from time to time.

One of the most famous possible sites stems from the discovery of the Kidd-Palmer Chart, a treasure map that pinpointed the location of Kidd's treasure in the South China Sea. This map produced such fervor that a group of investors financed an expedition during the 1950s. The whole venture fell apart when the map was proven to be a hoax.

Finally, on May 7, 2015, it was widely reported that part of the long-lost treasure of the notorious pirate Captain William Kidd had been found off the coast of Madagascar. One silver bar was recovered.

Perhaps the most intriguing legend, however, links the once richest man in America and the American fur trade with Captain Kidd's treasure. Did the whole Western movement of traders, trappers, and Rocky Mountain men begin with William Kidd? Without a great deal of corroboration—indeed, the only indication at all is one piece of circumstantial evidence—here's the story.

John Jacob Astor was once one of the richest men in the world. He was the first American multimillionaire. In today's dollars, his fortune would number in the billions, and he made it the hard way: earning every penny. Maybe,

He came from humble beginnings, being the son of a village butcher in Germany back in 1763. At the age of 16, he emigrated to England to work for his uncle, who crafted musical instruments. During a subsequent trip to Montréal, Canada, he became acquainted with a fur dealer from New Jersey named Alexander Henry, who advised him that the fur-selling business was the up-and-coming thing. He told vivid stories about Lake Superior and the other Great Lakes, going so far as to place Astor with a group of voyageurs canoeing along Lake Superior's North Shore to Fort William, which was the inland headquarters of the Montréal-based North West Company.

Astor wound up selling seven flutes, left over from his time making musical instruments, buying some furs, and shipping them to Europe. That marked the beginning of his accumulation of wealth.

Although soon headquartered in New York State, Astor began making annual pilgrimages to Montréal, staying with Henry and learning the fur business. The friendship moved to a business relationship. By 1792, the North West Company, consisting of Henry and two other Canadian investors, had partnered with Astor and a U.S. businessman in a voyage to sell furs to China.

The venture proved to be so lucrative that they followed it up with another trip in 1793, in which an outgoing cargo of 40,000 beaver pelts returned with a valuable cargo of silk and tea.

In 1794, when Henry proposed an international business relationship between his company and Astor, the North West Company, suspicious of being partnered with a U.S. company, refused the deal. By this time, however, Astor had learned so much and established so many contacts that he was able to purchase land on the U.S.–Canadian border, sell it for an enormous profit, and add to his growing wealth.

By 1800, John Jacob Astor was the leading fur merchant in the world, with an accumulated wealth in today's money of some $5.9 million. He founded the American Fur Company and followed that up in the next eight years with the Pacific Fur Company and the Southwest Fur Company.

You might wonder what the first successful American entrepreneur had to do with Captain Kidd's treasure. According to the *Ottumwa Courier* of February 4, 1904, and later the *Idaho Daily Star-Mirror* of June 7, 1923, an article entitled "The Story of How John Jacob Astor Obtained His Great Wealth" was gradually picked up across the country in sensational pieces with headlines such as "Captain Kidd Loot Basis for Astor Fortune."

It is no secret that Astor's fortune took a dramatic rise in value in the early 1800s. Was it because of his skill as a businessman, or was something else involved?

Supposedly, according to the newspaper accounts, Captain William Kidd's wife visited Kidd when he was held in solitary confinement at Boston's Court Street jail. He was said to have slipped her a piece of paper with the numbers 44106818 printed on it.

John Jacob Astor, the first millionaire of the famous Astor family, made his wealth in the fur trade, Chinese opium, and real estate, but it's been said his seed money was the lost treasure of Captain Kidd.

As it turns out, this is the latitude and longitude of Deer Island, off the coast of Maine. This fact was discovered in 1894, when an astronomer visited the island's current owner, who lived near a cave with a latitude 44 degrees, 10 minutes, and a longitude 6818.

In the early 1800s, Astor had supposedly sent a team of trappers to this section of the state. The speculation ever since has been that while trapping a beaver, they discovered a cave containing a treasure box with the initials W. K. on it. They were reported to have brought it back to Astor.

Was this the hiding place of Kidd's treasure? Had he buried it here so it would not be confiscated when he returned to Boston for his trial, where he had every hope of being acquitted? Remember, he still thought himself innocent of piracy because he had ventured forth in good faith, carrying letters of marque from a respectable group of Massachusetts businessmen who had commissioned him as a privateer.

> *The speculation ever since has been that while trapping a beaver, they discovered a cave containing a treasure box with the initials W. K. on it.*

The idea of those inclined toward conspiracy theories was that Astor sent the treasure to London, hidden in one of his fur trading ships, secretly sold it for some $32.8 million in today's money, and then deposited it in a New York bank, where he could launder it by pushing it through his fur company. This, according to the story, is how his income rose so quickly and dramatically. If so, much of the westward expansion of the United States, led by famous fur trappers and mountain men such as Kit Carson, Jim Bridger, and Jedidiah Smith, was, in fact, financed by Captain William Kidd and his buried treasure.

The whole story is considered by most people to be in the category of mythology rather than historical fact, but to this day, the inhabitants of Deer Island still have fun with it and the tourists it draws.

Whatever happened, Astor quit the fur trade in 1894 as the wealthiest man in America. He went on to build the first big commercial vessel to sail on Lake Superior, the 77.8-foot brig *John Jacob Astor*. The famous Waldorf Astoria hotel bears his name as well. He built a series of summer homes in New York State and died with an estimated wealth of $754 million in today's economy.

Sad to say, that wealth evaporated over the years. His descendants spent it all within a few generations.

Kidd is a polarizing figure today. Some believe the version of his story published by Captain Charles Johnson in his 1724 book *A General History of the Pyrates,* which is still in print. "Captain Charles Johnson" is said to be a pseudonym for one of London's writer-publishers.

Others swear by newspaper articles from the late 19th century, some of which swore that Kidd was innocent. One of them, called "The Virtuous Captain Kidd," took the position that Kidd was made a scapegoat by the East India Company to "avoid foreign imbroglios."

Whatever the truth of the matter, undoubtably, Captain Kidd has created an indelible mark on world history. He is, along with Edward Teach, the infamous "Blackbeard," one of the most well-recognized "pirates" from the Golden Age of Piracy.

Was his treasure ever discovered, or does it still lie buried somewhere along the east coast of the United States?

No one knows, but as long as his memory persists, the real treasure of Captain Kidd lies in the stories and legends. You can't spend them, but they're a lot of fun.

Who knows? Maybe the thrice-hung pirate is still getting a laugh when people search a thrice-cursed island, searching for a cursed treasure that might not even exist.

Blackbeard's Boast

If a notorious outlaw stood in front of you and claimed to have buried a treasure in an undisclosed location, you might be tempted to take his statement with a bit of skepticism and not consider him very trustworthy. If the same outlaw was rumored to have had 14 common-law wives and captained the *Queen Anne's Revenge*, a dreaded vessel that roamed the Spanish Main, you would probably listen a little more closely. If he was wearing a feathered tricorn hat and had pistols and knives stuck in his belt while festooned with burning hemp in his ears so as to surround his head with smoke and lit matches stuck in his enormous black, braided beard to produce a sulfur smell right out of hell itself, you might be tempted to pay attention. Such a

A model of *Queen Anne's Revenge* can be viewed at the North Carolina Museum of History in Raleigh.

man could obviously steal a lot of treasure just by showing up and looking fierce.

Whether he would bury it rather than spend it, well, that's a different story. But you would probably at least listen to him.

That is why treasure hunters from Chesapeake Bay to the Caribbean still look for the treasure that Edward Teach, better known as Blackbeard, boasted that he buried, maybe in multiple caches.

He was the prince of pirates, the most notorious buccaneer to ever have plundered shipping lanes and terrified seacoast villages during the Golden Age of Piracy. When he was finally killed by Lieutenant Robert Maynard on November 22, 1718, the whole eastern seaboard breathed a sigh of relief.

Many piratical terms are bandied about with great gusto even though people might not understand what they mean, so we'll start with a quick pirate tutorial.

First, what is a pirate?

When we looked into the buried treasure of Captain Kidd, we saw that privateers were basically pirates with a license to steal. They were issued writs from a government that allowed them to capture ships and steal loot from enemy countries as long as they shared the profits with the government that declared them their legal representatives. Most pirates started out as privateers, and Blackbeard was no exception. He was licensed by the British to prey specifically on ships that were financing Spain's fragile economy by stealing gold and silver from Central and South America.

This brings us to the term "Spanish Main." It refers to the Spanish Empire on the mainland of the Americas from Florida to Brazil. It eventually came to include much of the Caribbean, but since it first referred to the *main*land, Spanish Main was the name that stuck due to its marketing appeal, exploited by writers, poets, and eventually filmmakers.

The Spanish Main is indicated here along the coastline with the darkened line. Spanish territory is shaded.

Edward Teach—better known as Blackbeard—began his career as a pirate under Captain Benjamin Hornigold, eventually capturing a ship he renamed Queen Anne's Revenge and becoming the most notorious pirate of the Spanish Main.

Even pirates need to go to shore once in a while to regroup, make repairs, and restock their food supplies. In the 17th century, local governments in the Caribbean were not nearly strong enough to stand up to the kind of pressure pirates and privateers could bring to bear, so the area became known as a kind of pirate haven. The island of Hispaniola offered the best central ports pirates would regularly use. For years, hunters would reap the rewards of the wild boars and cattle that proliferated there. They would smoke the meat over a slow fire in little huts the French called *boucans* and make a type of beef or pork jerky called *viande boucanée*. It kept seemingly forever without spoiling and was a favorite stock of food to bring aboard for long voyages. Eventually, the name *boucanée* was applied to the sailors and was then Anglicized to become "buccaneer," so Blackbeard the "pirate" was a "buccaneer" who plundered the "Spanish Main."

No one knows for sure where or exactly when he was born. His birthplace is usually said to be Bristol, but claims have been made that he was born in New York, California, Philadelphia, or even Denmark. His name comes with a question mark as well. Most writers say it was Edward Teach, but it is sometimes listed as Edward Thatch or Edward Drummond.

He was issued privateer status by England during the War of Spanish Succession, which we will examine further when we study the origin story behind the wreck of the Plate Fleet of 1715, but when the war ended, Teach, like many other privateers who had learned their trade and had no desire to give it up, became a pirate.

He was known for his ferocity and cruelty, traits which he deliberately cultivated. After a running battle with the British

30-gun man-of-war HMS *Scarborough*, his fame began to grow exponentially.

But this brings up an interesting point. Naval historian David Cordingly has long had an interest in pirates. For 12 years, he was the official keeper of pictures and head of exhibitions at the National Maritime Museum in Greenwich, England. In his book *Under the Black Flag: The Romance and the Reality of Life Among the Pirates*, he points out that the logs of the *Scarborough* make no mention of this battle. Was the whole thing concocted to enhance Blackbeard's reputation? If so, it makes us wonder if his boasts about buried treasure are equally fictitious.

Yet another anomaly has been found in the Blackbeard story. He is remembered as being one of the most ferocious pirates who ever lived and was feared far and wide. When the *Queen Anne's Revenge* showed up on the horizon, flying the skull and crossbones flag called the Jolly Roger, most ships would just give up, letting the fearsome pirate board them and steal any valuables, food, liquor, and weapons they had aboard. They would then feel lucky if they could sail away with their ship empty but lives still intact.

A 1920 painting titled *Capture of the Pirate, Blackbeard, 1718* by Jean Leon Gerome Ferris.

Despite his reputation, however, no account of Blackbeard ever killing anyone was officially verified. Was his whole image a cleverly orchestrated marketing campaign?

If so, it worked. Unverified legends, including those included in newspaper articles, abound. One story, for instance, claimed that he once shot his first mate. No one ever came forth as a witness, but he was supposed to have said of his own legendary persona, "If he didn't shoot one or two of them now and then, they'd forget who he was." One would suppose a boast like that would tend to keep other pirates in line.

Other such stories grew up around him, and he seemed to have enjoyed them. One was the fact that he was supposed to have had 14 common-law wives. Would that many women have enjoyed his company if he was the beast that history claims he was? Granted, stories arose around his treatment of women as well, but still....

Blackbeard worked out of Nassau, in the Bahamas, but he also had a base in North Carolina, where he had a deal with Governor Charles Eden. In Nassau, he was given the title of magistrate over the "Privateers' Republic." In North Carolina, he bought off the governor in exchange for a free pardon.

His reputation on the east coast of the United States was enhanced when, using only the *Queen Anne's Revenge* and three smaller ships, he barricaded the port of Charleston, South Carolina, in 1718. No merchant vessels were allowed to enter or leave.

The blockade may have marked the beginning of the end for his career, however. Some prominent citizens were held for ransom. The prisoners were eventually released, but instigating a grudge against important political leaders probably wasn't his smartest course of action. He was now a hunted man, and this is where his alleged buried treasure enters the picture.

His fleet now numbered four vessels. He ran two of them aground at what is now known as Beaufort Inlet. One of them was the *Queen Anne's Revenge*. His crew became suspicious, and some began to accuse him of trying to downsize his followers and increase his own share of the treasure.

They might have been right. He removed treasure from three ships, marooned a large segment of his crew, and sailed to Bath, North Carolina, where he received a pardon under what was legally called an Act of Grace. He then sailed to Ocracoke Inlet in the remaining ship, a sloop named *Adventure*, presumably to enjoy a life of wealth and ease.

Apparently, that was his retirement plan, but the governor of Virginia, Alexander Spotswood, remembering how the prisoners from Charleston had been treated, became worried. He wasn't comfortable with a notorious pirate moving into the neighborhood, even if Blackbeard was, at least technically, outside of Spotswood's jurisdiction. He gave instructions to Lieutenant Robert Maynard to track down the notorious pirate and destroy him. Blackbeard's reputation, so fierce in battle, worked against him in retirement.

Maynard found him at Ocracoke Island on the evening of November 21. The next morning, the battle began. According to Maynard's official account: "At our first salutation, he drank Damnation to me and my Men, whom he stil'd Cowardly Puppies, saying, He would neither give nor take Quarter."

Many colorful legends surround the battle. One of them is the source of Blackbeard's Curse. He was defeated, and his severed head was placed on Maynard's bowsprit as grisly proof of his death, becoming a trophy that was viewed for years. But his headless body was said to have swum either three or seven times around Maynard's ship, dooming anyone who had participated in spoiling what was to be Blackbeard's quiet retirement.

What happened to his treasure? His boast was that he had buried it in diverse places. Was that just more of the legend?

Whatever the truth may be, treasure seekers are convinced that he was telling the truth and that his plan all along had been to terrorize and gather riches for his retirement. Does the money lie on the shores of Chesapeake Bay or on Ocracoke Island, where he sailed after deliberately marooning his crew? Were they correct that his intention all along was to save the bulk of it for himself? Did he stash it in Nassau, where it was better to reclaim it and share it with a small, handpicked number of friends?

Until someone finds a buried chest of treasure with a handwritten note that says, "Here there be Blackbeard's treasure," we'll probably never know.

Jean Lafitte and the Galveston Hoard

Although no one knows for sure, Jean Lafitte was likely born in France, probably in the year 1780, or possibly on the Caribbean island of Hispaniola as late as 1790. At the time, his name was spelled with two Fs, Laffite, but 20 years later, he wound up in the United States, and the resulting paperwork changed the spelling to Lafitte, with two Ts. That's the spelling that stuck with him for the rest of his life. He never dreamed what an important role he would play in the history of his adopted land.

In the early 1800s, he, his mother, and his older brother, Pierre, settled in New Orleans, and the two brothers soon became master smugglers. They grew rich by selling stolen goods that were at a premium due to the Embargo Act of 1807. His profits allowed him to acquire extraordinary amounts of money, ships, and weapons, which would soon stand him in good stead as the War of 1812 loomed on the horizon.

Legends say that he had an office on Bourbon Street, but his profession had made him familiar with the south Louisiana bayous and routes of port ships along the Mississippi River and its many inlets. He used this knowledge to great advantage when he became a privateer.

Jean Lafitte was a pirate whose territory was mostly in and around Louisiana, where he partnered with his brother, Pierre.

Soon, however, the U.S. government began to crack down on his business by enforcing the new embargo specifically in New Orleans. Lafitte countered by shifting his base of operations to a small island in Barataria Bay, about 40 miles south of the city.

He had become so familiar with the area that government officials couldn't find him. He had become, officially, a pirate even though the "golden age" of piracy was long over, and his wealth grew exponentially.

With the outbreak of war in 1812, Lafitte was considered a threat to national security. New Orleans was about to take on strategic importance as a central point of control along the Mississippi River. In 1814, a naval force was commissioned to destroy Lafitte's fleet. They were highly successful, but Lafitte managed to escape.

In times of war, however, compromises sometimes need to be made. The U.S. government recognized that Lafitte's specific knowledge of the area could be of vital importance, so they granted him legal authority to capture British ships as a way of gaining an advantage in the coming Battle of New Orleans.

He proved invaluable and was later recommended for pardon by General Andrew Jackson, who lauded his accomplishments during the war. When President James Madison granted the pardon, Lafitte had been promoted from pirate to national hero.

But where was all the wealth he had accumulated during his varied career?

No one knew. Rumors abounded, but that was all.

As for Lafitte himself, he managed to disappear. Some historians believe he returned to piracy, forcing the U.S. government to try to arrest him.

Legends are many and varied. Some believe the treasure was aboard one of his ships that was sunk.

Others insist that he hid his treasure, planning on coming back for it once he evaded capture. One rumor has it buried beneath an oak tree on the campus of what is now Mount Carmel Academy in New Orleans.

Another tale was so persistent that a swamp along the Natalbany River in Springfield, Louisiana, was drained because Lafitte's treasure was thought to be underwater there. Sad to say, a lot of money and time invested in the project produced nothing.

More than 200 years later, the verdict is still out, but citizens who live in Galveston, Texas, have no doubt. They say that Lafitte moved to the Texas Gulf Coast, buried his treasure for

Pierre Lafitte ran a blacksmith shop in New Orleans, which served as not only a legitimate business but also a way to launder money and move illegal goods stolen by his brother, Jean. The structure still stands and is used as a bar for tourists.

safekeeping, and returned to a life of piracy. To this day, the city of La Porte, Texas, holds an event called the "Annual Search for Lafitte's Gold."

This much is known.

Between the years 1817 and 1820, Lafitte seems to have based his smuggling operations on Galveston Island. At the time, it was part of part of Spanish Texas. He and his brother, Pierre, patrolled the Gulf of Mexico, armed with a letter of marque from Cartagena, a port on the coast of Colombia. It gave him permission to pillage Spanish shipping lanes. These were the valuable highways, so to speak, that linked the Gulf Coast to the rest of the globe. The brothers then sold their booty at auction.

To this day, behind a chain-link fence on the east end of Galveston Island, an old structure lies between a residential home and a metal-sided warehouse. In front of it stands a state historical marker with a small sign that graces an overgrown lot. The sign says this was once Lafitte's headquarters.

The village itself, which Lafitte called Campeche, is gone. He called his home there Maison Rouge because it was supposedly painted red. At its peak, an estimated 1,000 men lived in the encampment, but in 1818, a storm devastated much of the island and destroyed many of Lafitte's ships.

In 1820, after one of his vessels raided an American ship, the U.S. Navy attacked. Lafitte supposedly burned the village, set sail for the Yucatán, and survived until 1823, when he died just after dawn on February 5 from injuries sustained in a battle with a Spanish merchant vessel. He was buried at sea in the Gulf of Honduras. Others say he died of an unknown illness, but, as we shall soon see, these reports may have been fraudulent.

Did he bury the treasure on Galveston Island to ensure the U.S. government wouldn't confiscate it, or did he manage to escape with it? For that matter, did a treasure ever exist at all?

Whatever they think behind closed doors, the Laffite Society of Galveston (notice the original spelling of his name) keeps his memory alive, if slightly romanticized. Members dressed in period costumes parade on the Strand during Mardi Gras.

A housing development called Laffite's Cove is built with home models called Chateau Lafitte Townhomes.

A bar has been there for 45 years called Robert's Lafitte. Visitors can attend a movie called *The Pirate Island of Jean Lafitte* that is showed daily downtown at the Pier 21 Theater.

A museum called Pirates! Legends of the Gulf Coast chronicles Lafitte's life story and history in the area. It features a replica pirate ship, where actors portraying pirates mingle with guests.

The Jean Lafitte Historical Park and Preserve consists of a network of six sites—the Barataria nature preserve, three Cajun cultural districts, the Chalmette battleground and cemetery, and a New Orleans visitors center—in the Mississippi River Delta area that protect the historical resources of the region.

Ghost hunters make nighttime pilgrimages to the Harborside Drive lot, where Maison Rouge allegedly stood. They report unexplained sounds of arguing, gunfire, and a pack of howling dogs, thought to be the spirits of animals provided by a voodoo queen to protect Lafitte's home.

Reportedly, residents of the town thought of him as being handsome and the very picture of a gentleman. Women loved him because he could obtain the latest fashions and sell them below market value. He may have been a pirate, but he is remembered as a daring buccaneer.

Most historians, however, believe that Lafitte's background has been sugarcoated so that popular culture can make a hero out of a really bad guy. Lafitte participated in the slave trade. A lot of money was to be made selling humans he had captured on ships. Slavery was a very lucrative business, and he profited from it. Just as George Washington and Thomas Jefferson, two of America's founding fathers and slaveholders, had their stories cleaned up for the benefit of history books written to give a gullible public two heroes to look up to, Lafitte's work up and down the Texas coast and into the Caribbean was nothing to respect.

Sure, stories about buried treasure are romantic, and Galveston is full of them, but as more than one historian testifies, "Do pirates bury treasure? Nah. They're like addicted gamblers. They go to Vegas and win until they lose. But that doesn't keep people from imagining."

One Galveston antiques shop sells an unidentified skull said to hold clues as to where Lafitte's treasure is buried. A common tale is that the treasure is buried at a place once called Three Trees, near the Pirate Beach community.

> *M*ost historians, however, believe that Lafitte's background has been sugarcoated so that popular culture can make a hero out of a really bad guy.

In the Galveston & Texas History Center, one can find two letters purportedly written by Lafitte. The first, dated July 7, 1819, is addressed to General James Long. In it, Lafitte talks about Mexico and its desire for independence from Spain. The second is addressed to President Madison, in which Lafitte seeks compensation for ships and material that had been confiscated from him, arguing that his service during the War of 1812 illustrated that he was a changed man.

> My conduct since that period is notorious. The
> country is safe and I claim no merit for having,

like all the inhabitants of the state, cooperated in its welfare.

So far, the story we have told is straightforward and available to most historians, who might argue over details but would probably agree on the general thrust. In 2021, however, two researchers, the mother-daughter team of Beth Yarbrough and Ashley Oliphant, wrote a book called *Jean Laffite Revealed*. In it, they added what might prove to be a brand-new chapter in Lafitte's life. It's bound to make historians salivate a bit because it is meticulously researched and completely changes the familiar story found in most history books.

It makes the claim that he faked his death and spent the last 35 years or so of his life living under an assumed name in Lincolnton, North Carolina.

While in the Princeton library, poring over a bunch of boring ledger books, they came across letters written by and to a man who went by the name of Maison Rouge. That, you will remember, was the name of Lafitte's home on Galveston Island.

Further research led them to uncover the quiet history of a man named Lorenzo Ferrer, who moved to town and lived there for decades without ever holding a job or working a day in his life until he died and was buried in the local St. Luke's Episcopal churchyard in 1875.

If so, it seems a bit ironic that both the notorious pirate Edward Teach, also known as Blackbeard, and Jean Lafitte died in the same state, a century apart.

Who was Lorenzo Ferrer? Did he really exist? According to Yarbrough and Oliphant's search, not until he was 50 years old and living in Mississippi. No record of him exists before that at all, anywhere.

So how did Lafitte become Ferrer, and why did he wind up in North Carolina, living the life of a very wealthy man? It's a fascinating story and may help explain what happened to the mysterious Galveston hoard of Jean Lafitte.

The authors reveal in entertaining and thought-provoking detail how they came to their conclusions, but here's the basic story.

Lafitte was a man who liked to be surrounded by important, powerful men. One of his friends was a man by the name of Arsene Latour, who stayed in touch with Laffite's former attorney, Edward Livingston, after Lafitte had faked his death to take the pressure of government intervention off his shoulders. He was living undercover in Cuba.

Edward Livingston had become a trusted adviser to Andrew Jackson, who had become president after his victory at the

One rumor about the ultimate fate of Lafitte was that he changed his name to Lorenzo Ferrer and lived a comfortable life in Lincolnton (pictured), a small town in North Carolina.

Battle of New Orleans. Jackson owed some political favors to Lafitte because Lafitte had provided the weapons and firepower that brought about American victory.

In 1829, while visiting Havana, Cuba, and meeting with Lafitte, Latour wrote to Livingston in Washington, saying that a man who went by the code name Maison Rouge (Lafitte) needed help getting back into the country. Lafitte wanted to get back in the capitalistic game and become a player. He was good at making money and missed the action. Mississippi was experiencing a cotton boom, and Lafitte wanted in.

To make a long story short, Lafitte became Lorenzo Ferrer and secretly entered the country by using one of his old pirate routes, a tributary of the Mississippi River called Bayou Lafourche. That way, he escaped notice by the New Orleans port authorities.

He settled in Jackson, Mississippi, where he met a woman named Louisa, who was considerably younger than he was. She was originally from Lincolnton, North Carolina. No official record says that they married, but they did live together. She must have enjoyed the lifestyle he provided because he started doing what he did best: making money by trading in slaves and goods.

Eventually, Lafitte's nose for business paid off in that he foresaw the coming of the Civil War and the end of slavery.

When the Civil War raged on and threatened Lincolnton, stories surfaced that Lafitte once again decided to hide his wealth to keep it from the Yankees.

Wanting to go out on top, he left Mississippi and moved to Lincoln County in North Carolina. He remained there for the rest of his life.

His economic DNA somehow forced him to stay in the center of things. He joined the church where he was finally buried and even was a cofounder of Masonic Lodge #137. He apparently donated a decorative sword that hung in the Lodge for years and years.

Recently, the Masons decided to take a closer look at the sword that graced their meeting place. Knowing it was donated by a founding member, they contacted Oliphant and Yarbrough after becoming aware of their historical research.

When the authors studied it, they discovered that it had been manufactured for the War of 1812. That set off some alarm bells, so they took it to an antique metal expert. Upon closer examination under a blacklight, they discovered the name "Jn Laffite" scratched into the metal, partially obscured by several coats of varnish and sealant. That was the way the old pirate always signed his name.

It's not that Yarbrough and Oliphant's research took residents by complete surprise. Rumors did exist in town that Lorenzo Ferrer was Jean Lafitte, but few people believed them. Now, an actual paper trail existed and a real artifact that seemed to verify the stories.

When the Civil War raged on and threatened Lincolnton, stories surfaced that Lafitte once again decided to hide his wealth to keep it from the Yankees. Secondhand tales emerged that someone had heard from someone else that Lafitte, now Ferrer, had been seen ordering slaves to carry three locked chests either into or out of the courthouse. What happened to them? No one knew.

It was the story of Galveston all over again. Lafitte had to get out of town. Did he bury his treasure for safekeeping? The authors insist that absolutely no evidence exists to suggest such a thing. But treasure stories have a life of their own.

Whatever the case, the conspiracy breeds questions:

💰 What did Ferrer live on all those years? Did he bring his fabled treasure with him when he came to town? If so, where is the remainder of it? Is it hidden in some secret resting place, waiting to be discovered?

- Ferrer (Lafitte) was a Mason at the end of the war and very much pro-slavery. Did he have anything to do with the Knights of the Golden Circle? Was he a part of the secret organization that included such men as John Wilkes Booth, Jefferson Davis, Nathan Bedford Forrest, and Jesse James? Did he contribute to the legends of lost Civil War gold?

- Did a connection indeed exist between Ferrer and Lafitte that ran from France to Louisiana, Texas, Cuba, Mississippi, and eventually North Carolina, which included a host of aliases along the way?

The authors make no claim except that Ferrer and Lafitte were one and the same. But that doesn't stop others from speculating and developing conspiracy theories.

Thus, the story continues. To the area around New Orleans, to Galveston Island, to nearly every inlet and recess of the Texas coast, we can now add Lincolnton, North Carolina.

Where is Jean Lafitte's hidden hoard? Who knows? All we can do is keep looking.

Around the World with Captain Thomas Cavendish

L et's start with a quick history quiz. Who was the first person to sail around the world?

Most history books credit Ferdinand Magellan, the Portuguese explorer. They are wrong because Magellan died en route. He never made it, even though some members of his initial expedition did. And to be fair, we also have to say that his sponsors didn't order him to circumnavigate the globe. He was merely sent out to sail west across the Atlantic to try to find a route to the East Indies. But let's bow to tradition and give him his historical due.

Now, another quiz. Who was the first person to sail around the world on purpose?

Fewer people have heard of him, but his name was Thomas Cavendish. His ships were actually the third fleet to accomplish the feat but the first to set out with the deliberate intention of doing so. The voyage took place in the years 1586 to 1588, while Elizabethans such as Cavendish's fellow countrymen Edmund Spence, Christopher Marlowe, and William Shakespeare were

An engraving of Thomas Cavendish, the first person to navigate around the world with the intention of doing so. Cavendish was also a privateer not above stashing away his loot for later retrieval.

exploring a new world of poetry and drama that would map out the future of the English language.

Cavendish was a British privateer, which is to say that he was a pirate sanctioned by his mother country to commit acts of murder, mayhem, and plunder as long as he shared the profits with his government. But the trouble with most privateers is that at heart, they are nothing but legal pirates. Because they are forced to share the wealth when they get home, the temptation to cook the proverbial books in their favor is always in front of them. Since the crew works on shares, they are usually tempted to go along.

In other words, if a privateer steals $1 million worth of loot and gets to keep half, he and his crew split half a million dollars when the voyage is over. But if they bury half a million dollars somewhere on the way home and split the rest upon completion of the journey, they can then sail back to where they banked their stash, dig it up, and split it again. That means they are dividing three-quarters of a million dollars instead of half. All they need is a good place to make their bank.

Apparently, as least according to legend, either St. Helena Island in the South Atlantic west of Africa, Santa Catalina Island off the coast of California, or Palemano Point, an exposed reef off Hawaii's Big Island, might have fit the bill for the Cavendish expedition. If so, some $5 million in loot is still buried in one of those locations. Locals claim Hawaii, but who knows?

Many legends abound about buried Hawaiian treasure. Oahu alone is home to more than a few of them. A chest of gold and silver is rumored to be somewhere on Kaena Point. Chinese coins have washed ashore on Maili Beach, Aina Moana State Park is said to hide some $100,000 to $150,000 worth of gold coins, and enough money for anyone is rumored to be on Ford Island, just off the coast. A Peruvian treasure chest might be somewhere as well.

Captain Cook may have buried some loot on Kauai.

The caves on the north harbors of Kealakekua Bay on the Big Island are said to harbor some great wealth.

But the one that excites treasure seekers the most is Cavendish's stash on Palemano Point. This is his story.

Cavendish was born into a wealthy family in Suffolk, England. He eventually inherited a lot of money, and you wouldn't think he would ever have been interested in the hard life of the sea, but like many people who are given money rather than having to earn it, he blew through his inheritance rather quickly.

It was an era of adventure, so he decided to get on board with the times. Selling what property he managed to retain, he used the proceeds to join Sir Walter Raleigh's attempt to establish a North American colony in the new frontier that Raleigh had named Virginia after Elizabeth I of England. She had been dubbed "the Virgin Queen" because during her entire rule, she had decided not to marry in order to keep her personal control over the politics of the patriarchal era.

Cavendish captained one of Raleigh's ships and decided he liked the life. Upon his return, having then had at least some experience, he decided to set off with his own expedition. Both Ferdinand Magellan and Sir Francis Drake were household names at that time, and he wanted to add his to the list.

He decided to set forth with the specific intent to circumnavigate the globe, gathering treasure along the way. Being an official British privateer, he had the backing of the world's biggest and most feared naval fleets.

You've got to give him points for preparation for such an audacious endeavor. He studied navigation, gathered all the obscure charts he could find, and hired some of Drake's veterans to act as guides.

When he felt ready, he set off with three ships: the *Desire*, the *Hugh Gallant*, and his flagship, the *Content*. They left Plymouth in the summer of 1586, sailing south along the west coast of Africa to Sierra Leone. There, he scored his first victory when he attacked a village of natives before putting in at the Cape Verde Islands to restock. From there, he sailed west across the Atlantic and found himself off the coast of Brazil by early fall. For three weeks, they resupplied and rested at San Sebastian Island. He even took the time to build a small boat with a shallow draft in order to explore inland rivers.

He went on to explore the coast of Patagonia and, by the first of the new year, began the dangerous passage through the

Sir Walter Raleigh, the famous soldier, explorer, statesman, and author, financed Cavendish's first expedition.

Straits of Magellan, by now known as a treacherous graveyard for ships.

By February, he found himself in the welcome waters of the Pacific. Despite the hardships encountered by all such expeditions, he had been fairly successful up to now, having taken 19 ships, along with their treasure, but he had lost 12 men in doing so. Those losses mounted due to disease, and eventually he didn't have enough sailors to sail all three vessels, so he deliberately sank the *Hugh Gallant*.

While sailing north along the west coast of North America off the coast of the Baja Peninsula, he gained his greatest prize, the one that would secure his place in legends about lost treasure and may have brought down upon himself the curse that eventually took his life.

Privateers are always on the lookout for easy prey, so when Cavendish came upon the Spanish ship *Santos* after it left Manila headed back to Spain, loaded down with 22,000 gold pesos and 600 tons of precious silks and spices stolen from the Maya, he must have started to salivate. The ship was the personal property of Philip II of Spain and had been pushed way off course due to a storm coming up out of the south. After a six-hour battle, Cavendish emerged with the biggest prize of his life. Not only did he capture the ship and its treasure, he took two prisoners, one with a working knowledge of Chinese waters, which Cavendish knew he would need for future voyages, and one who was familiar with the Philippines, where he would soon be headed.

Everything was going his way until he ran into trouble with his crew. Sailors in those days were often recruited from the urban dregs of society. Most of them were fleeing something rather than being attracted to privateering or, more correctly, pirating, as a way of life. Discipline was brutal because captains felt they had to keep their crews in line with the lash. This, of course, led to the constant threat of mutiny.

Now, Cavendish faced such a threat. The crew thought they had been mistreated and were dissatisfied with the way the loot was divided. The ship named *Content* did not live up to its name. The crew either took over command of the vessel, or Cavendish sent it home on its own to quell a riot. No one knows for sure because the ship disappeared from history and was never heard from again.

Cavendish was now left with one ship, the *Desire*. It was too loaded down with stolen loot to continue on, so he decided to "bank" some of it.

The question is, where?

Some say he buried it on Santa Catalina Island, off the coast of what is now Los Angeles County in California. Others are convinced that he kept the bulk of it aboard until he was on his way home. It is known that he made a record voyage across the Pacific, cleared the Cape of Good Hope in May 1588, and stopped off at St. Helena Island, where he put in to refit and reprovision. He might have buried some treasure there. Either place would have been a remote, safe place to make his bank.

Many treasure seekers, however, believe he chose Palemano Point, an exposed reef off Hawaii's Big Island. Local people there still prowl the secluded beach with metal detectors, convinced that the latest storm will have uncovered a fortune.

All we know for sure is gleaned from his ship's journal, which says he had stolen what was called "a beautiful treasure" from the *Santos* and buried it on the beaches of "Ilhabela" in a region called "Saco do Sombrio." No one knows exactly what that means or where those places are located.

At this point, Cavendish sails out of our treasure story but apparently not out of the part about the curse that so often accompanies so many gold seekers.

> *Local people there still prowl the secluded beach with metal detectors, convinced that the latest storm will have uncovered a fortune.*

Whatever happened and wherever he banked his loot, he landed at what is today the Mariana Islands in January 1588, survived a local plot to turn him in on pirating charges, and made it home to a hero's welcome on September 9. Quite the showman, he decked out his ship in gold cloth and dressed his crew in silk for the homecoming. He brought home so much gold that the price of gold fell in London due to devaluation.

The entire voyage around the world had consumed 780 days and was so successful that he was the belle of the courts and songs were written about him, especially since his return happened to come right after the defeat of the Spanish Armada. National confidence was at record levels.

In the back of his mind, however, Cavendish must have been plotting to get back to his secret "bank" and cash in on his winnings, but little did he realize that the treasure curse was following him. He was about to confront it face-to-face.

Four years later, he set off on a repeat journey. On this trip, nothing went right. He had no official backing, so he had to pay expenses out of his own pocket. He planned to follow his old route, probably because it was the only way to recover his buried treasure, but this time, he decided to find the fabled, mythi-

One theory about the last days of Thomas Cavendish is that he sailed to Ascension Island, which is an isolated island in the south Atlantic Ocean, where he committed suicide.

cal Northwest Passage. It probably rankled him that Drake had received knighthood and he hadn't, so he sought fame as well as fortune. Whoever found the Passage was bound to become famous. Speculating about it was all the rage in both England and America.

For 26 days, he was becalmed off Ecuador. Diseases ran rampant through his crew. In true pirate fashion, he was able to pillage some Brazilian cities, but soon after, a storm decimated his fleet of five ships. The captain of the *Desire* mutinied and deserted. He was unable to navigate the Straits of Magellan and had to turn back due to ferocious storms.

Some might call it kismet. Others karma. Maybe it was the curse of buried treasure, but something certainly worked itself out on Cavendish. He headed back into the Atlantic and was never heard from again.

Did he die at sea as is commonly believed? Or did something else happen? Here's where conspiracy theories enter the picture.

- Some people speculate that a few of Cavendish's men deserted when he raided the Brazilian coastline. They became farmers, but they probably knew where any treasure was buried, dug it up, and used it to finance their futures as landlubbers.

- Cavendish returned to "Ilhabela," wherever that was, cashed in his treasure, and lived out his life in secrecy where no one knew him. Maybe he even perished at sea, proving that you *can* take it with you, at least if your destination is Davy Jones's locker.

- A corollary to the above is that perhaps he was lost at sea while on his way to St. Helena, which might have been the elusive "Ilhabela." Plotting his route when he left South America suggests that might be the case.

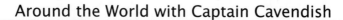 Many historians believe he made it as far as Ascension Island. There, he left a suicide note, which stated: "The failures of this unfortunate action weigh heavily on me ... of bad that happened in this trip the last of them is my death."

What was denied him in life was awarded after he died. He now has the official title of Sir Thomas Cavendish.

Shipwrecks

The Wreck of the "Ship of Gold"

If you are interested in obtaining gold from an authentic lost treasure, you don't need to leave the comfort of your home to get it. You can purchase authentic gold coins scavenged from the wreck of the SS *Central America*, the infamous "Ship of Gold," simply by googling the phrase and purchasing them for a low, low price. Supply is limited, so act quickly!

This is possible because the ship was located on September 11, 1987, in about 8,000 feet of water by an ROV (remotely operated vehicle). *Life* magazine called it "The Greatest Treasure Ever Found!" At the time, the treasure was calculated to be about 50 pounds of gold dust, 10,000 coins, and 577 gold bars.

In 2014, a second salvage attempt recovered 15,500 gold and silver coins, 45 gold bars, hundreds of gold nuggets, and more gold dust.

As of this writing, coins from this wreck are still very popular with collectors. But be careful! The gold from which these coins and artifacts were made is said to be cursed because it was stolen from Native Americans of California. You'll have to decide whether or not the curse is real, but strange events have followed it from the very beginning. Many people have died. When the "Ship of Gold" went down off the coast of South Carolina, it caused such financial hysteria in New York that that it led to the Panic of 1857.

Here's the story. You be the judge.

The SS *Central Amerca* was loaded with 30,000 pounds of gold when it sank during a hurricane in 1857. Of the 578 passengers and crew, 425 drowned.

In 1848, at a place near present-day Sacramento called New Helvetia or New Switzerland, a man by the name of John A. Sutter was running a mill that produced lumber. He had come to California in 1839 and was doing well enough to attempt to expand his operation. He sent a team led by James Marshall to search out sites for a possible sawmill on the American River.

On the morning of January 24, 1848, Marshall saw a little golden sparkle running through what was called a tail race in his operation. Reaching down, he picked up a small flake of gold.

What happened next sparked the great California Gold Rush of 1848. He is said to have shouted out one word: *Eureka!* ("I found it!")

That's how it all began, and the story grew so big and so fast, leading to such profound changes in U.S. history, that in 1849, the word became the California state motto. By 1865, Horace Greeley, editor of the *New York Tribune*, wrote an editorial in which he is said to have originated the phrase, "Go West, young man!" He probably wasn't the first person to have said it, but he usually gets the credit. The western rush, begun in 1848, was only intensified. Hollywood, the newest version of the old get-rich dream, was now on the horizon.

Sailing around South America by way of the Estrecho de Magallanes (Strait of Magellan), between the southern tip of South America and Tierra del Fuego, was a hazardous proposition.

It would take two years before people of means could get to California by the "civilized" method of steam or sailing ship. Sailing around South America by way of the *Estrecho de Magallanes* (Strait of Magellan), between the southern tip of South America and Tierra del Fuego, was a hazardous proposition. The only alternative was by ox-drawn wagon and a lot of walking, a journey that took about five months, depending on how much equipment you wanted to take with you and which route you traveled.

The principal destination was Yerba-Buena, or what would soon become San Francisco. Despite the hazards of the journey, more than 300,000 people could be found along the American River in the early years of the 1850s. Prospectors created an economic boom. Most of the people who got rich made their money by supplying essential, and often nonessential, needs to the prospectors. But banks invested in the area, and, of course, the Native Americans who lived there were driven off their land for good. They simply could not compete with the guns, germs, and sheer numbers of the civilian army, let alone the official one.

Law was often a do-it-yourself affair. Despite all this, a lot of gold found its way out of the mountains and into bank vaults.

Unfortunately, every boom produces a bust. The eventual lack of gold in California led to a lack of money in New York banks. The Ohio Life Insurance and Trust Company collapsed. Something had to be done, and quickly.

A few New York banks decided to band together and organize the transfer of a large shipment of gold from the San Francisco Mint in order to consolidate their reserves. The solvency of east coast business was at stake. The whole affair was supposed to be kept secret, but, of course, that didn't work. Pretty much everyone knew about the shipment.

On August 20, 1857, several hundred passengers boarded the SS *Sonora* of the Pacific Mail Steamship Line. They left San Francisco and headed south toward Panama City.

Besides the personal fortune of many of the wealthy passengers safely stowed away in the captain's cabin among other places, the ship's hold was loaded with $1.6 million in gold, consisting of freshly minted 1857-S Double Eagles, some $20 coins, and gold in other forms such as ingots and gold dust.

The first leg of the trip went very well. Rather than risk the long journey around South America, the plan was to land at Panama City. The passengers were transferred by a railroad line, built in 1855, which was about 48 miles across Panama. The gold was shipped separately, under heavy guard. It took only a matter of some four hours to cross the isthmus, and they arrived safely at Aspinwall, now called Colón, Panama.

Both passengers and cargo were safely stored away in the ship that would carry them across the Gulf of Mexico, around Florida, and then north to the New York Harbor. The ship chosen to make the last leg of this journey and rescue the financial economy of the east coast was the Steamship Central America, henceforth known to history as the "Ship of Gold." It was under the command of Captain William Herndon, who possessed a solid reputation in the naval service due to his service during the Mexican-American War. Previous to this, he had done notable work exploring the Amazon River.

All went according to plan until the morning of Thursday, September 10. Back in those days, weather reports didn't exist. The skies, which had appeared to be normal in the morning with only a following breeze, soon intensified into a raging gale. By nighttime, the ship found itself in the midst of a full-fledged hurricane.

On Friday morning, September 11, the crew still controlled the ship, but it had begun to take on water through the drive

Captain William Herndon, formerly a navy commander during the Mexican–American War, was honored by having a town named after him in Virginia, as well as two naval ships.

shaft and various broken windows. The ship listed so violently that the crew manned the boilers to keep up steam.

At 11 A.M., Captain Herndon informed the passengers that the ship was in danger. Crew and passengers were all engaged in bailing. At one point, the ship listed sharply to the starboard, and the captain ordered all passengers to the port side for balance.

At about 1 P.M. the next day, the sail of a brig called the *Marine* appeared on the horizon. Under the command of Captain Hiram Burt and 10 crew members, it, too, had been damaged. As the two vessels drew closer together, Captain Herndon ordered women and children on deck. They were instructed to leave behind all unnecessary baggage and prepare to board the lifeboats.

Historian Normand Klare later wrote that "as if to illustrate how little value was the gold, ladies brought out bags not entrusted to the cargo holds, and scattered coins on the floor, asking all who wanted money to help themselves."

A few picked up some coins, but none took more than two $20 coins in order to avoid weight that might carry them down should they be cast into the water.

Soon after 8 P.M., a huge wave struck, and the SS *Central America* started to break apart. It soon sank to the bottom.

Captain Herndon, true to his naval tradition, went down with his ship. Since then, two U.S. Navy ships were named the USS *Herndon* in his honor, along with the town of Herndon, Virginia. Two years later, his daughter Ellen married Chester Alan Arthur, who went on to become the 21st president of the United States.

Some survivors managed to cling to wreckage and a few life preservers. A Norwegian bark arrived in time to rescue about 50 people. Three more, adrift in a lifeboat, were picked up over a week later. The rest died: 425 passengers and crew members, buried at sea 160 miles off the shore of Charleston, South Carolina, along with the immense wealth the ship had carried. In today's dollars, it would be valued at more than $300 million. The money that had been destined to shore up the economy of the East was lost at sea. There, it would lie in the darkness, about 8,000 feet below the surface, for 130 years.

When news of the shipwreck filtered out to the New York establishment, the Panic of 1857 ensued, leading to a severe recession.

Was the gold cursed? Is that why the ship went down?

Well, probably not. It was the victim of a hurricane, a fate met by many other vessels. But what happened next makes you wonder.

In September 1988, the wreck was located by Tommy Gregory Thompson and his Columbus-America Discovery Group of Ohio by using Bayesian search theory. This is a technique that has been used successfully to locate other wrecks. In a nutshell, it employs sophisticated computer techniques to explore relevant search parameters, discarding ranges that will most like-

The loss of so much gold with the sinking of the *Central America* helped to trigger the Panic of 1857 and the subsequent recession.

ly not deliver the best solution. It's used when a lot of data is involved, using the speed of software programs to shorten the time and space required to search large areas.

An ROV was sent down to explore. It immediately located and recovered significant amounts of gold and artifacts scattered around the bottom. The efforts recovered gold estimated to be worth about $100 to $150 million, far short of the total cargo. The coins recovered were thought to be that of passengers who had emptied their personal stashes before going down. The main cargo was still at large.

Who financed the expensive recovery? ROVs and sophisticated technology don't come cheap.

The effort was probably funded by Harry John, an heir to the Miller Brewing Company fortune. Near the end of his life, he was known to have launched a few unsuccessful treasure hunts, and this might have been one of them.

But with the announcement of the discovery came other claims. No fewer than 39 insurance companies filed suits. Their

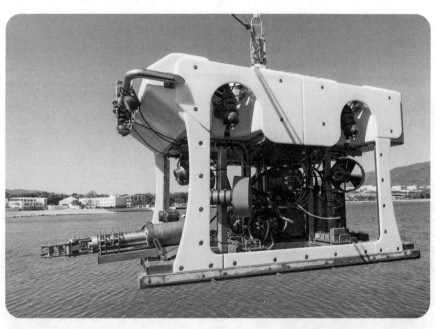

Remotely operated vehicles (ROVs) like this one were used by Tommy Thompson to find and recover the gold from the wreckage. It cost Thompson's investors $12.5 million to retrieve about $125 million in gold, so not a bad return on investment!

claim was that because they paid damages back in the 19th century for the lost gold, they had the right to it now that it had been found.

The team that found it, however, argued that the gold had been abandoned, so it was matter of "finders keepers, losers weepers."

A long legal battle ensued. Eventually, in 1996, 92 percent of the gold was awarded to the discovery team.

But that wasn't the end of it. In 2005, Thompson was sued by several of his investors, who had provided $12.5 million to finance his search. Then, in 2006, several members of his crew followed suit, claiming they had never been paid for their investment of time and energy.

Thompson disappeared. A receiver was named by the courts to oversee his company and, if possible, salvage more gold from the wreck in order to pay back his various creditors. They decided that the original expedition had only excavated 5 percent of the ship. This project was eventually carried out in March 2014 after a contract was awarded to Odyssey Marine Exploration to conduct archaeological recovery and conservation of the remaining shipwreck.

In 2009, it was discovered that Thompson had opened an offshore account in the Cook Islands for $4.16 million.

In 2015, he was located and arrested by U.S. Marshals Service agents. He was extradited to Ohio and ordered to provide an accounting of the expedition profits. Three years later, in November 2018, Thompson agreed to surrender 500 gold coins in his possession but claimed he had no access to the rest of the treasure. A jury awarded investors $19.4 million in compensatory damages. $3.2 million went to the Dispatch Printing Company, and $16.2 million went to the court-appointed receiver to be used to compensate the other investors.

Coins from the wreck were soon being advertised for sale by Universal Coin & Bullion, a precious metals dealer based in Beaumont, Texas. Heritage Auctions sold several gold pieces recovered from Central America at auction in 2019. The prize of the auction was a Harris, Marchand & Co. gold ingot, which sold for $528,000.

The ship's bell, weighing in at a whopping 268 pounds (122 kilograms), stood 2 feet (0.6 meters) tall and wide. It was engraved with the words "MORGAN IRON WORKS" and "NEW YORK 1853." When it was salvaged, it went on display at the Columbus Museum of Art in Columbus, Ohio, in 1992, and a year later, it was moved to the Columbus Zoo and Aquarium in Liberty Township, Delaware County. In 2021, it was shown at the American Numismatic Association's World's Fair of Money in Rosemont, Illinois. Finally, it was offered to the U.S. Naval Academy in Annapolis, Maryland. There, after a public ceremony held on May 23, 2022, it was put in place next to the Herndon Monument. The lost captain and his lost ship's bell were united once again.

Who knows what constitutes a curse? Is it a mystical pronouncement, supervised by spirits and ghosts? Is it some kind of supernatural judgment? Is it a result of divine vengeance? Or is it simply a natural process that follows in the wake of greed and avarice?

The latter certainly seems to be the case with the story of the wreck of the SS *Central America*, the "Ship of Gold." Everyone involved suffered, from the Indians who were killed, persecuted, and hounded from their lands to the hundreds of prospectors who worked and died, usually earning next to nothing, to those who went down with the ship and to the New York bankers, many of whom went bankrupt in the Panic of 1857.

Whatever constitutes the true nature of a curse, this treasure was cursed indeed. And the bulk of it still lies buried beneath 8,000 feet of water. People still want to salvage it. Maybe the curse isn't done working yet.

The Plate Fleet of 1715

Does a curse attach itself to certain objects? Is some kind of metaphysical, or even supernatural, force involved? Or is the nature of a cursed object simply the result of the human tendency to see patterns where none exist, an attempt to bring order out of chaos?

Humans see pictures in cloud formations, for instance, when obviously none exist. Is that what we do when the subject of treasure curses comes up? If people who seek such a treasure experience ill of any kind, do we tend to fabricate theories of a curse when, in fact, the real problem lies in the reality of human greed and, perhaps, self-fulfilled prophecy?

To illustrate this, it would prove profitable to examine the events surrounding the famous Plate Fleet of 1715. Ten ships, loaded with immense treasure, went down in a hurricane off the coast of Florida. On the surface, we could suppose a curse was involved, or we might just chalk it up to bad luck and being in the wrong place at the wrong time. After all, hurricanes occur every year, and ships often encounter them. Sometimes, they are destroyed and sink to the bottom of the sea. It happens.

We need not imagine a supernatural, metaphysical force as a curse, although it might be good to remember that the word "hurricane" is derived from a Taino Native American word (*hurucane*) that means "evil spirit of the wind." That might indicate an original belief in some kind of divine or spiritual energy.

The main question, however, is why does a fleet carrying immense treasure choose to tempt fate by sailing directly into a hurricane alley, knowing full well that the tropical storm season is about to begin? If the answer is greed and avarice, it opens a new dimension. The curse of ill-gotten gain and stolen wealth now comes into play. No supernatural force other than human covetousness is needed. We might as well call it a curse. The word certainly covers the situation. The devil is, after all, in the details.

On July 24, 1715, a convoy of 11 Spanish ships and one French merchantman set sail from Havana, Cuba, to Spain. It was called a "Plate Fleet" because their cargo consisted of valuable treasure looted from the so-called "New" World. *Plata* is

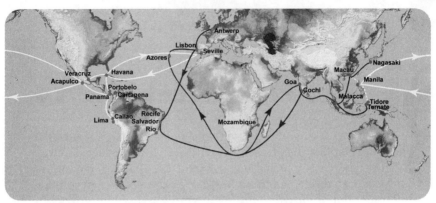

The Spanish trade routes (in white) include the Americas and the Philippines. The Portuguese (dark lines) traveled to what is now Brazil and to much of Asia.

the Spanish name for the silver coins that made up much of the wealth stored in their holds. Thus, it was a *Plata*, or "Plate," fleet.

Generally, two such fleets sailed every year. The *Flota de Tierra Firme* traveled from Spain to Cartagena de Indias and Panama, carrying various trade goods and necessities. The *Flota de Nueva España* went to Veracruz. For safety, the two fleets often stayed together until they reached the Caribbean.

It was on the return voyage that problems usually developed. The ships were by then loaded to the gills with gold and silver, jewelry, tobacco, spices, and indigo and were a rich prize for marauding pirates and privateers. By the time they sailed east, the crews were tired and usually sick from tropical diseases, malnutrition, and horrible hygienic conditions aboard. All this made them vulnerable to attack.

If all this wasn't bad enough, another unstable element was in the equation. The return trip was apt to run into the hurricane season. Traveling west during the summer, the Atlantic was usually calm, with gently prevailing winds, but in the fall, as anyone knows who lives anywhere near the southeast coast of the United States, tropical storm season can be a tough time beginning in late August. Especially in the days before accurate weather reports, hurricanes could blow up suddenly, without advance warning. The results were often devastating.

By 1715, the pattern was well known to seafaring voyagers. When the fleet sailed, it was only days before the hurricane season was set to begin, and all the captains knew it.

This year, the fleet, for a number of reasons, had been delayed by two years in the Caribbean, so their official excuse was that they were attempting to escape marauding pirates and privateers who were anxious to steal their valuable cargo, but they also had an unspoken and unwritten reason. To understand *that* reason, we need to review some historical background.

Between the years 1688 and 1715, Louis XIV of France had adopted a policy of rapid expansion. Europe was thus ravaged by two expensive wars. Because wars were often fought at sea, they naturally disrupted trade between the Americas and various nations of Europe, one of them being Spain.

The War of the Grand Alliance ended in 1697 with the Treaty of Ryswick. But another war soon began in 1701. This second war, the War of Spanish Succession, came about because of infighting over who was to rule Spain. Carlos II had died without producing an heir. On his deathbed, he named Philippe, the grandson of Louis XIV of France, as his successor.

This created a political problem. Leopold I, the Holy Roman Emperor, wanted his son, Archduke Charles, to wear the crown. He wanted to prevent an alliance between France and Spain.

British and Dutch allies capture a Spanish treasure fleet in this 1702 painting by Ludolf Bakhuizen, *Battle of Vigo Bay*. The fight for wealth brought in from the Spanish Main was a key strategy during the War of the Spanish Succession.

War soon broke out. England and the Dutch Republic were on one side. Spain, France, Portugal, Bavaria, and Savoy were allied on the other.

To finance these wars, Spain was extremely dependent on wealth from its colonies in the New World. Many of the battles were fought at sea, often by privateers who received letters of marque to attack and capture any vessels that might contain loot for the coffers of their sponsoring government.

The oceans were no longer safe for commerce. Trade between Spain and the Americas was virtually suspended. Spain suffered major defeats by the English navy.

This War of Spanish Succession came to a close in 1715 with a series of treaties known collectively as the Peace of Utrecht. England and France together agreed that Philippe, the grandson of Louis XIV of France, would, indeed, ascend the throne of Spain, but he would have to renounce his rights to any power in France. England would be given Newfoundland, the island of St. Christopher, and the territory surrounding Hudson Bay.

The fighting may have ended except for the marauding hordes of pirates who wanted to capitalize on the newfound trade routes opening up, but Spain needed money badly, and not just to bolster its sagging economy; Philippe, the new king of Spain, had a more pressing reason: his wife had died, and he wanted to marry Elizabeth of Parma, making her the queen of Spain.

Elizabeth was no shrinking violet. Utilizing the only power most women could employ back in those extremely patriarchal days, she requested ("demanded" might be a better word) a sizable dowry of precious jewelry and gems of various kinds. To put it bluntly, she wasn't going to come across without being well paid up-front.

Isabel de Farnesio (Elizabeth of Parma), Queen of Spain, demanded a huge dowry of precious gems, a treasure King Philippe hoped would be satisfied by the return of his fleet from the New World.

Her requests had included a heart made of 130 pearls, 14-carat pearl earrings, a pure coral rosary with large-sized beads, and an emerald ring weighing 74 carats. (Remember that ring. It's going to become an important mystery.) Philippe had thus requested more than 1,200 pieces of rare jewelry from the Americas as a dowry for Elizabeth. With the fleet delayed for two years, he was, perhaps understandably, anxious. They were under orders to hurry things along. That might explain the "unwritten reason" we mentioned earlier.

Whatever the case, Spain was in economic need of financial relief, so the 11 ships making up the fleet made ready to sail from Havana in the summer of 1715. The *Escuadrón de Tierra Firme*, under the command of Capitán de Mar y Guerra Don Antonio de Echeverz y Zubiza, and the *Flota de Nueva España*, under the command of General Don Juan Esteban de Ubilla, began preparations for the trip back to their home country.

After a two-year delay, the mighty Plate Fleet was finally ready to sail home to Spain. The fleet's cargo was estimated at 15 million silver *piastres* ("pieces of eight") and untold wealth in jewels and precious gems. Because Spain funneled so much New World wealth into the coffers of European countries, it might be said that the whole economy of Europe was held in the balance.

The fleet's cargo was estimated at 15 million silver piastres ("pieces of eight") and untold wealth in jewels and precious gems.

Little did the fleet commanders know that 200 miles away, their fate was forming in the south Atlantic.

On July 24, the ships put to sea, intending to round the coast of Florida, pick up the Gulf Stream east to Bermuda, and then head for Spain. Protected by two huge ships of some 200 guns each, they felt no great fear of pirates. They expected a safe passage as they left the Havana harbor in the early morning of a beautiful, calm day, blown forth on a gentle breeze.

The weather held for five days, and they had no indication of a rapidly approaching killer storm. On July 29, long swells started to appear from the southeast. The atmosphere was soon heavy with moisture, and the sun shone through a gathering haze. The ships began to dip and roll. Experienced navigators, pilots, and old hands alike started to be concerned. They knew that these were the early signs of an impending tropical storm, traveling northwest, and now southeast, of the convoy.

By nightfall, the hurricane changed course, heading west, directly into the path of the soon foundering convoy. On the morning of July 30, as the ships sailed off the coast of Florida, winds picked up. By midday, they had increased to over 20 knots and then to over 30 knots. The waves were some 20 feet high, driving the fleet closer and closer to shore.

All ships were commanded to head directly into the wind to stay away from the treacherous reefs, but it was too late. At 4 A.M. on July 31, the hurricane struck the doomed ships, driving one after another onto the deadly reefs. There they stacked up, helpless in the face of the storm.

The entire fleet was lost, and of the 2,500 passengers and crew, over 1,000 died.

One ship survived to tell the tale. The French warship *Griffon*, under the command of Captain Antoine d'Aire, had headed toward the northeast, directly into the storm, and arrived in Brest, on the coast of Brittany, on August 31, 1715. Even still, d'Aire was unaware that all the Spanish ships had perished.

A few people managed to survive being washed up onto

Pieces of eight were Spanish dollars worth eight *reales* of Mexican silver. Back then, people cut the coins into eight pieces to make change. The 1715 pieces pictured here came from the wreck of the Plate Fleet.

the shore of Florida, near present-day Vero Beach. To this day, that stretch of dunes and sand is called the Treasure Coast due to the valuable artifacts that still wash up on beaches when frequent storms wash away sand, exposing the treasure that lies beneath. In those days, however, the land was inhospitable, at least to Europeans unused to living under those conditions.

The survivors found themselves in a land infested with disease-carrying mosquitoes, rattlesnakes, wild animals, and hostile Indians, who saw the place not as an inhospitable wasteland but home. The Europeans were far from what they would call civilization, without food, fresh water, or badly needed medical supplies.

The morning of July 31 revealed the full extent of the disaster. The beaches of the land they called *la Florida* were littered with pieces of broken ships and bodies. The survivors could not really comprehend what had happened to them.

The wreckage was scattered over many miles, so it was impossible to immediately discern the extent of the tragedy. Many half-dead survivors died every day, adding to the already devastating number of casualties. Eventually, on August 6, it was decided to send Nicolas de India, a pilot, and 18 men in a launch toward the island of Cuba. Their mission was to contact the governor, Vicente de Raja.

The boat reached Havana 11 days later. Shortly afterward, ships were readied for the task of rescuing the survivors and salvaging what they could.

Right away, the rescue fleet showed some success. They dragged the bottom, bringing up chests of coins, jewelry, and gold. Ships from St. Augustine, some miles north, arrived to help in the recovery effort. By the early weeks of September, the salvage attempt was so successful that 25 armed soldiers were sent to guard the accumulating wealth.

By the end of October, over five million pieces of eight had been recovered along with gold, jewelry, and a great portion of the king's treasure. Salvage attempts continued for the next three years, but by then, the news had spread like wildfire, attracting unwanted scavengers.

In January 1716, the notorious pirate Henry Jennings attacked the camp from his 40-ton sloop *Barsheba*, and John Wills arrived on the scene with his 35-ton *Eagle*. Both were under orders of the governor of Jamaica. They commandeered the Spanish salvage camp at Palmar de Ays, detaining the defenders and looting the camp, making off with 120,000 pieces of eight and other valuables as well as two bronze cannons and two large iron guns.

> *In January 1716, the notorious pirate Henry Jennings attacked the camp from his 40-ton sloop Barsheba, and John Wills arrived on the scene with his 35-ton Eagle.*

When they returned to port with their treasure, so many people came down with treasure fever that it might be said their voyage gave rise to what is now called the Golden Age of Piracy. Notorious figures of the era, such as Edward Teach (Blackbeard), "Calico" Jack Rackham, and Charles Vane raided the Florida wrecks throughout 1716.

By 1717, the pirates had expanded their operations, working out of their center of operations in the Bahamas to cover the entire Caribbean Sea and north along the American coastline all the way to Maine.

Would these men have congregated in the Bahamas, forming a notorious base of piratical activities, had they not been tempted by the loss of the Plate Fleet? No one knows.

In any event, other such attacks were conducted, some by privateers and others by out-and-out pirates. The Spanish finally abandoned their operations in 1718, but immense wealth still remained on the ocean floor. Some of the rotted hulks were clearly visible, protruding above water at low tide. For years to follow, ships sailing these waters would "fish" for treasure, and even to this day, folks carrying metal detectors walk the beaches, some finding treasure, indeed.

Gary Drayton, who rose to fame as the chief metal detector on the television series *The Curse of Oak Island*, dowsed this area regularly and recently displayed for viewers what he calls his "precious," the emerald ring he believes was part of the dowry of Spain's Queen Elizabeth.

By the way, she did finally consent to the marriage and managed to establish quite a reputation, especially after the death of her husband. But the emerald ring she demanded now has another home. It belongs to Mrs. Drayton, the "queen" of Gary's home.

As often happens, the story eventually faded from memory. But 250 years later, it was brought back into the headlines, and the curse began to work once more.

It is known that three ships were never found by the Spaniards. General Juan Esteban de Ubilla's frigate, the *Santa Rita y Animas*, bought in Havana on July 15, 1715, was one of them. Two ships believed to have been part of the *Flota de Tierra Firme*, the *El Señor San Miguel* and the French *El Ciervo*, were the others. All three carried immense wealth down to the bottom with them.

No one can identify for sure which rotting hulk belongs to which name on the manifest back in Cuba, but it is known that more are out there, and treasure still washes up on the beaches from Vero Beach to Cape Canaveral. That's enough to keep real treasure seekers going, which explains why salvage operations sparked new flames in the 1950s.

Technology had made great strides by then, so when Kip Wagner, a building contractor from Ohio, discovered a Spanish coin worth eight *reales* on a beach near Sebastian Inlet, Florida, he spent several months combing the beaches between Sebastian and Wabasso on Florida's east coast. He managed to find and uncover the original Spanish salvage camp. Along the way, he discovered other coins and artifacts.

He even discovered the underwater hulk of the *Capitana*, another nearby wreck, across from the Sebastian River, then called the Ays River.

Wagner obtained a salvage permit from the state of Florida, and in 1961, along with his friend Dr. Kip Kelso, organized the

The Florida counties of St. Lucie, Martin, and Indian River (shown dark on the map) are part of the Treasure Coast where coins and other objects from the wrecks still sometimes appear.

Real Eight Corporation, also known as the Real 8 Company. He tells his story, and a lot more about the 1715 tragedy, in his book *Pieces of Eight*.

Every treasure worth its salt has at least one treasure map, and the lost treasure from the 1715 fleet is no exception. In 1781, a map claiming to be drafted by Bernard Romans in 1774 shows the Sebastian River in Florida with the following notation: "Opposite this River, perished the Admiral commanding the Plate Fleet 1715, the rest of the Fleet 14 in number. Between this & ye Bleech Yard." This note is accompanied by the place name "El Palmar" and features a drawing consisting of five palm trees.

The bulk of the remaining treasure to be found from the Plate Fleet of 1715 is probably beyond the reach of most casual treasure seekers, but the fact that some of it still occasionally washes up on the shores of Florida's "Treasure Coast" after a storm is enough to keep the hopes of seekers alive. Hurricanes, the "evil spirits of the wind," are a yearly reminder of the curse that plagued both the fleet and the fortunes of those who came under the spell of the gold it carried. Greed might very well be punished by spiritual forces that stand in opposition to human avarice. Is the curse still active, and does it shroud the lives of those who pursue lost treasure?

Every seeker must search their own motives to determine the answer to that question.

Caves &
Mines

Daniel Boone and the Dry Indian

Perhaps no one in modern times has done more to excite the popular imagination about the wonders of the caves of Indiana and Kentucky than Roger Edwin Turpen. Most everyone has probably heard about Mammoth Cave in Kentucky, the world's longest limestone labyrinth cave system, but, despite aggressive advertising, relatively few people have taken advantage of exploring the caves and caverns that lie beneath the feet of those who hike the area of southern Indiana. Turpen's documentaries are changing that. Now, thanks to television, even armchair enthusiasts are growing in number.

The area from Wyandotte Caves, north of Laconia, in Boone County, Indiana, population 50, continuing south across the Ohio River to Kentucky, is home to some of the most historic caves in the Midwest.

Squire Boone, brother of the famous Daniel Boone, is buried in one of them. While being chased by Indians, he is said to have remembered a cave he and his famous brother had discovered years earlier. He swung down into the cave on a sturdy hanging vine and hid there until his pursuers departed. Believing that the cave saved his life, he chose the spot for his burial place. Visitors today still visit the site.

Recently, explorers with the Indiana Speleological Survey (ISS) pushed the limits of endurance with a 17-hour trip through the Corydon Binkley Cave system. When they arrived back on the surface, they discovered that they had traveled a little more than 40 miles. That's not nearly as long as the 400 explored miles of Mammoth Cave, but it's still extremely impressive. This single group of cavers had discovered Indiana's longest cave system, now recognized as the 11th longest in the United States.

Roger Turpen has begun to introduce this whole system to an even larger public. In his beautifully photographed film *The Legend of the Ohio River Indian Cave (Southern Indiana)* (see Bibliography), he tells a story about the legendary Daniel Boone. Supposedly, in the late 1700s, Boone reported seeing an Indian in Kentucky on the banks of the Ohio River. A short while later, he saw the same Indian on the Indiana shore.

This in itself doesn't warrant much attention. Indiana means "the place of the Indians," so seeing an Indian, especially in the time of Daniel Boone, was not an extraordinary achievement, and the fact that at some points along this stretch, the Ohio River is so narrow that a good golfer with a seven iron could easily carry the opposite bank doesn't merit attention, either.

What struck Daniel's attention was that the man was completely dry, with no evidence of a canoe or watercraft of any kind in sight.

When questioned, the Indian replied that a secret cave, known only to the Shawnee, ran completely under the river and had been used by his people for centuries.

To date, no one has ever found it, but an ancient marker might still be around to show the way for those who recognize the signs.

It's time to take a brief detour into the mysterious realm of marker trees. Maybe it will help treasure seekers on future quests.

Marker trees, or bent trees, are trees that may have been trained to purposely grow in such a way so as to point to specific

The entrance to the Wyandotte Caves in Indiana seems humble enough, but inside are over nine miles of passageways on five different levels.

Frontiersman and
explorer Daniel Boone
was a folk hero for
helping to open up the
Kentucky wilderness to
settlers.

locations. You may have come across examples if you spend any
time walking in the woods. A tree will grow straight up out of
the ground until, about 4 or 5 feet up from its roots, it takes a
sudden turn to run parallel to the ground before turning again
to grow straight up once more.

The theory of such marker trees, authenticated by indigenous people who grew up in the tradition, is that their ancestors
trained young saplings in this way to point to significant sites
such as graves, holy places, bends in a trail, or caves.

Some scoff at the idea. They point out, for instance, that
Europe, China, and Siberia have their share of such trees that
have been shaped by natural means, and no such tradition exists
there.

It's true that natural forces do shape trees. Those who believe in the tradition of marker trees don't insist that every bent
tree is a marker tree, but they insist that some of them are.

A number of years ago, I came across the work of Don
Wells, who might be one of the foremost American authorities
on the subject of bent marker trees. Besides writing books (see
Further Reading in the back of this book) and articles on the
subject, he publishes a newsletter that keeps followers abreast
of his work. He has identified hundreds of such trees, photographed them, and, when given permission by property owners,
sometimes even reveals their location.

I have such a tree on my property. It points to a mysterious
rock pile where no such pile should exist because it's on a side
hill above a swamp. Agriculture never existed here that would
have necessitated clearing land, and it's an inconvenient place to
store rocks for future use.

I was curious about it and contacted Don. He was kind enough to invite me to join him in a research trip he was taking in my area. When he told me that he explores these areas with his dowsing rods seeking earth energy hotspots, I was hooked. Having written a successful book on the subject, I jumped at the chance to pick up my dowsing rods and join him.

Huge gullies and washouts still dot the now forested landscape to illustrate the catastrophic results from destroying centuries-old, hard-won topsoil creation.

After a wonderful and fruitful day together, I invited him to bring his wife, Diane, to my place sometime soon for a morning of dowsing and research.

It wasn't long before they came to spend a day out in my woods. With their help, I discovered a lot of information that helped fill in the cracks about what I believe happened on my property long before Europeans arrived with their greedy tobacco and cotton fetishes that once caused this entire area to become a federally designated disaster area as tragic as the Dust Bowl in the Midwest. Huge gullies and washouts still dot the now forested landscape to illustrate the catastrophic results from destroying centuries-old, hard-won topsoil creation.

When we came in for lunch on my back porch, Don, Diane, and I spent a delightful afternoon sharing stories and experiences.

When I learned that the mysterious cave that runs under the Ohio River might have such an ancient marker tree pointing to it, I contacted Don right away. At the time, he was preparing a talk that he was scheduled to present at a gathering in Colorado, but he took time off from that project to look into my question.

Don Wells, who is also into dowsing, is an authority on the study of marker trees. Along with his wife, Diane, he is the author of *Mystery of the Trees*.

Although he has never visited the site, he said he plans to go someday if time and circumstances permit, but he was able to point me to one of Turpen's films, which shows a picture of the tree. It points directly to a cave opening, which has been explored and doesn't seem go under the Ohio River. That doesn't necessarily mean anything, however. Unexplored openings, sometimes disguised by natural or man-made rock walls, are frequent. The cave does point down toward the river, and it could connect with caves on the Kentucky side, so who knows for sure?

All this draws attention to other caves in the area and one in particular. The story is told in Turpen's film *Dark Silver: Legend of the Lost Southern Indiana Silver Mine*.

According to local sources, between 1810 and 1812, just prior to the last significant Indian Wars in Indiana, tensions ran high during an uneasy peace which existed between the Shawnee and the European white settlers. A few whites were trying hard to build cultural bridges rather than walls between the peoples, but it was becoming increasingly difficult to do so.

Indians had been trading with whites for some years, exchanging forest goods for the milling of their corn, but they were especially eager to obtain firearms. Although whites were reluctant to sell guns, sometimes the temptation was overwhelming because the Indians brought silver to trade. They refused to say where they got it.

One of those who was trying to reach out across racial barriers was a man by the name of Absolom Fields. He had lived near McBride's Bluff in what is now Martin County since at least 1807 and had forged a friendship with a band of Indians who lived near what was then called Indian Creek, a tributary of the White River.

He was awakened from sleep one night by two Shawnee, who told him they wanted to show him something.

Not knowing what to expect, he simply went along with their instructions. They placed a blindfold over his eyes, turned him around several times to disorient him, led him some distance, then placed him in a canoe.

The current was slight, so they could have been going either upstream or down. Fields couldn't tell which. Eventually, they grounded the craft and guided him a short distance along what felt like a trail. When they took off his blindfold, he found himself in a large cavern. Several Indians were there waiting for him—men, women, and children—so apparently, their intentions were peaceful. Absolom began to breathe a little easier.

They showed him a large amount of silver ore and some cast silver bars as well, which were about six inches long, two inches wide, and half an inch thick. They had apparently been cast in a mold.

Without explanation, they gave him three of the bars, then blindfolded him again and took him back to his cabin.

Needless to say, after the Indians moved west following the wars, he spent days trying to retrace the route to the hidden cave, but he could never find it again.

The closest he came was years later, when on a flatboat trip down the Ohio River to the Mississippi and then New Orleans, he met an Indian who had lived near McBride's Bluff.

"If white man only knew it, he could shoe horses as cheaply with silver as with iron," the Indian said.

Fields asked where the silver mine was but was met with typical Indian humor.

"You stand on Big Bluffs, look away to south over big bottom. Maybe it that way. Maybe not. Don't forget to look down under you. Maybe down there. Maybe not. White man never finds. He heap too big fool—digs till he most finds it and quits. Paleface never find."

Given the "Lone Ranger and Tonto" Hollywood dialogue, the conversation sounds a bit contrived. But stories circulated that symbols were chiseled on a large rock below the highest point in the Bluffs to indicate where the silver was hidden. Somewhere, it was said, you could find a half moon, a star, and a crawling snake with its head pointed toward the treasure cave.

It sounds far-fetched, but the fact remains that Absolom Fields kept the three silver bars. They remained in his family for years until one of his descendants finally cashed them in.

The rest of the silver, if it ever was there in the first place, remains hidden.

When the story eventually made its way to the ears of a state geologist who was surveying land in Harrison County, he decided to investigate. He deduced that the silver mine must have been located beneath the farm of Philip Blume, who worked land in Scott Township, just to the west of Indian Creek.

When he investigated the site, he found an old excavation that had been abandoned for years, but no silver was to be found.

Had someone found the fabled mine and dug it dry? Was this the site of an abandoned silver mine at all? Were the original miners digging for something else?

To this day, the questions remain unanswered, but that doesn't mean that people have stopped looking, for many other Indiana treasure stories exist to keep them occupied.

Josiah Hite, for instance, was a counterfeiter in the town of Charlestown in the 1800s. He was arrested but managed to escape and was never seen in the area again. Stories abound that he buried a cache of silver coins somewhere near his home, intending to return for them when things died down, but he never came back.

A group of ruthless criminals who operated throughout the Midwest both during and after the American Civil War was called the Reno Gang, or sometimes the Reno Brothers Gang, or the Jackson Thieves. They gained fame by pulling off the first three peacetime train robberies in U.S. history. Supposedly, they buried some of their loot in the vicinity of Little Goss Cave, near Greenville, about three miles off present-day Highway 150, near Route 335.

When the story eventually made its way to the ears of a state geologist who was surveying land in Harrison County, he decided to investigate.

If the stories are true, it would be a good hiding place. The cave has two entrances and three interior levels. From a lookout point above the lower entrance, one man with a rifle could hold off an army. Outlaws must have loved it.

During the gang's brief but brutal reign of terror, they accumulated a vast sum of stolen treasure. When the Pinkertons and local vigilantes finally closed in on them, none of them had spent much of it despite bribing the jurors they supposedly bought off during their court trials. What became of the rest? It very well could be hidden in a dead-end cave somewhere. The Little Goss Cave is as good a guess as anywhere.

Another cache of Civil War coins said to be worth around $5,000 is said to have been buried somewhere near what is now the George Rogers Clark National Historical Park by Brigadier General John Hunt Morgan, a Confederate cavalryman who gained the nickname "the Thunderbolt of the South." He led a troop of 2,000 men, who terrorized the countryside on both sides of the Ohio River.

Indiana was a Northern state with a lot of Southern sympathizers. In 1863, while the Battle of Gettysburg was being fought, those who identified with the North panicked when they heard the cry "Morgan's coming!" Southern sympathizers hung portraits of him in their homes.

Morgan and his troops rode through seven counties in southern Indiana. For six days, they looted homes and towns, cut telegraph lines, burned railroad bridges, and created fear and

John Hunt Morgan was a brigadier general in the Confederate army who was nicknamed "the Thunderbolt of the South" for his aggressive raids in Indiana and Ohio.

consternation. They became the Confederate force that penetrated the farthest north into Union territory during the Civil War.

Eventually, Morgan was hunted down and killed, but not before Governor Oliver P. Morton gathered gold deposits from Indianapolis banks and quickly transferred them to Chicago for safekeeping. Most of the men that Indiana could field for the war effort were off fighting, but Morton ordered church bells to be rung in Indianapolis to gather anyone who had a firearm of any kind. A day later, 20,000 men gathered to defend the capital, sleeping on the lawn of the State House. Martial law was declared, but Morgan was reported to be in several different locations.

Eventually, on July 8, 1863, only a week after Lee's disastrous battle at Gettysburg in Pennsylvania, Morgan camped five miles north of the Ohio River. By then, he must have been aware of how the tide of battle in the war had turned.

The next day saw the only "major" military action in Indiana during the war. What is now called the Battle of Corydon was fought a mile south of the former state capital, near what later became Old Indiana Route 135.

Morgan's men won a major victory in just half an hour, capturing 450 members of the Indiana Home Guard. He set them free after they promised not to fight again. Morgan then sacked Corydon, leaving that afternoon.

On July 10, Morgan continued his raids, stealing a large treasure. Eventually, he was forced to flee into Ohio, but it was not before he supposedly buried a good deal of his loot for safekeeping, to be retrieved, he thought, at a later date.

That date never came. Morgan was eventually arrested by Union brigadier general Edward Hobson and 4,000 cavalrymen.

Upon hearing that General Morgan was approaching Indianapolis, Governor Oliver P. Morton secretly took the gold deposits there and shipped them to Chicago.

Surprisingly, he and six of his raiders managed to tunnel into an underground airshaft, escaped, and rejoined the Confederate Army. But he was killed on September 4, 1864, in Greenville, Tennessee.

Three years later, the Indiana state treasurer received claims totaling $497,400 in damages caused by Morgan and his raiders.

Where was the money? No one knew for sure, but people still look around whenever they travel to the George Rogers Clark National Historical Park. After all, you never know what might turn up.

Rumors abound of other treasure to be found in the environs of southern Indiana. Gold is said to be buried near the scene of the Harris Farmhouse, now called Bear Farm. This area was a stop on the underground railroad, smuggling slaves north before the war.

Subordinates to Al Capone are thought to have hidden 2,000 cases of whiskey, worth about $300,000, in a cave near Michigan City. They were hunted down and killed before the whiskey could be found. Be careful if you go after this cache, however. The entryway of the cave was supposedly sealed with explosives to prevent anyone getting it.

Speaking of gangsters, mobster Jim Genna is believed to have buried a huge sum of money locked in a steel box underneath a pile of rocks in a pasture near State Road 6 near Bremen. Neither treasure hunters nor the FBI has found it yet.

A bank employee who embezzled roughly $95,000 in paper currency committed suicide after supposedly burying his fortune on a farm outside of Terre Haute.

A passenger train was robbed of $80,000 in coins, gold bullion, and paper currency in 1928. The robbers were caught and hung four days later, but they are believed to have hidden their stash somewhere near Marshfield, in Warren County.

On and on the stories go. You might get the idea that if you want to get rich quick, all you need to do is move to Indiana. Enough hiding places certainly exist, given the rich hunting grounds of unexplored limestone caves found in the vicinity. It's enough to stoke the rumor mill for a long time, and it all started when Daniel Boone saw a dry Indian across the Ohio River.

The Lost Dutchman Mine

The Superstition Mountains, located about 60 miles east of Phoenix, Arizona, are aptly named. Because of the curse of the Thunder God, even the Apache Indians avoided them, knowing full well that gold aplenty could be found in "them thar hills."

The Yavapai had villages within the area, however. Although often coupled with the Apache, sometimes even being confused with them due to the name Yavapai-Apache Nation that was placed upon the two tribes by white Europeans, the two nations are separate entities.

The Yavapai call themselves *Wipuhk'a'bah* and speak a language with Yuman roots. The Apache refer to themselves as *Dil'zhe'e* and speak an Athabaskan language. When they were

Superstition Mountain can be found about an hour's drive east of Phoenix, Arizona, and today is a popular place for hikers and rock climbers.

both defeated by the armies of the United States, they were forced to relocate first to the Rio Verde Reserve and then to San Carlos.

According to the legends, the Apache name for the Superstitions is "Wee-kit-sour-ah," which means "the rocks standing up." In Apache folklore, it is the place where all must pass after death. The mountains are a kind of purgatory. Warriors who are considered martyrs, giving their lives for the sake of the tribe, are said to be buried in a sacred area deep within the confines of the mountains.

The Yavapai and Apache are not the first to inhabit the area, however. Evidence seems to indicate that ancient cliff dwellings and caves show signs of former habitation. No one knows for sure who these people were. They may have been the ancestors of the Pima, Salado, or Hohokam. Did they have even earlier legends about the curse, legends that were inherited by the Indians who were in the area when the Spanish first showed up?

I will always remember an incident that happened to me when I lived in Arizona a little south of this location. I visited an archaeological dig that was investigating the site of an ancient Hohokam village. An archaeologist was getting ready to close up shop for the day when I greeted him, and we started a lively conversation about his work. Glancing down, he stooped over, scooped up a pottery shard with his shovel, and deposited it in my hand.

"You're the first person to hold this piece in your hand for more than 1,600 years," he said.

I was properly in awe when suddenly, out of a clear, blue sky without a cloud in sight, we heard the distant sound of thunder coming from the north.

We looked at each other, the scientist and the romantic, and both said at the same time, "Whoa!"

Was it the Thunder God? Of course not!

Most days, I believe that. But ...

The Yavapai tell stories about the "curse of the Thunder God" that are still very much in the minds of those who live in the area. Even those who don't believe in curses, however, are forced to face some pretty convincing statistics that sometimes strike fear into the hearts of those who venture into the mountains, and because legends place the famous Lost Dutchman Mine in this area, plenty of people do just that. The simple fact is that people disappear there more often than other places. When they do, their death is usually blamed on the curse of the Thunder God, who is protecting his territory.

In point of fact, the Superstition Wilderness Area, and specifically Superstition Mountain, is famous for the very violent thunderstorms they experience during the summer months. It's called the "monsoon season." When people die during these storms, it is only natural to believe that the Thunder God has struck again.

According to Apache legends, the Thunder God lives within Superstition Mountain and makes his presence known especially during the hot months of summer. For those who intrude upon his solitude, he sometimes places the curse of death on those who violate his sacred domain. He is protecting the gold that lies there, which he considers a sacred source of being, and he's been doing it for a long time.

Francisco Vázquez de Coronado attempted to search for it, but his men began turning up dead and mutilated. He was the one who gave the mountains their ominous name and was the first European to experience the curse.

> *Don Miguel Peralta allegedly found a vein of gold and worked the site until 1848 ... His party was ambushed by Apaches while carrying what turned out to be his last shipment of gold back to Mexico.*

During the 1840s, Don Miguel Peralta allegedly found a vein of gold and worked the site until 1848. According to legend, his party was ambushed by Apaches while carrying what turned out to be his last shipment of gold back to Mexico. Everyone except for a few family members, who managed to escape the trap, was killed. To this day, the area is known as the Massacre Grounds.

Gold was found strewn throughout the area, and the entrance to his mine was destroyed, but despite the danger, the region became a goal for those who sought to get rich quick.

Sometime between 1949 and 1956, a man stopped by the side of the road at Apache Junction in the Arizona desert and, quite by accident, discovered a group of stones on which were etched a sort of treasure map. These stones have been since named the Peralta Stones. Many have studied copies made from them, and a few have claimed to have deciphered them, but the location of the mine remains a mystery.

Although they are the subject of intense debate, it is known that such stone carvings were often used by the Spanish, who used coded symbols to point the way to their many mines and buried treasures. The land in question was granted to the Peralta family by the Spanish Crown for mining purposes, so it is entirely possible that the stones are authentic.

In later years, a descendant of Peralta even claimed to have found gold there.

Apache Junction is just to the west of Superstition Mountain in Maricopa County, where the mysterious Peralta Stones were uncovered.

Remember these Peralta Stones. They will become a key to other treasures as well, especially when we explore the mystery surrounding Montezuma's lost fortune.

The name that makes the area famous, however, is not Peralta but rather that of the Lost Dutchman. Not only has he been credited with the most well-known mystery in the lexicon of American treasure hunters, he is also responsible for the curse that protects his secret mine.

Jacob Walz, usually spelled Waltz, wasn't a "Dutchman" at all. He was from Germany and, therefore, a *Deutchman* to those who lived on the American frontier. That became the name by which he was known.

In the 1870s, the Dutchman began to show up at irregular intervals at nearby towns, paying for supplies with gold nuggets. This wasn't uncommon at the time, but the nuggets showed unusual purity. People began to talk.

It turns out that Waltz claimed to have discovered his claim with the aid of a Peralta descendant. He and his partner, Jacob Weiser, worked the mine for years, allegedly hiding their findings in caches throughout the Superstitions.

In the area of the Superstition Mountains, follow Peralta Trail (named after the Peralta Stones) and it will lead you to Weavers Needle.

Some believe that Waltz never found a mine at all. Some say he discovered the cache of gold hidden by Montezuma's followers, but that is a tale we will get to in a moment.

Most stories place the gold in the vicinity of Weavers Needle, an obvious landmark. Weiser was eventually killed by Apaches, although some say that Waltz himself did the deed in order to keep the riches for himself.

Twenty years later, Waltz began to suffer from poor health. He moved to Phoenix, where he died in 1891. But on his deathbed, he was said to have given the location of the mine to Julia Thomas, a neighbor who took care of him while he lay dying. Beneath his bed, according to legend, was found a box containing gold nuggets.

Thomas tried to find the mine herself, but neither she nor dozens of other seekers in the years that followed were able to locate it. Since then, many have died trying, furthering the legend of the curse.

In 1931, a treasure hunter named Adolph Ruth disappeared while searching for the mine. His skull was found two years later, along with a note which read *Veni, Vidi, Vici* ("I came, I saw, I

The grave of Jacob Waltz can be viewed at Pioneer & Military Memorial Park's Masonic Cemetery in Phoenix.

conquered"). This suggests that he might have had success, but no one knows for sure.

As late as 2012, a bellhop from Denver named Jesse Capen disappeared while searching for the lost mine. His body was eventually found three years later.

In 2015, a group of explorers who called themselves the Arcana Exploration claimed to have determined the location of the lost mine, but details remain elusive, and no official claims have been filed.

To this day, aside from the fame of the Oak Island treasure that has had the benefit of 12 seasons of television to help its popularity, the Lost Dutchman Mine remains the best-known cursed lost treasure trove in North America.

The Old Spanish Treasure Cave

Having looked at the journeys of Coronado and his search for the Seven Cities of Cibola, it's time to take up the saga of legends concerning the conquistadors who didn't go back to Mexico with him. As some stories have it, they stayed on, searching and looting as they went, until they came to a cave in what is now northwest Arkansas. Supposedly, a treasure worth $40 million in today's dollars is buried there.

If the stories are true, when Coronado turned back after his unsuccessful search for Cibola, some of his army liked the freedom they had found in looting, pillaging, and generally behaving in a manner civilized society denied them. They decided to keep going west through Texas, Oklahoma, and finally Arkansas. They had by then accumulated many gold coins, a few gold and silver bars, and lots of valuable artifacts they thought would enhance their position when they finally returned home.

The local population of Indians disagreed with their ideas and began to track them.

Eventually, as the Spanish approached what is now Gravette, Arkansas, they encountered a blizzard. Caves are plentiful in that region, and they found one that seemed to offer ideal protection. They discovered a large, roomlike cavern that came equipped with a natural chimney so they could build a fire and wait out the storm.

Fires, however, produce smoke, which was soon spotted by the pursuing Indians. Once that happened, the conquistadors were trapped and, as it turned out, doomed. In the attack, the party was slaughtered.

At least one, however, must have escaped and survived the journey back to Mexico because some 300 years later, in October 1885, an old Spaniard arrived in the area of the cave by stagecoach from Mexico. He carried three old maps made of parchment. They seemed to pinpoint a particular cave among the many that existed in that area. He began asking questions among the locals, seeking a cave with its opening partially concealed by a large, flat rock that had carvings pecked into it.

Such a rock was well known in the area, but no one had paid it much attention. When they guided the old man to it, he became very excited. The owner was more than happy to grant permission to move the rock, and when they did, they exposed a large cave.

The Spaniard was understood only with great difficulty because of his language and accent, but he soon managed to hire a team to begin excavating. They uncovered a large opening with many side passages, some of which were purposefully disguised. Whenever a decision was needed to figure out where to go next, he would consult his maps and then make decisions based on landmarks described in a language only he could read. His choices were always spot-on.

This went on for a year. Soon, winter set in, and the old man, because of his health, felt he needed to head south for warmer weather, but he left enough money and detailed instructions behind so that the work could continue in his absence. He cut the bark off a large tree to produce a smooth surface, on which he carved a map of where they had been and where he wanted them to go. Upon reaching a certain point on the map, the workers were told, they were to immediately write two letters, one to Madrid, Spain, and the other to Mexico. People would come, he said, who would guide the conclusion of the excavation.

The old man then gathered up his maps and left. He was never seen in that area again.

Thirty-five years later, his story was finally told. One of the locals who was familiar with the Arkansas story got a job in

Not far from Gravette, Arkansas, and just off Highway 59, you can find Old Spanish Treasure Cave, a tourist attraction that has been open since 1908, when it was purchased by George Dunbar. It offers tours and activities such as panning for gold.

Oklahoma, working in Paul's Valley. There, he met someone who casually asked about caves near the Missouri-Arkansas border. It seems as though an old Spaniard had stopped by that area three years earlier. He had a bad case of pneumonia and was forced to stay for a while, hoping to recover sufficiently to continue his journey. Although it was very difficult to understand much of what he said, he had some old maps with him and made it clear that if he were to die, they should be sent to Madrid, Spain.

The old man died, and for whatever reason, either lack of communication or general neglect, the maps were never sent. They seemed to be of an area in northwest Arkansas, but that's all anyone knew. Eventually, the maps were lost and the excavation abandoned. All that remained was a great story that could be told around a roaring fire on a winter evening.

Today, though, a cave called the Old Spanish Treasure Cave is visited every year by tourists, scouts, and school groups. Its temperature remains at a steady 60 degrees, give or take five degrees either way, so it remains open all year long. People marvel at the stalagmites and stalactites, columns, and other features that awe people regarding living caves everywhere, but this cave tells a story about conquistadors, Indians, old Spanish men, and mysterious maps. It definitely adds to the allure.

The large central chamber is called the Council Room and seems to feature a natural chimney. No treasure has ever been found there, but artifacts, including conquistador helmets, weapons, and armor, have. Could this be the place? Are the legends true?

The cave has been used by everyone from outlaws to Indians, so one would think any treasure would have been reported long ago, but because it has so many unexplored side tunnels and natural hiding places, that might not be the case. It has plenty of unexplored nooks and crannies.

Ownership of the cave has passed through many hands over the years. In 1908, it belonged to George Dunbar, who allegedly found some gold coins and a bracelet. In order to explore the cave further without onlookers, he opened a front company called the Sulphur Springs Cave Company. That gave him an open purpose, but privately, he had caught the gold curse. He was really looking for treasure. Whether or not he ever found any seems to be a mystery.

A local newspaper article from 1926 relates that serious excavation was going on at the time. A new owner named W. W. Knight from Kansas City hired a team of scientists to conduct a survey, but apparently, the newspaper never followed up on the story.

The Council Room is one of the more interesting chambers in the Old Spanish Treasure Cave. No gold has been found there in modern times, but there has been evidence of Spanish conquistadors.

Another possibility, however, might explain why the treasure, assuming it is really there, has never been found.

Paul and Tracy Linscott are the current owners of the cave. Although they run the place as a tourist attraction and tell the story of conquistadors, Indians, old Spaniards, and missing maps many times a day, they don't claim that a treasure exists there. They just hint at it.

But they have a few interesting add-ons to the local history. The couple has found a sword blade and a belt, but more than that, when they bought the property, the Spaniard's map tree was still there. Over the years, the carvings have succumbed to the ravages of time, and the tree has since been destroyed by a lightning strike, but Paul Linscott had photographed the tree before it happened.

Even more interesting, though, is the fact that recently a severe drought in the area drew down the water levels that cover part of the cave. Linscott was able to penetrate portions of the cave that had been underwater and never explored.

On one trip, he discovered symbols that looked like a candy cane and an eyeball with some "squiggly lines" above it. He interpreted this to mean that if you looked where the eye was looking, beneath the water, symbolized by the squiggly lines, you might see where the treasure was.

Following those directions, he found a small room with a long pool in it. In a crevasse in that room, he dug out clay and mud until he found some wood.

Then, apparently, the curse hit. It started to rain. As water poured into the cave, Linscott was forced to flee before escape became impossible.

Currently, he's waiting for another drought.

Linscott recently announced the opening of another tunnel he calls the Lost Miner's Tunnel. No one yet knows where that will lead.

Whatever the case, however, it appears that some treasure is yet to be found as well as historical confirmation of what, up until now, was only legend.

Mystery of the San Sabá Mine

When it comes to the existence and location of the San Sabá silver mine, legends abound. This version is probably the most popular.

In the middle of the 1700s, Indian rumors of deposits of a "white metal" near the San Sabá River reached the ears of Spanish officials in Texas. In 1756, Jacinto de Barrios y Jáuregui, the governor of Texas, sent an officer named Bernardo de Miranda y Flores to look into them.

Records show that 16 soldiers and six civilians left San Antonio de Béxar on February 17, returning on March 10 with three pounds of ore, which was sent off to Mexico City to be assayed. Officials at the mint ordered a bigger sample. This time, 30 mule loads were brought back and again transported to Mexico City.

Ruins of the Presidio de San Sabá (formerly known as the Presidio San Luis de las Amarillas) are still available to be seen in central Texas.

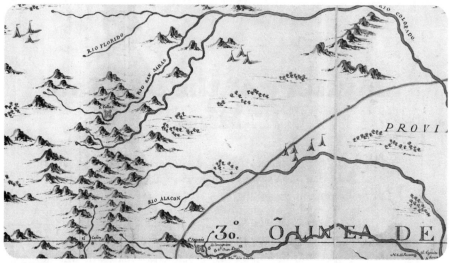

A 1769 map shows San Sabá in relation to Apache populations and, to the south, Spanish towns.

As a result of this second trip, the Spanish decided to build the Presidio San Luis de las Amarillas in 1756, near present-day Menard, Texas. A presidio is basically a fort housing Spanish troops. They followed that up with the Mission Santa Cruz de San Sabá in 1757. Both were located near the San Sabá River. As was almost always the case, such projects were attributed to missionary work, but ever since the Cortés invasion, few were fooled by this excuse.

The samples the expeditions brought back were called *almagre*, which is a red-colored earth that is often referred to as red ochre. It is created when alluvial deposits of red granite are weathered, oxidizing any iron or hematite. This gives the deposits a reddish appearance, but silver is often found in this type of soil.

The region where these *almagres* were found were said to be located about 75 miles northwest of San Antonio. What this meant was that it wasn't practical to send ore all the way to Mexico City for smelting, so it was decided to set up smelters on-site and produce silver bars.

What was still called a mission to the Apache Indians now included two full-blown mine sites with smelters. Needless to say, this stretched resources a bit. Supporting two mining camps was beyond the budget of most missions.

To make matters worse for the Spanish, the Apache tribe in the immediate vicinity was not really interested in converting to Christianity. They had only aligned with the Spanish to protect themselves from the Comanche, who had been outfitted by the French with guns and horses. Both tribes claimed this land as their own.

On March 16, 1758, 2,000 Comanches sacked and burned Mission Santa Cruz de San Sabá. The Spanish were forced to leave.

Little did they know at the time that this moment in history marked a turning point in the Spanish involvement in what is today Texas. This was the first and, as it turns out, only time that a mission was completely destroyed. It was also the first time the Spanish found themselves battling Native Americans who were armed with guns and mounted on horses. The Spanish were used to being outnumbered, but they could plan on defeating a much larger force because of their firepower and battle tactics. Spears, bows, and arrows were no match for muskets. But after this defeat, the Spanish no longer felt safe in Texas.

Legends were told about a rich deposit of silver, but no one felt brave enough to enter the area and check it out. The Comanche were fierce warriors, and it wasn't worth the risk.

Time went by and the exact location was forgotten, but the legends lived on.

The first to act on them was Stephen F. Austin. His family had owned a lead mine in Missouri, so on his first visit to Texas, when he learned from Erasmo Seguín, his guide, about possible silver deposits, he was immediately interested.

Later, as Austin's political star rose and he wanted to entice settlers to his new colony, he included on his 1829 map of Texas

A 1758 painting by Mexican artist José de Páez depicting the sacking and burning of Mission Santa Cruz de San Sabá by the Comanches.

the location he thought might have been the place the old Spanish mine had been. He was guessing, of course, but it made for great marketing.

In 1836, his cousin, Mary Austin Holley, wrote a book about Texas, claiming that "tradition says that a silver mine on the San Sabá River was successfully wrought many years ago, but the prosecution of it was arrested by the Indians, who cut off the workmen."

That fanned the flame a bit more, and one person who picked up on it was Jim Bowie. Yes, *that* Jim Bowie.

Bowie's public life was sandwiched between two famous fights. The first was on a sandbar in 1827, when he defended himself with the knife that would forever after bear his name. The second was when he died at the Alamo alongside Davy Crockett and William Travis in 1836. In the meantime, he took some time off to search for the San Sabá Mine. That involved a fight as well, this time with a large force of Indians in 1831, but his adventure became so noteworthy that San Sabá is sometimes called the Lost Bowie Mine.

Like almost everything else in his life, this episode is shrouded in mystery, but all the events just mentioned are, in a kind of weird way, connected.

Let's start with the sandbar fight that made him famous.

It began as a duel, to be fought on September 19, 1827, just north of Natchez, Mississippi, on a sandbar in the Mississippi River, and it really shouldn't have involved Bowie at all.

Samuel Levi Wells III and Dr. Thomas Maddox had issues. They decided to solve them by fighting a duel. Bowie agreed to be Wells's second. His job, according to the rules of combat followed in those days, was simply to ensure that proper etiquette was followed.

The famous Jim Bowie—known for the knife named after him and his contributions to the Texas Revolution—led an unsuccessful expedition to find the lost San Sabá mine.

Attending as spectators were Major George McWhorter and General Samuel Cuny, who supported Wells, and Major Norris Wright, Colonel Robert Crain, and brothers Carey and Alfred Blanchard for Maddox.

There were other spectators as well, who had just gathered for the show.

At the first exchange of bullets, nobody was killed, but things quickly got out of hand. From the crowd, who were just supposed to watch, Crain, for some reason, fired at Cuny. Bowie, in retaliation, shot at Crain but missed. Norris then shot Bowie in the chest, but Bowie was far from finished. Drawing his soon-to-be-famous knife, he began to chase after Wright. The Blanchard brothers shot Bowie again, one of them hitting him in the thigh, while both Wright and Alfred Blanchard shot him as well.

Bowie, however, managed to fight on. Armed now with only his knife, he severely wounded both Wright and Blanchard. The Blanchard brothers both decided that discretion was the better part of valor and ran, but Cary was shot and wounded by Major McWhorter as he fled the scene.

The whole brawl took less than 10 minutes. General Samuel Cuny and Major Norris Wright were dead, and Bowie and Cary Blanchard were wounded. Neither of the principles who were there to duel with each other suffered a scratch, but the spectators who survived were so impressed with Bowie's "big butcher knife" that his fame, and that of his knife, was spread abroad. By the time he recovered from his wounds, he was famous as the South's most feared knife fighter, and men began to ask their local blacksmith to make them a "Bowie knife." Nine years later, when he died at the Alamo, he had it in his hand, at least according to Walt Disney and the thousands of kids who watched his version of the battle back in the 1950s.

Bowie eventually recovered from his wounds but began a series of activities that sent him into a downward economic spiral. He engaged in some questionable land deals that soon caught up with him. He and his brother Rezin decided it best to move to Texas, which was then controlled by Mexico. He was given Mexican citizenship under the name Don Santiago Bouie. Part of his deal with Mexico was that he was to build an agricultural mill in San Antonio.

Soon after that, he became engaged to the daughter of a government official named Juan Martín de Veramendi, but before the official marriage could take place, a substantial dowry was required. This created a problem. Most of Bowie's wealth was tied up in the suspicious land deals for which he had been forced to leave the States. In other words, he was just about broke, so he approached his future father-in-law for a loan.

Like many Americans who were beginning to move to Texas, Bowie wanted to acquire vast tracks of land in the newly developed region. Had he been able to hold on for a few years, he might have done it. But fate has a way of nudging history aside from time to time.

In short, Bowie needed some fast cash. Since his father-in-law was connected to the Mexican government, he would have been able to access information about Spanish silver mines in the area. Certainly, the San Sabá Mine would have been near the top of the list, but the Comanche still controlled the area.

Nevertheless, his father-in-law agreed to finance an expedition of exploration to search for evidence of minerals, especially the silver, which was still on everyone's mind. Bowie put together a crew of friends, including his brother Rezin, and headed north on a treasure hunt.

From the record, it appears that Rezin might have had some inside information about the lost mine. He had been given an oar sample that assayed well, and Jim and Rezin planned to put together an outfit to establish a mine.

The warring Comanche, however, were justifiably angry that white explorers were intruding on their territory. Knowing an attack was coming, Bowie's party raced to get to what they later called abandoned "houses" on the San Sabá River. This might have been the old, abandoned presidio built by the Mexican government back in 1756.

Unfortunately, they couldn't find any trace of their target, so they were forced to head north of the San Sabá and throw up a makeshift fort.

Jim Bowie's brother, Rezin, was a land speculator and also founded a sugar mill in Lousiana with Jim and took credit for inventing the famous Bowie knife. He accompanied his brother on the search for the mine.

They finished their work just in time. The very next day, the Comanche attacked. The battle became well known, and Bowie's partners managed to survive while suffering only one death and a few injuries.

Deciding to rest after the Indians retreated, they ventured forth in small parties and eventually found the remains of the old presidio along with what might have been the old smelting pits.

When they recovered sufficiently from the battle, they made their way back to San Antonio, arriving home soon after they had all been given up for dead. They reported that they had not been able to find the mine nor the minerals.

In 1832, Bowie gathered a force of volunteers to go back north, saying he wanted to punish the Comanche who had attacked them and killed one of his followers. At least, that was the official reason for the trek. Most people figured he wanted another chance to find the San Sabá Mine.

Again, he was unsuccessful, although he did report that the mine had probably been filled in and hidden by natives to keep foreigners from moving to the area.

That's the official story as it appears in the records of what is now the state of Texas, but problems are associated with that account.

💰 First: According to Bowie's logs, the group, especially handpicked because of their experience, took at least a week longer to get to the presidio than it should have. Its general location was known to be north and east of San Antonio. What had they been doing during this time? Had they detoured through the old Los Almagres Mine, located some 75 miles to the northwest? Had they found the silver rumored to be there, already smelted into silver bars, and then hidden it for later retrieval? The split-per-man certainly would have been more profitable if the government authorities didn't get their hands on it. Bowie and his men may have been Mexican citizens, but, as history would soon prove, they were Americans through and through. They might have felt under no obligation to share with what they considered to be a foreign country whose time was short anyway.

💰 Second: Where exactly did the famous fight take place? They claimed to have built their makeshift fort in a grove of trees, but any evidence of its location would

This illustration, published in an 1833 issue of the *Saturday Evening Post,* depicts what Rezin Bowie said happened in their battle with the Comanche. The only problem is that there is conflicting evidence and testimony about where the fight occurred.

soon have been weathered away. Had they even been near the old presidio at all, or was that a fabrication hatched to cover up where their first expedition had been? In other words, were they really after the San Sabá Mine all along and simply wanted to deceive their sponsors?

The entire area was controlled by the Comanche for the next 10 years. If the Bowie expedition had really found the old cache of silver bars and hidden them away, their secret died with them, probably at the Alamo.

All this is, of course, conjecture bordering on conspiracy, but some evidence still whets the appetite of those who believe the silver from San Sabá is still out there.

In 1936, for instance, the state of Texas officially decreed that Bowie's famous battle with the Comanche took place in McColloch County on Calf Creek. Archaeologists discovered some artifacts, and the local residents claim to have found many arrowheads and lead bullets when they gathered firewood there.

The problem is that this location is almost 20 miles away from where Rezin Bowie and Caiaphas Ham, one of the people on the Bowie expedition, said the battle took place.

Both witnesses also said they buried some things at their campsite to protect them from Indians should they lose the coming battle, but what did they bury? No one knows.

Bowie was not the last to look for the mysterious San Sabá Mine. Once the most famous of lost mines, it seemed to melt away from popular interest until it was recently featured in an episode of The History Channel's *Beyond Oak Island*, which quickly brought it back to folks' attention. But that doesn't mean that everyone forgot about it. Quietly, some have devoted a lot of their time and energy to finding it.

In his 1930 book *Coronado's Children*, J. Frank Dobie talks about the time back in 1868, when Wiley Stroud, Greenberry Ezell, and a Colonel Dixon obtained a Mexican map that pointed them from an old Spanish fort, presumably the original presidio, to the San Sabá Mine. There, they found a quantity of silver bars.

As is often case, their story was that they were not able to excavate it but planned to return. Years later, the mine flooded, and it took more than 20 years to pump the water out.

Thus it went, with similar stories surfacing from then until 1990. Colorful characters searched and failed, sometimes dying under mysterious circumstances. My personal favorite is Wenonah Learn, a former pet shop owner who became a "vaudeville rattlesnake dancer," whatever that is. If Wenonah died, it probably wasn't from the gold curse.

Every so often, new locations arise based on recently uncovered evidence. The problem is that even though the original Spanish presidio and mission might be found, mule pack trains hauling that much silver must have been seen and noted, and no historical records indicate that that was the case. Also, the San Sabá Mine and Los Almagres pits are often confused. Which one actually held the silver bars, if they were ever cast in the first place?

No, this story lives on in popular imagination because of its unique cast of characters. Spanish missions, Apache and Comanche Indians, and Jim Bowie are hard to beat. Plus, we're talking Texas here. The bigger the tale, the better!

Treasures of Kings

Montezuma's Revenge

The missing gold of Montezuma: the Aztecs buried it, the Utes protected it, the Spanish killed for it, and the Mormons looted it. At least, that's the common story. To this day, people die looking for it. Is it still out there? And is the curse still working?

On November 18, 1519, Spanish conquistadors under the command of Hernán Cortés entered the Aztec capital of Tenochtitlan, now Mexico City, overthrowing indigenous control and imprisoning Montezuma, the ruler of the empire.

Cortés had sailed east from Cuba before marching his soldiers overland from Veracruz. Despite what church leaders wrote about missionary endeavors, their objective was gold and riches. With the capture of Tenochtitlan, their objectives were realized almost beyond belief. The amount of gold they discovered surmounted their wildest dreams.

But avarice is fueled by the word "more." The amount of riches bestowed upon them by Montezuma, who hoped to buy

The Aztec capital of Tenochtitlan was located on an island in the middle of Lake Texcoco. Today, that lake has long been drained, and the ruins of Tenochtitlan are to be found in the center of Mexico City.

One of the carvings of Quetzalcoatl gracing the pyramid at the Teotihuacan ruins.

the Spanish invaders off, didn't satisfy, it merely inflamed. Cortés wanted more.

The reason his military objectives were at first so easily obtained was because of a historical mystery that he didn't, at least at the time, understand. Mesoamerican cultures have different versions of this story, but the common understanding goes something like this.

Quetzalcoatl, the "feathered serpent," was chief god of the Aztec religious system. He was represented by Venus, the solar light and morning star.

His twin brother, Xoloti, was the evening star.

In Catholic biblical imagery, Venus is called the "morning star." According to Isaiah 14:12, however, the "morning" star of light became a "fallen" star of darkness: "How art thou fallen from heaven, O Lucifer, son of the morning! How art thou cut down to the ground, which didst weaken the nations!"

In other words, the mixture of Jesus and Lucifer, good and evil, was about to come into fruition in the persons of Quetzalcoatl and Cortés.

According to many historians, Quetzalcoatl, the "feathered serpent" or "plumed serpent" whom many Mesoamerican peoples claim was their ancestor, was an *hombre blanco*, a white man, with a flowing beard. He condemned sacrifices that polluted the people. He taught them how to use proper cooking fires and showed them how to "live together as husband and wife." He arrived from the sea "in a boat that moved without paddles" and "taught the people to live in peace." Under different names, he is found in Olmec, Maya, and Inca oral history as well.

Quetzalcoatl was thought to be the inventor of books and calendars. He was the one who had given them maize, or corn. In some religious systems, he had become the symbol of death and resurrection.

If all that didn't give him enough to do, he was also related to the gods of wind, dawn, merchants, arts, and crafts. He was the patron god of learning and knowledge. He went to the underworld and created humankind in this, the fifth, or present-day, world.

Wind, fire, and earthquakes had destroyed humankind in the previous worlds. According to Aztec legend, the destruction came about because their inhabitants did not worship the gods.

Because of the jealous impulses of indigenous priests, who felt threatened by Quetzalcoatl's success as a religious leader, he was eventually forced to sail away "toward the rising sun."

But he left a final message: "I'll be back."

According to some scholars who are members of the Church of Jesus Christ of Latter-day Saints, Quetzalcoatl was the resurrected Jesus Christ, although this is not the official doctrine of the church. LDS doctrine simply teaches that after his resurrection in Jerusalem, Jesus appeared in the New World, carrying on the ministry he had begun in Jerusalem, but it's hard not to paint Quetzalcoatl into this picture.

According to the Mormon story, the "good guys" who followed his teachings soon found themselves opposed by the

In the Book of Mormon, Joseph Smith receives golden plates from the Angel Moroni. The plates had text that Smith later translated into the Mormon book.

"bad guys" who were happy with the old ways. Eventually, the final battle between the two warring factions ended in a fierce struggle all the way up north on a plain below Hill Cumorah in New York State. There were buried the golden plates, later discovered and translated by Joseph Smith, who recorded the whole saga. You can read his translation for yourself in what is now called the Book of Mormon.

But before we go on, think about those golden plates. Where did the gold on which the story was etched come from? Could they have been part of Montezuma's lost treasure, carried all this way by his ancestors?

Or, as an alternative, it is thought that during the Utah War of 1857, Mormon leaders hid a large treasure near an old Spanish road where it crossed the Santa Clara River, just a few miles southwest of St. George in Washington County. Brigham Young is also said to have ordered gold treasure to be hidden away in Bloomington Cave, which is the fifth-largest cave system in Utah. Where did all this treasure come from? Had Mormons discovered the Aztec stash after they settled in Utah?

Either way, the church is connected in some way to the Aztec treasure tale.

Many other stories exist about Quetzalcoatl. Some believe that he was a survivor of the great cataclysm that destroyed Atlantis and that he was a member of a small group of missionaries from that civilization who dispersed around the world to spread the forgotten wisdom of a lost, advanced culture. Some of them went to Egypt and Turkey. Quetzalcoatl journeyed to Mesoamerica.

Others claim that his followers produced the Mound Building cultures of the Ohio Valley.

Still others believe the whole story to be an Aztec myth.

At any rate, when Montezuma saw a bearded man with advanced technology sailing to his land in "a boat that moved without paddles," it was the equivalent of the Christian return of Jesus Christ. Cortés was welcomed as the second coming of their long-lost divine benefactor.

But he soon proved himself to be far different from the peace-loving Quetzalcoatl. If Quetzalcoatl was considered to be the "morning star" of light, Cortés would be the "star of darkness" that fell from heaven, bringing death and destruction with it. Seven months later, on June 30, 1520, Montezuma was dead, and angry crowds had attacked the Spanish conquistadors.

The Spanish had the advantage of having greater firepower, horses, and defensive battle gear, but they were hopelessly outnumbered. Their only option was to retreat and flee the city.

Cortés and the Spaniards teamed up with the Tlaxcala people to lay siege to and conquer the Aztec capital of Tenochtitlan in 1521. But although Cortés gained the city, he lost the treasure it was said to contain.

Attacked on all sides under a constant bombardment of rocks and spears, they were forced to leave their treasure behind, littering their escape route with gold and silver they had stolen from Montezuma's palace. Many of them died, but Cortés escaped with one thought foremost in his head: "I'll be back!"

A year later, on August 13, 1521, he returned in force. He had rebuilt his army and recruited a large number of Tlaxcala indigenous fighters who were enemies of the Aztec. With this army behind him, he recaptured the city, expecting to reclaim the gold he had briefly possessed in such abundance.

It was gone, along with many of the Aztec people.

Cortés commanded his men to search every cave, hole, lake, pond, and potential hiding place, but the treasure and gold they had abandoned during their retreat was nowhere to be found.

The people who remained now had a new emperor named Cuauhtémoc, who was captured before he could flee the city. He and his closest courtiers were tortured to learn where the treasure had gone, but the best Cortés could find was a few baskets of minor gold items and trinkets.

As it turned out, Cuauhtémoc and his court, deciding to stay rather than leave, had not been trusted any further by the people after Montezuma's death. Cuauhtémoc had forfeited the trust of the old order of priests and was kept in the dark about where the people were going when they fled. As a result, all Cortés was able to obtain was a direction. It had been "taken north."

Those words taunted treasure seekers for the next 800 years.

The treasure had been there: tons of gold, silver, and sacred religious objects that symbolized a great civilization. That was a known fact. Now, it was gone. That, too, was a known fact.

That leaves two big questions:

- 💰 Where had it come from?
- 💰 Where had it gone?

Let's take them one at a time.

To tackle the first question, and maybe even the second, we need to take a short detour through Aztec history.

About 1,800 years ago, a group of people from the north began to settle in what is now called the Valley of Mexico. They were a Nahuatl-speaking culture, who soon began to build an extensive system of canals and dikes that were needed to control water levels for agriculture.

We call them Aztec, a name derived from the word *Aztlán*, which means "White Land," the "home of the seven caves." This might refer to their ancestral homeland. We don't know where it was for sure, but many anthropologists believe it to be in what is now northern Mexico. Others place it much farther to the north, but we'll get to that in a minute.

By 1428, Itzcoatl, their ruler, allied his people with Tlacopan and Texcoco, forming what is called the Triple Alliance, which controlled the nation until the arrival of the Spanish in 1519.

That's what is written in most history books, but it's not what you'll hear if you talk to native Aztec historians. Their story is much richer, a lot more intriguing, and takes us back to ancient times.

A page from the Aubin Tonalámatl, the early 17th-century Aztec manuscript that relates the history of these people. It is now preserved at the National Institute of Anthropology and History in Mexico City.

The *Tonalámatl of the Aubin Collection* (or *Aubin Tonalámatl*), more commonly referred to as the *Aubin Codex*, reveals quite a different tale than what is commonly found in history books. In pictures and texts, it outlines a migration story that traces the Aztec nation all the way back to its roots in the almost mythical Aztlán and concludes in 1608, after the Spanish invasion.

Surviving texts are written on European paper, so they are undoubtedly copies made by Spanish translators, a few of whom secretly wanted to retain whatever they could of Aztec tradition after their church had burned everything else of value. Still, the language used is alphabetic Nahuatl, a transliterated Aztec text, so the translators had obviously gone to the trouble of learning the language in order to record the story as accurately as possible. Presumably, they received it right from the lips of Aztec elders.

According to the codex, the Aztecs believed that their ancestors came from the north but not northern Mexico. It was someplace farther away than that, a land of red rocks that gave birth to four rivers.

Some scholars place the location near Phoenix, Arizona, but that's just a guess. It really doesn't connect all the dots of the text. Red rocks are scarce by the time you get to Phoenix. But if you continue farther north, you will come to the Four Corners country, the junction of Utah, Colorado, Arizona, and New Mexico. This area is right in the heart of the Canyon Lands.

Cecilio Orozco of California State University and Alfonso Rivas-Salmon, an anthropologist at the Universidad Autonoma de Guadalajara, believe this to be the mythical Aztec homeland. The "four rivers" refer to the Green River, the upper Colorado River, and the San Juan River, which merge to become the lower Colorado River.

V. G. Nair, in his book *Buddhism in America before Columbus,* relates the story of a priest named Quatu Zacca. He lived such a long life in a small house on an island in the Colorado River that the natives revered him as a god, entrusted to care over an ancient cave going back to the time of the ancestors of the Aztecs. He was appointed the Watcher, who would preserve the place until they returned to renew their empire. In this story, we encounter some native mythology that might confirm the Aztec legend.

When Orozco and Rivas-Salmon went into the field to inspect the area, they discovered ancient paintings and pictographs on the canyon walls of Utah that are strikingly similar to symbols found on surviving Aztec calendars, but those samples of Barrier Canyon-Style Rock Art date back well before the

Utah is home to a number of sites where native peoples have left behind petrographs. Some believe that the ancestors of the Aztecs were among those whose stories are written on these rocks.

1200s. They go back in time to at least 502 B.C.E. and maybe quite a bit before that.

In other words, if the Aztecs settled in Mexico 1,800 years ago, their migration took some seven centuries to complete.

In his book *The Book of the Sun*, Professor Orozco states it very succinctly: "Utah is sitting on a treasure, a missing link in the prehistory of man in this hemisphere. It's right there on the canyon walls. Utah is the home of Quetzalcoatl."

Most Utah archaeologists reject his findings. If they were to accept them, they would be forced to throw out what is commonly believed by accredited experts, most of whom are academics of European ancestry, not Aztec elders.

To make matters even more complicated, Orozco believes that the Utah rock art reveals a connection to the four- and eight-year cycles of the planet Venus. Venus is often recognized in mythology as representing duality because it is both the morning and evening star. It fits in perfectly with the opposing history of Quetzalcoatl and Cortés.

The legends reveal that the ancestors of the Aztecs were forced from their homeland by what they called a "rain of fire." This cataclysmic event prompted a series of migrations. The people moved south to escape tumultuous conditions, believing they were led by spirit guides to travel until they found an eagle fighting a serpent on a "barbed tree," perhaps a cactus. When they did, indeed, come across this exact sign, they settled down to build their capital city, called Tenochtitlan.

The modern Mexican flag features this event. The place where they settled is now Mexico City.

This raises some interesting questions. What if, like so many myths, a kernel of truth is at the bottom of it all?

Take, for instance, the "rain of fire" that caused the initial migration. What was it?

Some anthropologists who think outside the box associate it with what is now called the Younger Dryas Impact Event. Some 12,800 years ago, a segmented comet rained down fire on Earth from North America to Siberia, bringing on the Younger Dryas Ice Age, which brought about the end of megafauna all over Earth as well as the paleolithic Clovis culture.

If this is the event they meant, the Aztecs are far more ancient than traditionally believed.

Think of it this way. Aztec astronomy is noted by its intricate use of calendars. This was a skill they attributed to Quetzalcoatl, who is thought by some to be a survivor of a catastrophic event such as a "rain of fire" on Earth. Did this "rain of fire," which prompted the great migration, coincide with the event that brought about the legend of Atlantis? Is it all connected?

This theory doesn't sit well with academics. The Anasazi and Fremont cultures of the American Southwest are known for their accurate knowledge of the heavens, but here is evidence that the Aztecs may have preceded them by thousands of years.

Academic prejudice aside, two obstacles to doing research in this area are evident.

First of all, the comet destroyed much of the traces of any early civilization that might have existed. It destroyed the Clovis Culture, for instance. This is a known fact. Could these people from Aztlán be survivors of the Younger Dryas Impact Event, as was Quetzalcoatl himself? The Aztecs would have been more primitive than the civilization of Quetzalcoatl. Indeed, they were probably Clovis people who still worked with stone implements. But if a more advanced civilization existed simultaneously with them, as more and more experts are beginning to suspect, this reinforces the idea that Quetzalcoatl was a missionary of sorts, who went forth following the cataclysm to spread the rudiments of an old knowledge, thereby prompting a new beginning for a renewed civilization.

The remains of the supernova that exploded around 1054 C.E. left behind what we now call the Crab Nebula.

Most academics reject this hypothesis. They speculate that the exodus may have been prompted by two other events.

According to Aztec legend, their southward migration began on May 24, 1064. Ten years before that date there occurred a rare celestial event. It consisted of the supernova explosion that created the Crab Nebula.

The Aztecs were gifted astronomers after they arrived in Mexico and maybe before. If a brand-new star suddenly appeared in 1054 that outshone all the others, only to dim and disappear a few months later, it would certainly have been seen as a prophetic symbol.

Then, in 1064, a volcanic explosion created the Sunset Crater in Arizona, obliterating hundreds of square miles of arable crop land. If this was where the Aztecs lived at the time, it would have reduced their ability to grow sufficient quantities of food.

They had no choice, according to this theory. They had to move away.

Then, in 1066, Halley's Comet appeared in the sky. Surely, this would have been interpreted as an omen from the gods.

Whatever the cause, the migration was successful. When the scribes of Cortés described what they found at Tenochtitlan, they painted word pictures of a clean city, beautifully decorat-

The volcano that created Sunset Crater in Arizona exploded in 1064, which may have been a reason for the ancestors of the Aztecs to migrate south around that time.

Franciscan friar Bernardino de Sahagún is sometimes called "the first anthropologist" for spending 50 years studying the Aztecs, learning to the Nahuatl language, and documenting the culture of the civilization. He also translated the Gospels into Nahuatl.

ed and meticulously laid out, that housed more people in more comfort than the squalid, rat-infested cities of Europe. What they discovered, before the Spanish destroyed it, was a paradise.

This brings us to the second, almost unforgivable, obstacle to research. The Aztecs, unlike many ancient civilizations that archaeologists try to understand, were a literate society. They wrote books, but representatives of the Catholic Church burned every textual record they could find, believing them to be pagan superstition and the work of the devil. Is it any wonder that this information has been suppressed? It accuses the Catholic Church of a terrible historical sin, and rightly so.

Once again, quoting Orozco: "We must re-evaluate much of our thinking about the greatness and antiquity of Native American civilization."

As if this immoral travesty wasn't enough, in 1529, a Catholic priest named Fray Bernardino de Sahagún was sent to Mexico with a twofold task.

First, he was to convert the indigenous people. This was, after all, only eight years after Cortés brutally murdered many of them in order to establish complete control over the population by means of terrorism. By 1529, they were deemed ready to convert or die.

But de Sahagún's attack had a second prong to it. Rumors had surfaced that many Aztec legends were very similar to Jewish and Christian religious stories. Could it be that the Aztecs were familiar with the god of the Bible? If so, it would create problems because the reason the Spanish church felt so ready to rule the Aztecs with a rod of iron was because the natives were considered subhuman pagans. Some theologians believed they didn't even possess souls. But what if they were God's creations, just like Europeans? How could the church justify treating their own in this fashion?

De Sahagún decided that the best way to convert the people was to establish some common ground, so he wrote a book. That's what scholars do. The result was what is now called *Historia general de las cosas de nueva España* ("General History of the Things of New Spain"), now commonly called the Florentine Codex. It tells the story of Nahua history, religious beliefs, and culture in the common language of the people, but it also includes a running commentary in Spanish.

One of the most intriguing sections of the book concerns Nahua migration mythology. They spoke of a mysterious place called Tamoanchan, which they claimed was, in effect, the birthplace of all Mesoamerican cultures. It was an Eden of sorts, a paradise from which they came following a great flood. According to the Codex, the original inhabitants, the ancestors of the Aztecs, had come from the sea:

> They say they came to this land to rule over it.
> They came from the sea on ships, a multitude
> of them, and landed on the shore of the sea, to
> the North. From there they went on, seeking
> the white mountains, the smoky mountains, led
> by their priests and by the voice of their gods.
> Finally, they came to the place that they called
> Tamoanchan, and there they settled.

In other words, this story actually precedes the Aztec migration saga, taking it even further back in history. It seems to say that the ancestors of the Aztecs arrived on the east coast of the Americas, crossed the Appalachian Mountains, the "smokey

The battle between eagle and serpent in Aztec mythology is an obvious metaphor for the conflict between Heaven and Earth.

mountains," and then continued west across the plains until settling in Tamoanchan, wherever that was.

Unfortunately for de Sahagún, his illustrations let slip the fact that the Spanish soldiers were not paragons of Christian virtue. That caused a certain amount of embarrassment, so the book was never widely distributed.

It is at this point that coincidence, if such a thing exists, might enter the picture. Consider some worldwide symbology:

- Remember the Aztec ancestors' veneration of Quetzalcoatl and his association with the planet Venus? The same acknowledgment is found in cultures as far distant as Egypt and Sumeria.

- They venerated the star Sirius, also called the Dog Star. Sirius is found in the constellation Orion. The belt stars of Orion are said to be represented by the positioning of the pyramids on the Giza Plateau, among other places. Orion is also associated with Osiris, a principal deity of the Egyptians.

- The eagle is a soaring creature of the heavens; the serpent, a slithering denizen of Earth. Together, the two symbolize the duality of Heaven and Earth, spirituality and materialism. The eagle fighting the serpent, the heavens at war with Earth, formed the symbolic image that indicated to the early Aztec pioneers where they were supposed to settle down. The symbolism is plain to see. Spirituality is constantly engaged in a war with materialism. Earth is the battlefield.

All these images—the morning star; the battle between the creature of the heavens, the eagle, and the creature of Earth, the serpent; the people being led to a new home, similar to the exodus accounts found in many religions; the persecution that followed the initial migration—they all tell the same story. It's happened again and again, as recounted in numerous mythologies.

Could it be that the human race is still an unknowing pawn in a cosmic battle that continues beyond our perception? Were the ancestors of the Aztecs any different from the early Jews or the Sumerians, who have similar exodus stories? Is something going on that is much bigger than we realize, and did the ancients understand it? Is the history of humankind a revelation of one continuous battlefield of that war, being fought on planet Earth? Is that why so much of our history is suppressed: to keep us from putting the pieces together? Have we forgotten our past?

We refer to the "battle between good and evil." Is that more than a metaphor? Are we pawns on a cosmic chess board bigger than we can perceive, and is it our task to rise to the occasion, pulling ourselves up by our own intellectual bootstraps?

It seems as though the Aztecs might have thought along these lines.

That might deal sufficiently with the question, "Where did the *Aztecs* come from?" It doesn't, however, answer the question, "Where did their *treasures* come from?"

Although it is probably impossible to know for sure, some "best guess" theories have been put forth over the years.

First and foremost is that they got most of the gold from areas they occupied after they reached present-day Mexico, provided in trade for items they produced. Trade networks were extensive in those days. Copper from the Great Lakes region was traded for everything from chocolate and pottery to cornmeal, which was used to make tortillas, their principal food. They also grew beans, peppers, avocadoes, tomatoes, squash, cotton, sweet potatoes, amaranth, pineapple, and flowers. Tropical bird feathers were traded all the way to the east coast.

Because of the advent of satellite photography, long, wide, perfectly straight road systems have been identified that connect Central America with places in Arizona, Colorado, and beyond.

The legend of the humpbacked, flute-playing Kokopelli goes back at least 3,000 years, according to dates connected with the first stone petroglyphs that depicted him. Although he is often identified closely with Hopi and Zuni traditions, some see him as a trader, often associated with stories typical of traveling

Kokopelli is usually thought of as the god of mischief in Native mythology in the Southwest, but the god was also associated with the business of trade.

salesman jokes. Undoubtedly, the Aztecs had an extensive trade system that would have seen precious metals streaming down to Mexico.

The possibility also exists that during their long migration south, the Aztecs would have almost certainly become familiar with regions rich in gold, silver, and copper where these metals meant nothing to the people who knew of their location but had no practical use for them. If the Aztecs lived in such areas for a sufficiently long period of time to have built up a stable, refined society, they probably had learned where gold was found, mining it and caching it in huge quantities, which they eventually returned to claim. The Anasazi, Mimbres, Mogollon, and Hohokam might even have been assimilated into their ranks to form strong family ties.

At the very least, the Aztecs' journeys would have made them familiar with rich northern areas unknown to the Toltecs and other tribes native to Mexico and Central America.

However they accumulated their precious treasures, and with Cortés at least temporarily defeated, the Aztec rulers knew their time was short. He had promised to return.

As it turns out, they had only one year. It wasn't much, but apparently, it was enough. During that year, they organized, packed up an immense amount of wealth, and disappeared from the face of the Earth.

In the fall of 1520, a group of exiles that exceeded 2,000 men, women, children, and slaves began a mass exodus north. The best guess is that they meant to return to their traditional homeland. The directions would almost certainly have been preserved. These were a literate, intelligent people. Surely, they would have passed on to succeeding generations the location of the now almost mythical Aztlán.

They had no draft animals or wheeled carts. Slaves could carry only a limited amount of treasure. But legends recall that after traveling northwest for what might have been a year or even more, they reached their destination, buried the treasure, and put the slaves to death to eliminate most of the witnesses.

This leads us to ponder the question, "Where did it go?" And even more importantly, "Where is it now?"

In 1789, Francisco Javier Clavijero, a Jesuit priest and historian who was born in Veracruz, Mexico, studied the ancient history of the Aztecs and decided that Aztlán lay in an area along or near the Colorado River, most likely in present-day Arizona.

More recent theories place it in the Grand Canyon and the fabled lost Egyptian city that supposedly is hidden away in the labyrinth of its caves.

Francisco Javier Clavijero penned important histories on the peoples of Mesoamerica, including *La Historia Antigua de México.*

Others choose the Superstition Mountains east of Phoenix. The Lost Dutchman, they insist, didn't find a mine. He found Montezuma's lost gold.

A theory even exists that they somehow made it all the way to Oak Island, in Nova Scotia, where they hid their treasure in an elaborate money pit, protected by booby traps.

This last theory seems a bit far-fetched, considering they had no way to transport such a hoard some 3,000 miles overland and having no recent history with ships. The biggest plank in this theoretical edifice is the Aztecs' ritual fondness for the color blue, which could have been supplied by Oak Island's blue clay deposits.

But that very idea, their fondness for the color blue, might point to a possible destination: Utah! Some of the rock art there contains out-of-context blue figures that might have been carved by a non-indigenous population.

Anthropologists believe that the Ute Indians are related to the Aztecs. At the time of European contact, the Utes virtually ruled parts of Colorado, New Mexico, California, and Utah. Their language contains many words that seem to echo Aztec vocabulary. When the Aztecs returned to their homeland, did people welcome them home?

To explore that question, we need to revisit the Peralta Stones we looked at in connection with the Lost Dutchman Mine. This time, we need to listen to the Dillman family.

The story is told in the History Channel's series *Lost Gold of the Aztecs.* It recounts the story of three generations of a family who were determined to locate Montezuma's treasure and break the curse that has followed it for more than 500 years.

Dan Dillman, a third-generation treasure hunter, tells the story of how his grandfather, Raymond, regaled him with dinner-table talk about the four Peralta Stones that many believed led to the Lost Dutchman Mine. Raymond, however, came to believe that the Horse, Priest, Heart, and Trail stones pointed in a different direction.

Treasure hunting in general was a hobby in the family. Raymond, plus Dan's uncles, John and Paul Dillman, pursued other interests until 1965, when while helping a neighbor clean out her basement, they discovered a 1964 *Life* magazine that had an article in it about the Peralta Stones. The stones soon became a special obsession.

Raymond researched them for 18 years, even going so far as to practice vision quests. His dreams and meditations eventually pointed him to Utah, not the Superstition Mountains. He believed the stones were created by two Spanish explorers, Álvar Núñez Cabeza de Vaca and Estevenico, survivors of the 1527 Narváez Expedition to Florida. These were the two men who staggered into Mexico after a nine-year ordeal, prompting the Coronado Expedition.

The story is told in detail in the History Channel video series. According to Dan Dillman:

> My grandfather's research into Álvar Núñez Cabeza de Vaca and Estevenico is extensive. He studied the personal diary of Álvar Núñez, which describes Núñez's nine-year adventures lost in the Americas and gives some details about the indigenous tribes, the animals, plant life and the treasures they witnessed while in captivity during their first two years in the Americas. It was my grandfather's theory that the two lost explorers witnessed and learned much about the lost Aztec treasures from the indigenous tribes, but they were not allowed to write about it in the diary because knowledge of any hidden treasure would have been meant for the Spanish king only. So, my grandfather's theory was that de Vaca and Estevenico created the Peralta Stones as a guide to lead them back to the treasure locations that were revealed to them to be in what is now southwest America. Unfortunately, they never made it back to the Americas.

In 1982, Raymond Dillman believed he had finally cracked the Peralta Stones code. He discovered to his own satisfaction that they didn't point to the Superstition Mountains. They pointed to Kanab, Utah. Following his dream, he traveled there and discovered what he believed to be Aztec ruins and artifacts, including arrowheads, weapons, pottery, bowls, fishing nets, llama hair, tools, and a large sacrificial altar of the kind the Aztecs would have used.

Following a dispute with the landowner, he was forced to give up his search and died 10 years later.

Treasure hunting can be a frustrating business. Searchers for Aztec treasure have encountered strange orbs of light in the sky. Divers who worked the Three Lakes Ranch, owned by the Child family for more than 30 years, have experienced unexplained problems, such as their scuba tanks being turned off, a feeling of being strangled, and hearing eerie screams over their communication systems.

The theory is that the Aztecs employed a diabolical strategy called a water trap to hide their treasure. They dug 35 feet deep under the water and then built a tunnel that would lead inside a cavern next to the pond. After building a room that was higher than the water level, they drained the lake, transferred the gold, and then allowed the water to fill the lake again. In order to protect the hoard, they killed the workers or, perhaps, even allowed them to drown when the water level rose. Aztecs, after all, were known for human sacrifice. Was this the fate of the slaves who transported the gold all the way from Mexico? Were they destined to guard the treasure in death as they carried it in life?

> *Was this the fate of the slaves who transported the gold all the way from Mexico? Were they destined to guard the treasure in death as they carried it in life?*

If so, whoever finds the treasure might also find another surprise waiting for them.

In the words of Lon Child, son of the original owner of the Three Lakes Ranch, "If there are curses, this is cursed. Every time there's been an attempt, bad things would happen."

Is the lost treasure of Montezuma to be found in Utah, and is his curse still at work, even in these modern days?

If so, it hasn't slowed Dan Dillman down one bit:

> I feel strongly connected to finding this quest to find treasure, not only because I am a de-

scendant of Aztec and Maya peoples, but also because I was born with 12 fingers, which is called being "polydactyl." My grandfather said that my ancestors who were born with 12 fingers were the spiritual leaders of the family. He told me as a child that being born with 12 fingers, six on each hand, was a gift from God, and that if I followed the Great Spirit, I would one day lead our family in the quest to find treasure.

If we find Montezuma's Treasure, I imagine I would be excited beyond words, but I know I will be humble and grateful at the same time, because the treasure wouldn't be just for my family, this treasure is meant for all. I believe it is meant to be a tool to help heal and unite the world.

This long and involved story has come to an unsatisfying conclusion. Here is a simple fact, however: When Cortés and his troops reentered Mexico City in August 1521, most of the Aztec gold and treasure that had been there when he initially raided the city but had to leave behind was gone. It was already on its way north, perhaps even in the process of being hidden, some 1,500 miles away. The best we can say is that it was probably in present-day Arizona, New Mexico, or Utah.

Bottom line? Five hundred years later, it's still missing.

The Seven Cities of Cibola

In the 16th century, Spain established a colonial empire in the New World that funneled gold from the Aztecs in Mexico and the Incas in Peru directly into the coffers of the monarchy, but the northern frontier of their holding was only a few hundred miles from what is now Mexico City. Beyond that lay terra incognita.

Rumored riches had drawn Hernán Cortés to Mexico in 1519. Very soon after that, Parfilo de Narváez explored Florida, and Francisco Pizarro voyaged to Peru. Their avowed purpose was to spread Christianity to the "heathen," but that was just a smokescreen to cover their real objective. They were after loot and the political advancement that comes from fame.

Other expeditions attempted the same thing. Most of them failed, but a few provided either some treasure or tales about more for the taking. It was enough to fuel the hopes and aspirations of many a conquistador.

One shining example of these tales occurred in 1536. That was the year Álvar Núñez Cabeza de Vaca and three half-dead companions, the only survivors of the Narváez Expedition to Florida, straggled into Mexico City, eight years after being shipwrecked and forced to endure a long and painful journey through what is now the American Southwest.

One of the many stories they told described land to the north of Mexico. There they claimed to have seen seven "large cities, with streets lined with goldsmith shops, houses of many stories, and doorways studded with emeralds and turquoise!"

Some believed that these Seven Cities of Cibola, as they came to be known, were the home of the lost treasure of Montezuma, but this has never been historically documented. Cabeza de Vaca has since been rumored to be the one who carved the original Peralta Stones, but this, too, is conjecture.

In 1539, Antonio de Mendoza was the viceroy of New Spain, now known as Mexico. He naturally wanted to know how much truth these stories conveyed, so he sent a party north. Fray

A 1720 map published by Henry Chatelain shows the supposed location of Cibola, one of the "Seven Cities of Gold."

Marcos de Niza was in charge, and with him he took Estevanico, who had been one of the survivors of the Narváez Expedition.

Fray Marcos returned a year later, bringing with him the news of Estevanico's death after being attacked by Indians. But he also said that before being forced back south, he had seen the fabled Seven Cities of Cibola.

Was the report a mistake or an outright lie?

We'll never know for sure. With Estevanico conveniently dead, the only one who knew the truth was Fray Marcos, and he's way beyond our ability to question. Given what happened as the result of the next expedition, it seems reasonable to believe that he didn't want to come back with bad news, so he might have forced himself to believe that somewhere near the far distant horizon, when he saw the morning sunlight reflecting off an adobe village, he saw gold. Or he decided to deliver news that he knew would be appreciated by the political forces in charge of New Spain at the time.

Whatever the case, Viceroy Mendoza convinced himself that another expedition was in order. For its leader, he chose his friend, Francisco Vásquez de Coronado.

Coronado had been in Mexico since 1535, so he was at least somewhat familiar with the task he was about to undertake. He had held some political offices and was even appointed governor of the northern frontier province of New Galicia.

His expedition was set to commence on February 23, 1540. Before he left, Mendoza instructed him to claim all the lands he discovered for New Spain but counseled him that the quest was to be a missionary undertaking only with no military conquest (wink, wink)!

History doesn't recall how Coronado reacted to this charge, but it is probably safe to say it was the Spanish sarcastic equivalent of "yeah, right!"

Records reveal that Fray Marcos and several other priests accompanied the expedition, along with 300 Spanish soldiers, several hundred Mexican-Indian allies, and 1,500 stock animals. Needless to say, it was a well-armed missionary endeavor.

They set sail from the west coast of modern-day Mexico, reached Culiacán, disembarked, and headed north overland.

Coronado and 100 soldiers, anxious to behold Cibola, marched swiftly ahead of the slower-moving main army. Eventually, they would make it all the way into what is now northern Kansas. They didn't find the seven cities, but it wasn't for lack of trying.

On July 7, 1540, they arrived at Háwikuh, just south of present-day Gallup, New Mexico. It was said to be the first of Cibola's fabled cities, but instead of a golden city, they found only a rather poor adobe pueblo occupied by Indians who were, quite rightfully, prepared to fight for their hometown.

Because his orders specified a missionary effort only, Coronado first tried peaceful negotiations. When that didn't work, he martialed his forces. The Indians fled before Coronado's superior forces and firepower, and the expedition obtained some much needed supplies but no gold.

Coronado made the village his headquarters for the next few months, but Fray Marcos, whose tales had raised many hopes of wealth and fortune, was ordered back to Mexico City amid a rising tide of anger and bitter resentment.

Coronado sent forth smaller groups to explore the surrounding countryside. One of their members, Garcia López de Cárdenas, became the first European to report seeing the Grand Canyon of the Colorado River.

Did he actually descend from the south rim, perhaps following what is now a well-traveled donkey path used by modern-day tourists? No one knows, but rumors persist to this day that he might have found gold somewhere, somehow, and chose to hide it where no one but himself could ever find it again.

In 1540, Hernando de Alarcon, one of those designated to

question Indians they came across, wrote an entry in his journal about interviewing some natives along the Colorado River:

> When asked about gold and silver, the Indi-
> ans said that they had some metal of the same
> . color as the bells which the Spaniards showed
> them. This was not made nor found in their
> country, but came "from a certain mountain
> where an old woman dwelt." The old woman
> was called Guatuzaca.

Where was that "certain mountain" that might have contained gold and silver? Was it a mine? Could it have been the scene of an Aztec treasure cache? It certainly sounds like an interesting possibility.

It causes us to speculate about the persistent rumors of gold that might have been found by Garcia López de Cárdenas. Did he really give vent to avarice and the curse of buried treasure?

The painting *La Conquista del Colorado* by Augusto Ferrer-Dalmau shows Coronado's explorers, led by Garcia López de Cárdenas, overlooking the Grand Canyon as they go in search of the city of Cibola and its supposed treasures.

Do tourists of today ride right by his buried hoard, not knowing that a great wealth of Spanish gold lies hidden from sight?

No proof exists that they do, only rumors and legends, but as we have seen, rumors and legends have an extremely long shelf life.

The main expedition, however, didn't fare very well. One of Coronado's subordinates happened to come across a Plains Indian they named the Turk. He wove fantastic stories about towns to the east in an area he called Quivira. Was this part of the lost Seven Cities of Cibola?

The army left the region of the Grand Canyon, perhaps leaving behind a fabled fortune, or perhaps not, on April 23, 1541, and journeyed all the way to the site of present-day Salina, Kansas. Once again, they found only disappointment. Villages were there, to be sure, but they consisted only of primitive grass huts.

The Turk finally confessed that the whole story of Quivira was nothing more than a plot conceived by the Pueblo Indians to lure the Spaniards out onto the plains, hoping they would become lost and eventually die of starvation.

The Turk finally confessed that the whole story of Quivira was nothing more than a plot conceived by the Pueblo Indians to lure the Spaniards out onto the plains, hoping they would become lost and eventually die of starvation.

Coronado was furious. The Turk was executed, and Coronado began the long march home, bitterly disappointed because, in his eyes, the mission had utterly failed. No gold, no jewels, no silver, and no honor was bestowed on him upon his return. The fact that he had discovered the Grand Canyon and was able to supply precious information about the American Southwest didn't mollify him one bit. He was much too materialistic for any of that. He wanted treasure and power.

Coronado arrived back at the capital in the spring of 1542. He was publicly scorned and discredited. Although he again resumed his position as governor of New Galicia, he and his captains were subsequently charged for their actions during the quest, perhaps because they were held in suspicion. Did they find the fabled riches and hide them so they could later be retrieved? It's very doubtful. Too many witnesses were present. But if that was the case, the records were never preserved. Ten years later, he died at the age of 42.

Coronado never understood that he would go down in history as the man who set the stage for what was to become the great saga of the American West. That was the real treasure.

Although he might not have seen the Grand Canyon himself, members of his expedition became the first European tourists to visit the attraction and stand in awe at the spectacle of the great gorges that disappear into seeming nothingness. He opened the way for later Spanish explorers and missionaries who would populate the Southwest, developing the distinctive Hispanic-American culture we know today. Whenever you eat Mexican food or enjoy the music of a Mariachi band, you can, in a sense, thank Coronado.

Hidden Relics of Egypt

Another American legend continues to generate almost as much interest as that of the underground labyrinth beneath the Egyptian Giza Plateau. It hints of an underground complex, full of mysterious treasures, that is said to exist somewhere in the labyrinth of the Grand Canyon. This one doesn't have the endorsement of old authors such as Herodotus and Pliny the Elder, who swore that what amounts to an underground city lies hidden beneath the pyramids, but it involves Egyptian and Asian artifacts and has generated a lot of ink. It's a story that involves the Smithsonian Institution's Department of Archaeology which, to this day, swears it's a total fabrication.

The story began with the April 5, 1909, edition of the *Arizona Gazette*. It told the strange story of Professors S. A. Jordan

Marble Canyon's expanse is now traversed by Navajo Bridge. S. A. Jordan and G. E. Kinkaid explored Marble Canyon in 1909, finding a cavern that contained tunnels and chambers chiseled out by people, and there were also treasures to be found there.

and G. E. Kinkaid, who were allegedly funded by the Smithsonian Institution to carry out explorations in the Marble Canyon region of the Grand Canyon. They emerged from the canyon with a tale that they had discovered a vast cavern system that contained evidence of a long-lost ancient civilization.

When the two men, supposedly with bona fide scientific credentials and representing the august Smithsonian, revealed their alleged discovery, the story quickly gathered momentum.

The area in which it was located was remote and almost inaccessible. In Kinkaid's words, as quoted by the piece in the *Gazette*:

> First, I would impress that the cavern is nearly inaccessible. The entrance is 1,486 feet down the sheer canyon wall. It is located on government land and no visitor will be allowed there under penalty of trespass ... I was journeying down the Colorado river in a boat, alone, looking for minerals. Some forty-two miles up the river from the El Tovar Crystal canyon, I saw on the east wall, stains in the sedimentary formation about 2,000 feet above the river bed. There are steps leading from this entrance some thirty yards to what was, at the time the cavern was inhabited, the level of the river.

After many trials and errors, he claimed to have found a whole system of tunnels and caverns which were chiseled out by hand. Eventually, it opened into doorways that led a mile farther under the surface:

> The main passageway is about twelve feet wide, narrowing to nine feet toward the end. About 57 feet from the entrance, the first side-passages branch off to the right and left, along which, on both sides, are a number of rooms about the size of ordinary living rooms, though some are 30 by 40 feet square. These are entered by oval-shaped doors and are ventilated by round air spaces through the walls into the passages. The walls are about three feet six inches in thickness. The passages are chiseled or hewn straight, as if laid out by an engineer. The ceil-

Kinkaid reported that he found idols—some resembling Buddhas—and pottery and weapons that appeared to have come from somewhere in Asia.

> ings of many of the rooms converge to a center. The side-passages near the entrance run at a sharp angle from the main hall, but toward the rear they gradually branch out at right angles.

How could such a story not be taken seriously? It's got exact measurements, precise locations, and scientific-sounding descriptions. He went on to talk about artifacts such as weapons, copper instruments, idols, pottery, and urns that Kinkaid said looked as though they came from the Orient. His account was riveting:

> Over a hundred feet from the entrance is the cross-hall, several hundred feet long, in which are found the idol, or image, of the people's god, sitting cross-legged, with a lotus flower or lily in each hand. The cast of the face is oriental. The idol almost resembles Buddha, though the scientists are not certain as to what

religious worship it represents. Taking into consideration everything found thus far, it is possible that this worship most resembles the ancient people of Tibet.

Surrounding this idol are smaller images, some very beautiful in form; others crooked-necked and distorted shapes, symbolical, probably, of good and evil. There are two large cacti with protruding arms, one on each side of the dais on which the god squats. All this is carved out of hard rock resembling marble. In the opposite corner of this cross-hall were found tools of all descriptions, made of copper. These people undoubtedly knew the lost art of hardening this metal, which has been sought by chemicals for centuries without result. On a bench running around the workroom was some charcoal and other material probably used in the process. There is also slag and stuff similar to matte, showing that these ancients smelted ores, but so far, no trace of where or how this was done has been discovered, nor the origin of the ore.

The people who read the article, obviously, were hooked. But Kinkaid went on in even greater detail:

Among the other finds are vases or urns and cups of copper and gold, made very artistic in design. The pottery work includes enameled ware and glazed vessels. Another passageway leads to granaries such as are found in the oriental temples. They contain seeds of various kinds. One very large storehouse has not yet been entered, as it is twelve feet high and can be reached only from above. Two copper hooks extend on the edge, which indicates that some sort of ladder was attached. These granaries are rounded, as the materials of which they are constructed, I think, is a very hard cement. A gray metal is also found in this cavern, which puzzles the scientists, for its identity has

not been established. It resembles platinum.
Strewn promiscuously over the floor everywhere are what people call "cat's eyes," a yellow
stone of no great value. Each one is engraved
with the head of the Malay type.

By this time, people who read the original article were no
doubt planning an immediate trip to the caverns themselves,
though Kinkaid had reassured them that they would not be allowed in if they did manage to find the place.

Still, he offered more proof when he revealed that all the
mummies found there were male. No children or females had
been buried in the many crypts. This led him to authoritatively
assert that the place was a "warrior's barracks."

Back in 1909, no one had yet seen the *Indiana Jones* movies,
but Kinkaid certainly set the stage for the future blockbusters:

There is one chamber of the passageway
to which is not ventilated, and when we approached it a deadly, snaky smell struck us. Our
light would not penetrate the gloom, and until
stronger ones are available, we will not know
what the chamber contains. Some say snakes,
but others boo-hoo this idea and think it may
contain a deadly gas or chemicals used by the
ancients.

Kinkaid offered his opinion that the place had been there
for millennia, that it was home to an ancient, lost civilization
which had occupied it for thousands of years, and that it had
developed a very sophisticated technology and way of life.

The *Arizona Gazette* even got in on the speculations. Its editorial board believed that Kinkaid and the Smithsonian had:

almost conclusively proved that the race which
inhabited this mysterious cavern, hewn in solid
rock by human hands, was of oriental origin,
possibly from Egypt, tracing back to Ramses.
If their theories are borne out by the translation of the tablets engraved with hieroglyph-
ics, the mystery of the prehistoric peoples of
North America, their ancient arts, who they

were and whence they came, will be solved. Egypt and the Nile, and Arizona and the Colorado will be linked by a historical chain running back to ages which stagger the wildest fancy of the fictionist.

The newspaper sold out as soon as it hit the stands. Most of Arizona, it appeared, was abuzz with excitement. The legend had taken root and was soon flashed across the country.

But then, things started to fall apart. The Smithsonian denied ever financing such an expedition. The institution knew nothing about any artifacts that had supposedly been shipped to them. The response was succinct and clear:

> Well, the first thing I can tell you, before we go any further, is that no Egyptian artifacts of any kind have ever been found in North or South America. Therefore, I can tell you that the Smithsonian Institute has never been involved in any such excavations.

That, of course, set off the conspiracy theorists. They accused the Smithsonian of a cover-up for reasons that were never made clear. No "Professor Kinkaid," or "Jordan," for that mat-

The officials at the Smithsonian Institution denied that there ever was a Kinkaid or Jordan or that they every funded an expedition to Marble Canyon.

ter, was found on the rolls of the Smithsonian Institution's Department of Anthropology, and no documentation, including pictures, could be located.

Then, it was discovered that the original article that had been published in the *Gazette* was written by an anonymous writer who had, it seemed, used a pen name to disguise his identity. People began to suspect that the paper had published this piece of fake news in order to sell copies and increase circulation.

But the damage had been done. The legend was now here to stay. Kinkaid had disappeared, if he ever existed, and has never resurfaced.

That didn't stop the true believers, however. They believed then, and continue to believe, that the storage rooms of the Smithsonian are hiding great treasures that the institution doesn't want to reveal to the world.

The fact that, if they had such treasures, people would flock to the museum in droves doesn't seem to matter. The final scene in the first Indiana Jones movie *Raiders of the Lost Ark*, when the Ark of the Covenant is placed in a wooden box, the lid nailed shut, and wheeled into a nameless, label-less corridor and hidden away for all eternity is shocking proof to some people that such things happen. Government cover-ups are a weapon in the hands of conspiracy theorists, and they employ them with great regularity.

The story continued, and now it seems to have a life of its own.

Jack Andrews, for instance, in 1972, claimed to have rediscovered the hidden complex:

> I think the "cave" described in the headline story of the *Arizona Gazette*, April 5, 1909, and its fantastic underground installation was, and still may be, located above an approximate six-mile stretch of the Colorado River in Marble Canyon, at the border of Marble Canyon and the Navajo Nation, above an area near Kwagunt Rapids.

Likewise, John Rhodes, a U.S. representative from Arizona for 30 years and former minority leader in the House of Representatives, although very secretive about the whereabouts of the entrance, says he not only knows where it is but that an armed guard stands ready to repel all intruders should anyone attempt to enter.

David Icke's 1999 book *The Biggest Secret* makes the claim that reptilian humanoids are in the process of taking over Earth and that the Grand Canyon is their secret base of operation:

> In 1909 a subterranean city which was built with the precision of the Great Pyramid was found by G. E. Kincaid near the Grand Canyon in Arizona. It was big enough to accommodate 50,000 people and mummified bodies found were of oriental or possibly Egyptian origin, according to the expedition leader Professor S. A. Jordan. My own research suggests that it is from another dimension, the lower fourth dimension, that the reptilian control and manipulation is primarily orchestrated.

Brent Swancer, whose February 3, 2018, article for *Mysterious Universe* provided much of the research for this segment, probably sums up the whole mystery best of all. It's only appropriate to give him the last word:

> It is clear that the tale of Kincaid's mysterious caves continues to incite speculation and debate, and is a spectacular story that captures the imagination, and shows no real signs of waning. Is there anything to it or is this all a pure hoax or half-truths? If the caves ever did exist, then where were they and who were the inscrutable people who supposedly inhabited them? Were they made by ancient out-of- place Egyptians, some sort of other lost civilization, or underground goddam reptilian monsters? Such a place and its relics would be absolutely groundbreaking, rewriting history itself, but considering the lack of articles talking about them and the complete lack of any evidence, the story is a dead-end at best, and will probably remain mysterious, and fuel for conspiracies, just as buried in mystery as the city itself.

Barring further proof, it seems as though this story must remain one of the many legends surrounding the mysteries of the Grand Canyon.

King Kamehameha's Burial Chamber

Hawaii is a land of contrasts. Beautiful beaches and deadly volcanoes. Beckoning, green mountains and vast, black lava fields. It is the land of *aloha*: of respect, love, and harmony. It is also the land of *kapu*, meaning sacred, and consecrated to the point of sacrificial death. *Kapu* also means forbidden and, most definitely, no trespassing, whether that is interpreted to mean literally or figuratively.

Island history is steeped in happy, dancing, childlike, innocent people. It is also littered with the mutilated bones of fierce warriors who fought to the death, with heads and limbs brutally cut off so the victor could inherit the *mana*, or spiritual life force, of the fallen enemy.

First settled by brilliant Polynesian navigators, the islands of Hawaii were not unified until 1810, when King Kamehameha, who embodied all the disparate, conflicting, emotional attributes of a typical Hawaiian, fought a long and brutal campaign that eventually brought Hawaii, "The Big Island"; Kahoolawe, "The Target Isle"; Kauai, "The Garden Isle"; Lanai, "The Pineapple Isle"; Maui, "The Valley Isle"; Molokai, "The Friendly Isle"; Niihau, "The Forbidden Isle"; and Oahu, "The Gathering Place" under one political roof.

The Hawaiian islands were unified as a single kingdom by King Kamehameha I in 1810. When he died in 1819, he was supposedly buried with a treasure of gold and jewels, but no one knows where he was buried to this day.

At the end, Kamehameha was revered as Hawaii's first unifying king and was buried in typical island fashion, with gold and jewels that numbered in the millions of dollars. But no one knows where. His burial chamber has never been found. A Hawaiian proverb states, "The morning star alone knows where Kamehameha's bones are guarded."

The rules and regulations of *kapu* were strict and punishable by death if anyone broke them. Commoners bowed their head in the presence of the king. Even his morning bowel movement was taken away and buried in secret, lest an enemy *kahuna*, or preeminent spiritual practitioner, capture any of his *mana* by using it to work a spell.

Some people believe that the king is buried in the royal burial ground at the palace of Moku'ula in Maui. Others think he was secretly hidden away in a cave on Maui in the Iao Valley. Other chiefs were buried there, so it is certainly possible.

Wherever the grave chamber is, most traditional Hawaiians agree that it would be terrible *kapu* if his remains were ever to be found and disturbed. They are cursed by a spell that lasts forever.

A historical marker plaque by the Naha Stone in Hilo, Hawaii, explains the legend of Kamehameha lifting the stone to prove himself worthy of ruling over the islands.

Kamehameha was destined for greatness, but it did not come easy for him. Prophecies foretold that a light in the sky anointed with bird feathers would herald his birth. He was born in 1758, the year that Halley's Comet passed over Hawaii. It seemed to be a powerful omen.

Because of his importance, he was hidden away shortly after his birth so he could grow up in obscurity, safe from enemies who were quite understandably upset that a leader was born who was destined to take their kingdoms from them. He was given the birth name Pai'ea and grew up in the secluded Waipi'o Valley, trained for leadership by his uncle, King Kalani'opu'u of the Big Island. He excelled in games and warfare. He learned the complicated oral history of his people. This was necessary because Hawaiians didn't have a written language. He learned the skills of navigation and religious ceremonies. Of course, he was also trained in the hula, although it is said of him that he didn't favor the dance very much. When he was old enough to take his rightful place in relative safety, he took the name Kamehameha, which means "the lonely one."

Trained as a warrior, he possessed legendary strength and skill. If you visit Hilo on the Big Island, you can still see the Naha Stone. It weighs between two and three tons and is said to possess a huge amount of *mana*. Whoever lifted it would be a king, but you had to be pretty confident to try. The punishment for failure was death.

Kamehameha stood seven feet tall and possessed enormous strength. Some say he lifted it and moved it several feet. Others say he rolled it over.

In 1778, Captain James Cook arrived in Hawaii at an opportune time. Kamehameha was 20 years old and ready to get about with his life's mission to unite the islands. Because he was able to obtain Western weapons and advisors, he had a leg up on the competition. First the Big Island, then Maui and Oahu; island by island, he was able to bring them all under his control. With the fall of Kauai, his victory was finally complete, and the prophecy of his birth and mission was fulfilled.

World history would have unfolded in a different manner if he had not accomplished unification when he did. A divided, fragmented Hawaii would almost certainly have fallen victim to competing world powers. Who knows how World War II would have turned out if Japan had settled the western islands?

Four commemorative statues honor him today. One is featured prominently in each episode of television's *NCIS Hawaii*, but they show up in other TV series as well. On June 11 each year, the statues are draped with flowered leis to celebrate his accomplishments.

Will his burial chamber and all its riches ever be discovered? Probably not—at least, not for the foreseeable future. But even if they were, the curse of *kapu* is so strong that few would want to risk it.

Gangsters & Robbers

Civil War Gold

Wars are expensive: payrolls to meet, armaments to build, ammunition to supply, people to feed, and so much more. The Pentagon is reported to have commissioned a detailed analysis attempting to determine how wars are won and lost. Although that report has not been verified, it was said to have determined that the nation that makes the most steel wins.

That may or may not be true, but it definitely makes us ponder the amount of money involved in carrying on a war. History is replete with stories about how wars can jump-start an entire economy. The Interstate Highway System of the United States, for instance, initiated by President Dwight D. Eisenhower, provided so much work that the national GDP flourished for many years, soon canceling out the money spent on World War II. Its justification was that if another world war broke out, we would need a rapid way to transport goods from coast to coast.

These days, if the military wants to make a payment of some kind, someone at the Pentagon issues an order for a low-level clerk to type in a computer code instructing someone to push a button that instantly transfers digital money into a bank account somewhere in the world so a check can be printed. That is an obvious simplification, but it's not far off the mark.

During the Civil War era, things were not that easy. Payments were backed by gold and silver that had to be deposited and held somewhere. If a deposit was in jeopardy, treasure had to be physically moved from one place to another.

The process of transporting such wealth was fraught with danger. Trains, ships, and wagon trains were vulnerable to attacks of many kinds. Sometimes, they simply disappeared.

That was the case for the three examples of missing Civil War gold that we are about to examine. In each case, the missing shipments led to circumstances that can only be described as the machinations of a curse of some kind. As we shall soon see, some of those curses seem to be active right down to the present day.

Pennsylvania

The first such example involves a federal shipment of gold that disappeared in the state of Pennsylvania. Although it took place in 1863, the FBI got involved in 2018. The mystery is still a matter of intrigue: a story filled with accusations, lawsuits, and conspiracy theories.

In 1863, Confederate general Robert E. Lee felt that the time had come for an invasion of the North. During the month of June, he moved up the Shenandoah Valley toward Pennsylvania, attempting to use the Blue Ridge Mountains to mask his approach. Federal spies soon spotted him, and the pursuit began. In an ironic twist of fate, because the Union army was following him north when Lee attacked at Gettysburg, it was one of the few times in the war that the Confederacy attacked from the North and the Union defended from the South.

Lee's plan was to draw the Federal Army out into the open, get between them and Washington, pull off a major victory, and then head south toward the Yankee capital in Washington,

The pivotal Battle of Gettysburg lasted three days and resulted in over 40,000 casualties. It forced the retreat of General Robert E. Lee's army and marked the end of the South's advances into the North.

D.C. A letter had been prepared to be delivered to Abraham Lincoln demanding terms and the end of the war. If the plan had worked, the United States would have been severed into two countries: Lincoln would be the president of the United States, and Jefferson Davis would be president of the Confederate States of America, ruling from his capital of Richmond, Virginia.

Because of the disastrous defeat now called Pickett's Charge, on July 3, 1863, Lee was forced to retreat back into Virginia, but this was by no means apparent before the battle began. With a string of victories behind him, Lee, and many in the North as well, felt the South was invincible. As it turned out, this was to be the turning point of the war, but no one knew it at the time.

In the aftermath of this great battle, one of the deadliest in American history, in June 1864, President Lincoln ordered a large transfer of gold bullion from Wheeling, West Virginia, to the U.S. Mint in Philadelphia. It was, of course, supposed to be a secret, but stories surrounding the event recall that the transfer involved two covered freight wagons, each pulled by four mules, and a small wagon. They were accompanied by eight armed men on horseback. The wagons contained 26 bars of partly refined gold, "disguised" by painting them black, that weighed 50 pounds each. They were stored in wagons containing false bottoms and covered with hay. Given today's value, they would be worth between $27 and $55 million. They headed north to avoid Confederate spies who were still active in the area.

The officer in charge was a Lieutenant Castleton. He was descended from a distinguished military family but was not at his best during this portion of his career. He had missed a lot of action while fighting both a hip wound and a severe case of malaria. As a result, he was a sick and frustrated man.

Accompanying him was a man of a quite different character. Sergeant Mike O'Rourke had been arrested by the police for many river port brawls, at least one involving a murder, but he had the reputation of being extremely shrewd. Perhaps his aggressive personality was seen as a counterpoint to Castleton's.

If that mix wasn't volatile enough, a man named Conners accompanied them. He was said to be mean, unfriendly, and sullen. Because he had been previously wounded in battle, he was available only for limited duty.

It wasn't an ideal combination of men to be trusted for a shipment of this size, but most able-bodied soldiers were needed at the front lines, so these were the three who had been appointed. Secrecy, not valor, was supposed to be the key to this mission.

Lieutenant Castleton and Sergeant Mike O'Rourke were charged with leading a wagon party loaded with millions of dollars in gold bullion for the war effort from Wheeling, West Virginia, to the U.S. Mint in Philadelphia (pictured). Along the way, the treasure somehow disappeared.

For three days, things went well. The entourage camped along the old Clarion River Trail and then near Ridgway, Pennsylvania. Both Castleton and O'Rourke found the people of Ridgway to be very hostile and quite abusive.

Castleton tried, unsuccessfully, to buy some quinine for his fever, which was getting worse and bothering him excessively.

Meanwhile, O'Rourke, true to his nature, visited a tavern, where he was accused of trying to enlist men for the army. A brawl ensued, probably started by O'Rourke. He and Conners were both glad to put the dust of the town behind them. Indeed, they were happy to escape with their lives.

The next day, the wagon party made a great detour around the town and followed a road that headed east toward Philadelphia. The route they followed ran pretty much along the present-day Route 120.

Two days later, they came to the village of St. Mary's. There, they obtained a map of a possible road through what was then called "Wild Cat Country." It had been drawn by surveyors back in 1842.

Today, this road is rough and only a little better than a four-wheel-drive path. It crosses two mountains, both some 2,000 feet high, and the west branch of Hicks Run before becoming an unimproved dirt road that eventually branches off in three different directions, each culminating at a different place on the Sinnemahoning River.

At this point, apparently, Castleton and the others got impatient, headed off through the timber in the general direction they wanted to go, and got lost in a maze of swamps and creeks.

Castleton was growing increasingly weak from his fever, tempers were short, and the company decided to divide up. The

wagons were worthless in this type of terrain, so they unload-
ed the gold and transferred it to pack saddles, fashioned from
discarded canvas wagon covers. In this way, they formed a mule
train that would start south whenever Castleton's physical condition improved enough to permit him to travel.

Meanwhile, Conners was given a report of the trip and a
Federal Army order to requisition supplies and men for help.
Before he left the group on his own, he was reported to have
heard Castleton and O'Rourke arguing over whether to bury
part of the treasure to cut down on weight or attempt to transport the whole thing.

The group that kept the treasure was never seen or heard
from again.

Conners returned 10 days later, bringing with him a rescue
party composed of a detachment from the Lock Haven Army
Post. They found the wagons but determined from trail signs
that the group apparently split up and departed to the southwest.

They searched for days but eventually had to give up and
return to Lock Haven.

At this point, the curse reared its ugly head into the political
arena.

A court of inquiry was held in Clearfield, Pennsylvania.
They charged both Castleton and O'Rourke *in absentia* with the
crimes of treason and theft.

Castleton's distinguished family, however, still maintained
some political clout, and the charges were eventually dropped,
pending further investigation.

This investigation was carried out by the Pinkerton Detective Agency under secret orders from the War Department.

The Pinkertons, found-
ed by Alan Pinkerton
(pictured), was a secu-
rity guard and detective
agency that became the
largest of its kind from
the 1870s to the 1890s.

Dents Run in northern Pennsylvania is a wild and wooded place where it could be quite easy to hide a treasure of gold bullion.

Pinkerton agents, disguised as prospectors and lumbermen, infiltrated the area, watching for signs of sudden ostentatious wealth. They searched the entire area from the Driftwood Branch to the Benezette Branch of the Sinnemahoning River and as far west as St. Mary's.

Two years later, in 1865, two Pinkerton detectives named Donavan and Dugan found two and a half bars of gold buried under a pine stump about 4 miles south of where the wagons had been abandoned. From this, they deduced that the treasure had been stolen.

The following year, two of the mules, still bearing their army brand, were located in the possession of an old man in Chase Run, who said he found them wandering in the woods.

Apparently, the curse grabbed ahold of detectives Donavan and Dugan. Retiring from the agency, they built a cabin in this area in 1871 and continued to search for the treasure on their own.

In 1876, during a survey of the Elk-Cameron boundary, a crew found the remains of three to five human skeletons near a spring at the head of Bell's Branch, which flowed into Dents Run. This was about seven miles from where the wagons had been abandoned.

Apparently, the gold is still being sought by the government. In 2018, the FBI obtained a court order to excavate in the area.

Why the sudden interest? Well, it seems that Dennis Parada, a treasure hunter, had heard folktales alluding to the lost gold for his whole life. He had spent over 40 years searching for it, finally forming a team that included his son, Kem.

They believed they had finally located it in the almost inaccessible recesses of what they called a "turtle-shaped cave" near the community of Dents Run, Pennsylvania.

Playing by the rules, they notified the proper authorities.

FBI agents visited the site twice and ordered geophysical surveys that indicated an object "with a density of 19.5 g/cm³." That's the density of gold. It was found to be "consistent with a mass having a weight of approximately 8½ to 9 tons."

The court order obtained by the FBI prompted a dig, which they claimed produced no treasure. But the dig was conducted in secret. Dennis and Kem Parada were banned from the area and forced to wait in their cars until about 3 o'clock in the afternoon, when they were finally permitted to survey what was now a large, empty hole. Even though a good amount of daylight remained, it was decided to continue the hunt the next day.

Those who live nearby, however, swear they heard heavy machinery operating all night long. When the Paradas returned to the site in the morning, they were told that the expedition was a bust, and it was closed down.

Quite rightly, the Paradas questioned the whole thing. The metal detection readings after the FBI finished were totally different from those that his team had previously reported.

Nevertheless, the affidavit that the agency lodged on March 9, 2018, asking a court for permission to dig up a Pennsylvania hillside in search of Civil War gold produced an "official" negative result.

As is so often the case, when a government-sanctioned report, such as the assassination of President Kennedy, Project Blue Book, and the real reason for the beginning of U.S. involvement in the Spanish–American War, is released, some question whether or not a cover-up is in play. Dennis Parada and his team are no exceptions to the rule. They feel cheated out of their long years of search and discovery, and, perhaps, rightly so. They filed a complaint. As of this writing, the issue remains unsettled.

Evidence seems to point in their favor. Despite the discovery of gold bars and mules, in spite of the evidence of the missing funds, abandoned wagons, and human remains, some connected with the government still say the whole story is nothing more than a conspiracy myth. A transfer never occurred, they insist. The whole story is a fabrication. Others believe the treasure has been illegally confiscated by the FBI. Still others insist it still lies in a secret location in the woods outside of Dents Run, Pennsylvania.

Supposedly, if a treasure hunter ever finds it, the government will give the finder 10 percent. Of course, that amount will be subject to taxes.

Still, given the price of gold these days, it might be worth looking into, but beware of the curse.

Michigan

Of all the treasure stories that deal with lost Civil War gold, the theory that a sizable hoard of Confederate wealth, destined to renew the South's lost cause, ended up beneath the waters off the shores of Muskegon in Lake Michigan might just take the cake. It's easy to brush this one off as just another wacky conspiracy theory, but enough evidence existed to interest both the History Channel and famed treasure hunter Marty Lagina of *The Curse of Oak Island* fame, who has invested in the hunt. Being a down-to-earth businessman, he is not about to waste money chasing ghosts, and for two seasons, the History Channel invested considerable resources in producing a wonderfully entertaining series of reality TV shows on the project called *The Curse of Civil War Gold*.

Season 3 was cancelled, and no one seems to know exactly why, but while the show lasted, it rivaled the 10 seasons of *The Curse of Oak Island* for its ability to hook viewers in and keep them coming back.

Mark W. Hollkey, Kevin Dykstra, and Al Dykstra scuba dive in Lake Michigan in search of treasure in the 2018–2019 documentary series *The Curse of Civil War Gold* that aired on the History Channel.

This story has it all: lost treasure, history, intrigue, plot twists, and an unfolding list of evidence and facts that are rooted in reality, not fantasy.

The modern part of the story couldn't begin in a more dramatic fashion. It came to light with a deathbed confession; that's a great way to start a treasure hunt.

Frederick J. Monroe is a scuba diving instructor and treasure hunter from Muskegon, Michigan. In 1973, a friend told him that his grandfather lay dying when, just before he passed away, he said, "There's $2 million of gold bullion sitting in a boxcar (at the bottom of Lake Michigan) and there's only three people that know of it, and two of them are already dead."

That's the kind of thing that gets a treasure hunter's attention. Hundreds of stories involving lost treasure are located in and around the Great Lakes. They can be treacherous bodies of water, as anyone knows who is familiar with the story of the freighter *Edmund Fitzgerald*, which capsized and sank in Lake Superior in November 1975.

> *Hundreds of stories involving lost treasure are located in and around the Great Lakes. They can be treacherous bodies of water ...*

The story of the Civil War gold, as told to Monroe, was that in 1892, it was starting to become economically practical to place railroad boxcars on car ferries to cross Lake Michigan. The alternative was to travel by rail around the bottom of the lake through the labyrinth of Chicago switchyards and then on to their final destinations.

It may have saved money, but it opened the possibility of weather-related accidents. Such was the case when a lighthouse keeper witnessed a boxcar being pushed off a ferry during a bad storm. The weight might have taken the ferry down with it, so the boxcar had to be jettisoned. The lighthouse keeper protected the secret, which would have led to everything from insurance claims to reputations being ripped apart almost to the grave. Only on his deathbed did he share what he saw that night.

Monroe carried the story with him for over 40 years until he eventually shared it with Kevin Dykstra.

"I started to search and search," said Dykstra, eventually triggering a massive research project that he came to believe proved that the boxcar contained stolen Confederate treasure that was smuggled into Michigan almost 150 years earlier. Along the way, it insured the family fortunes of at least two prominent Muskegon bankers named Hackley and Hume.

After the Confederates lost the Civil War, the South's president Jefferson Davis fled to Georgia with about half of his government's treasury money.

"If there was $2 million of gold bullion at the bottom of Lake Michigan, it had to be missing from somewhere," said Dykstra. "I needed to figure out where this gold was missing from."

What follows is what he discovered after years of meticulous research. Let's start at the beginning.

On the afternoon of April 9, 1865, following the Battle of Appomattox Court House, General Robert E. Lee, commander of the Army of Northern Virginia, surrendered his army to Lieutenant General Ulysses S. Grant, who commanded the federal forces of the Northern states.

For all practical purposes, the Civil War was over, but some in the Confederacy refused to accept that fact.

One of them was Confederate president Jefferson Davis. He still held out hope that he could relocate to Texas or Mexico and rally support for a southern confederation of countries that would continue the practice of slavery.

But taking on such a project required a lot of money. Splitting the Confederate treasury into at least two parts, he fled south into Georgia with a good portion of it, right ahead of advancing Union troops of the 4th Michigan Cavalry, led by Colonel Robert Horatio George Minty of Jackson, Michigan.

💰 Caveat #1:

> In the interest of full disclosure, we must stop here to point out a historical fact. Union Army records indicate that Minty was not at the scene

of Davis's capture. Soldiers from the 4th Michigan did participate in the event, but they were commanded by Colonel Benjamin Pritchard. Minty was a brigade commander who seems to have been over 100 miles away at the time.

Dykstra agrees with that historical fact but disagrees with the assessment that eliminates Minty from the plot to steal the gold. He was, after all, Pritchard's commanding officer. It would be natural to assume that when Minty received word of the gold, which, quite naturally, would have been kept secret from anyone else in order to cut down the possibility of looting, he hatched a plot with a trusted confidant to hide it. As we shall see in a minute, some tokens were presented to Minty by Pritchard. One of them was a gold coin that would eventually be made into a necklace. The purpose of this gift, unnecessary from a military perspective, might have been to instigate the secret plot to steal the treasure.

With this first caveat, we continue.

That Jefferson Davis was captured near Irwinville, Georgia, on May 10, 1865, about a month after the fall of Richmond, by members of the 4th Michigan Cavalry is historical fact. Newspapers of the time reported, with gleeful abandon, that Davis attempted to avoid recognition by donning a woman's shawl. Many accounts had him completely dressed as a woman.

In those days, this was salacious news, indeed—so salacious, in fact, that little mention was made of the missing treasury, which was estimated to be more than $1 million worth of gold, silver, and jewelry from the rebels' hard currency reserves.

Official reports suggest that at the time of the capture, no treasure was found. This begs the question: what happened to it?

Dykstra thinks that Colonel Minty, accompanied by a few others from the Michigan Cavalry, stole it and buried it so they could come back later and secretly take possession of it (which they did 11 years later with the help of a banker from Michigan). If this is true, Minty was guilty of treason.

Upon discovering that Colonel Minty, during an unrelated trial in 1864, was wrongfully court-martialed, effectively end-

On December 29, 1876, the Pacific Express was crossing the Ashtabula River in Ohio when the bridge collapsed, killing 92 of the 159 passengers. Also lost was, perhaps, $2 million in gold bullion.

ing his advancement in the military, Dykstra came to believe he had further motive that added revenge to the desire for personal greed.

If this theory is correct, Minty would have buried the treasure somewhere in the vicinity of Lincoln County, Georgia.

This fits in with later events. After the war, Minty worked for the Detroit railroad. Other rail positions followed, and eventually, he become superintendent of freight for the Atlantic and Gulf Railway in the southeastern corner of Georgia. One line of this railroad passes very close to where the gold had been hidden.

Following this thread, Dykstra's theory proposes that in 1876, 11 years after the capture of Davis, with the help of a Michigan benefactor, Minty, and, perhaps, Pritchard, returned to the scene of the crime, dug up the buried treasure, and smuggled it north toward Michigan on the rail system with which by now he was so familiar.

Now the conspiracy plot thickens.

On December 29, 1876, a railroad bridge in Ashtabula, Ohio, collapsed, causing 11 boxcars to fall into a river gorge.

One hundred fifty-nine passengers aboard the train plunged into the river below. Ninety-two of them died in the tragedy.

Newspaper accounts claimed that one of the boxcars was carrying $2 million in gold bullion. Naturally, thousands of people began to search for the missing gold. None was ever reported found.

As it turns out, Robert Minty had been the superintendent of construction on that railway bridge. This seemed like too big of a coincidence. According to Dykstra, "I believe that Minty needed a diversion, so with his credentials, I believe that he started a rumor of the $2 million at the bottom of the river gorge to keep everybody away from the gold that was en route at the time."

Shortly after this, newspaper accounts indicate that during a coin show in Traverse City, Michigan, a necklace containing a gold sovereign was displayed that three experts confirmed was part of the missing Confederate gold shipment that disappeared near Lincoln County, Georgia. Although Minty himself could not be traced to Traverse City, that was the hometown of his wife, Grace Ann Abbott, who was seen wearing the necklace.

💰 Caveat #2:

> Rand Bitter is the author of a 2006 self-published biography about Robert Minty called *Minty and his Cavalry: A History of the Sabre Brigade*. He believes that the reports about the necklace are probably real, but that it was given to Minty following Davis's capture. Along with the necklace, Minty was also given Davis's revolver and holsters. They are currently on display in a museum in Richmond. In his book, Bitter states that Minty never received a monetary reward of any kind.
>
> He justifies his opinion by pointing out that the great scandal of Minty's life happened at this time.
>
> In the 1870s, Minty moved to Indiana. He was alone. That in itself is not scandalous; marriages break up all the time. But Minty deserted his family in order to marry his wife Grace's sister, Laura Abbott, after which he was disowned by much of the remaining Abbott family.

This story becomes even more intriguing when we return to the deathbed confession that began this whole theory. The one who divulged the story about the boxcar being pushed off the train was none other than George Alexander Abbott, Minty's brother-in-law, who had previously made it very clear that he didn't like Minty or what he had done to the Abbott family name. Given his feelings toward his brother-in-law, he doesn't seem a likely candidate to know details about Minty's gold.

Assuming Minty did manage to smuggle Confederate gold into Michigan, how did he do it and what happened to it? A retired, court-martialed, disgraced, Union soldier-turned railroad engineer can't simply start flashing a lot of cash. People, especially small-town, Midwestern people, are bound to gossip about something like that.

Now the story takes yet another twist. Enter the millionaire 19th-century philanthropist patriarch of Muskegon, Michigan, whose name was Charles H. Hackley. He was a lumber baron and banker who, according to his family, made his wealth the old-fashioned way: he earned every penny of it.

According to his descendant, "My grandfather didn't need any of that Civil War gold. He had already proven his ability to make millions of dollars as a lumber baron. It's ludicrous to think that he would stoop so low as to have to steal something from some entity. He wouldn't have been party to that."

Dykstra is not so sure. He acknowledges the great debt that

Charles Hackley was a lumber baron in Michigan and a philanthropist who was quite wealthy, so why would someone like him want to steal government gold? Some speculate that Hackley was actually in debt and desperate.

Muskegon owes Charles Hackley. A visit to the city today reveals Hackley Library, Hackley Church, Hackley schools, Hackley Hospital, and, most importantly, as we shall soon see, Hackley Park. He was a much beloved philanthropist, taking a small lumber town and putting it on the map. The Hackley-Hume Lumber Mill on Muskegon Lake was a going concern until Michigan was effectively logged over, closing the mill in 1894 and drying up the lumber business in that area. By then, he was a wealthy banker.

But his wealth seems to have grown exponentially after 1870. What happened to infuse his working capital so greatly?

Did Hackley see the writing on the wall concerning the deforestation of the state of Michigan? While many lumber mill owners moved their operations to the Pacific Northwest, Hackley remained in Muskegon after his mill closed in 1894. He zeroed in on the urban revitalization of his hometown.

Where did he get the money? Had he simply saved it over the years? Or were other factors at work?

Dykstra believes that Charles Hackley was the kingpin of a small group of people who conspired to transport fellow Michigander Minty's stolen Confederate gold to the Muskegon vault at the Hackley bank. It was Hackley, according to Dykstra, who financed building the railroad that sent Minty back to Georgia. It was Hackley who built the secret Muskegon tunnels through which Confederate gold was transferred to various places around town. It was Hackley who concocted the plan to launder the money through his various businesses, eventually reminting it so it could be used out in the open, free from the taint of scandal.

Thus, it was stolen Confederate money, according to Dykstra, that, for all practical purposes, built the city of Muskegon, Michigan.

If all this is true, Hackley certainly made good use of Jefferson Davis's stolen treasure. Hackley died in Muskegon on February 10, 1905, but his legacy lives on. His home still stands on Webster Avenue, maintained by the Lakeshore Museum Center. His statue sits on a bench at the corner of Clay Avenue and Third Street.

§ Caveat #3:

> Hackley's great-grandson claims to have watched every episode of the television reality series *The Curse of Civil War Gold*, featuring Dykstra, his team, and Marty Lagina, a wealthy

resident of Traverse City, Michigan, and, for the last 11 seasons, star of *The Curse of Oak Island.* Lagina made his money in business but still confesses to be a treasure hunter at heart.

Although Hackley III was "enthralled" by the show, he also thinks it is "phony" and seriously flawed when it comes to historical accuracy.

Anyone familiar with what Los Angeles calls "The Business" knows full well that when TV cameras move into a local environment for filming, they tend to dominate with considerable arrogance. Apparently, that's what happened in Muskegon. "The crew came in like a bull in a China closet," Hackley's grandson said. "There's been no proper etiquette shown. They just run roughshod like they own the place. They haven't put up $12 million to make Muskegon a wonderful place like my grandfather did."

The TV crew demanded complete confidentiality so as not to give away any of the plot of the series before it was shown. Town officials said they denied permits because they were not told anything about the content or how their town would be presented. In at least one instance, a crew member was said to have snuck into a building to film without permission. He was, quite understandably, thrown out.

"Charles H. Hackley does not deserve to have his name and reputation desecrated. They're spreading rumors," said a spokesman for the Hackley family, "and they need to learn some manners."

Dykstra was apparently disturbed to hear about the Hackley family's opinion of the show. "Hackley did great things for Muskegon—no question," Dykstra said in an interview with

(Left to right) Mark Holley, Kevin Dykstra, Fred Monroe, and Al Dykstra in a scene from *The Curse of Civil War Gold*. Dykstra's program about looking for the lost gold in Michigan has ruffled the feathers of Charles Hackley's descendants.

the MLive.com/Muskegon Chronicle. "If the funds were ill-gotten, only he has to answer for that. Everybody in Muskegon and West Michigan are indebted to Hackley. What he did was so far above and beyond what anyone else has ever done and probably will ever do."

But what about the treasure itself? Does any more wealth lie hidden, not only in a sunken boxcar in Lake Michigan, but perhaps in other places as well?

If it does, the answer may lie in a treasure map. This map isn't drawn on paper, but it might lie hidden in plain sight, built into the structure of Hackley Park in downtown Muskegon. The park was designed by Hackley himself, who was a high-degree Mason with ties to the Knights Templar, who were famous for architectural designs built into their creations.

Dykstra believes he can identify a Confederate battle flag superimposed over the park's layout when viewed from above. This doesn't mean that Hackley was a Southern sympathizer. Far from it! He was a staunch Republican who held several public offices, such as Muskegon County treasurer, member of the Common Council, member of the Muskegon Board of Public Works, and president of the school board. But Dykstra thinks he might have superimposed a Confederate flag over the design of the park as a kind of tongue-in-cheek, inside joke with those in the know as a way of reminding them all where the money came from to build it.

It is also possible that some architectural clues could be in the location of various buildings he built surrounding the park. They might have Masonic implications, just as in the case of the Founding Fathers and Washington, D.C. This is, of course, sheer speculation.

Whatever the case, the two seasons of *The Curse of Civil War Gold* on television has certainly generated excitement in the population in and around Muskegon. Lakeshore Chamber of Commerce president Cindy Larsen was quoted as saying, "What is of great interest to the Chamber is the fact that it has given (Muskegon) national exposure. The visuals used in this program have been very positive for attracting people to the community."

> *The Lakeshore Museum Center holds annual "scandal tours," which involve a mock jury trial. Evidence is put forth, and people get to decide whether Hackley stole Confederate gold and hid it in Muskegon.*

The Lakeshore Museum Center holds annual "scandal tours," which involve a mock jury trial. Evidence is put forth, and people get to decide whether Hackley stole Confederate gold and hid it in Muskegon.

Aaron Mace, assistant program manager for the Center, claims, "We do not believe that Charles Hackley was connected to any plot to steal Confederate gold or that any plot existed at all. We get people coming here to visit because they've seen (Muskegon) on the show. We view it as an opportunity to educate people about the real history."

Jon Rooks, who owns the former Hackley Union National Bank building, now called the Highpoint Flats apartments, let a film crew inside to demolish walls in search of tunnels that would have been used to move gold around the city. He appointed them part of his demolition crew during the rebuilding process. In the process, they looked through old safety deposit boxes for hints of treasure. None was found.

According to Rooks, "The show has done a pretty good job at making a long-shot theory interesting. I also think that they've highlighted, to some extent, some of the fantastic things that Hackley has done for the community. The show could very well end on the note that Hackley was nothing but the great guy that we all pretty much know that he was."

Perhaps Hackley's great-grandson best summed up his family's opinion of the theory: "The bottom line for Muskegon is that they have always been so gracious and so wonderful to welcome us as Hackleys. All the entities that my grandfather established—the hospital, library, art gallery, and others—they've all been so professional in keeping the legacy going to make sure there's still value. Today, 100-odd years later, it's still going strong."

So much for the TV show. What about the treasure theory?

Frankfort superintendent Joshua Mills likes the whole idea. He's probably motivated at least somewhat by the economic possibilities that hordes of treasure seekers might bring into the area. Gold fever once sparked an economic boom in California for those who profited off those who came to town hoping to get rich. Maybe it could happen to the hotels and restaurants in Muskegon.

Civil War historians and authors such as Rand Bitter aren't convinced. "It's all a bunch of hogwash," he said. His research has convinced him that Minty's railroad employment following the war never placed him in a position that would have enabled moving secret boxcars full of money all the way from Georgia to Michigan.

Even Dykstra acknowledges the possibility that any gold found in the lake might not necessarily be from the Confederate treasury. His research is based on a lot of conjecture. "It's a long stretch," he says.

After all, the search began with hearsay evidence of a deathbed confession and worked out from there. Minty was presumed to be in command of the men who captured Jefferson Davis even though he was physically at least 100 miles away. He was from Michigan, and he worked on railroads for the rest of his life after the war, but it's still a long way from there to a boxcar pushed off a boat into Lake Michigan.

A lot of shipwreck divers are active in the Great Lakes region. Many of them wonder if the real treasure to be found involves income from a reality TV show.

Aside from the history, which, after all, is as much a part of treasure seeking as finding actual treasure, the fact remains that the state of Michigan would probably claim the gold if it was found. At the very least, lengthy ownership claims would keep it tied up for years.

So, where does that leave us? Alas, Season 3 of *The Curse of Civil War Gold* has been canceled for unknown reasons. That, too, could be part of the conspiracy. Who knows for sure?

Until somebody finds something specific, we'll all just have to wait and see.

But that's part of the fun of lost treasure.

A Stagecoach and a "Blood-Soaked Treasure"

In the April 30, 2019, edition of the *East Idaho News*, reporter Robert Patten asked an interesting question: "Can you find east Idaho's blood-soaked treasure?"

It's probably buried somewhere near the old Portneuf Road, which ran through the Idaho Territory from Virginia City, Montana, to Pocatello, Idaho. How the treasure got there is quite a story and captures the essence of the Old West that existed out on the frontier in 1865.

In the days before the railroad was built in those regions, stagecoaches were the preferred manner of transport for all manner of freight and trade goods, including gold from the Montana mines back to so-called civilization. It was a romantic and useful but dangerous mode of transportation. People were well informed about schedules and such and depended on them.

Long-distance travel back in the late nineteenth century typically involved a ride in a stagecoach. They were also used for shipping freight, but they were easy prey to attacks from bandits.

But outlaws are people, too, and in those wild regions, with vast spaces between stops and rest areas, stagecoaches were easy prey for robbers.

Sitting beside the driver was usually one man who rode "shotgun." Sometimes passengers were armed and ready to fend off attacks, but they were often outmanned and outgunned by bands of desperadoes.

One of those bands was called the Picket Coral Gang. They had a reputation for being particularly prolific and experienced when it came to holding up stagecoaches, and in May 1865 they set their sights on a gold shipment said to be aboard a coach of the Overland Stage Line.

The gang consisted of four outlaws who operated in and around Boise City, Idaho. The leader, Brockie Jack, had recently broken out of an Oregon jail and was hiding from authorities at a ranch not far from town. Next in line was Big Dave Updyke, who had just been elected sheriff of Ada County. He was, of course, officially an upstanding citizen, but because he was known to have contacts with felons and assorted riffraff, he was being closely monitored by the Payette Vigilance Committee. The rest of the gang consisted of sharp-shooter Willy Whittmore, recognized as a man with a very short fuse, and Fred Williams, about whom history has recorded next to nothing.

> *One of those bands was called the Picket Coral Gang. They had a reputation for being particularly prolific and experienced when it came to holding up stagecoaches . . .*

Boise City was about 200 miles west of the Portneuf Stage Route in eastern Idaho, but the four men left town, rode through the backwoods to escape detection, and camped out at Ross Fork Creek. Fred Williams, the one least apt to be recognized, went to Virginia City, Montana, to gather information about the stage schedule for the suspected gold shipment. His job was to relay the information to the gang and then book passage on the stage. He was the inside man.

The other three outlaws scoped out the route the coach would take in order to pick out the right place to stage an ambush. They found their spot just a few miles south of what is now Pocatello, Idaho, the home of Idaho State University. It was perfect: a narrow canyon, heavily timbered, and rocky. They built a roadblock out of boulders, forcing the stage to slow down as it passed through. Willy Whittmore, the best shot in the group, was armed with the new Henry repeating rifle, released

From 1856 to 1913, there were a recorded 458 stagecoach robberies in America. The one perpetrated by the Picket Coral Gang was one of the more unusual. The gang members were all either killed or they disappeared, and the gold from the stage vanished as well.

in 1860. His job was to shoot the lead horses if the driver found a way through.

It took two weeks of waiting for things to commence, but on July 21, 1865, the stagecoach finally left Virginia City. Charlie Parks, a veteran hand, was the driver. Besides the gold, it contained seven passengers, including Fred Williams. They crossed the Ruby Mountains on schedule and spent the first night at the Corral Station near present-day Dillon, Montana. Three days later, the stagecoach traveled along the route of the future Union Pacific Railroad. At the Sodhouse Station, they stopped to rest for the night. Williams snuck away from the stage, and no one seems to have missed him.

At the outlaw band's camp at Ross Fork, he was able to report that the stage was carrying two strongboxes full of gold. He then made his way back to the stage.

The ambush took place the next day, on July 26, but it didn't go as smoothly as planned. When Whittmore showed himself, carrying his new Henry rifle, it was obvious what was about to transpire. One of the passengers was a professional gambler named Sam Martin. Spotting the ambush, he pulled his revolver and began firing, shooting off Whittmore's left index finger.

Whittmore, famous for his short temper, yelled, "It's a trap!" He then proceeded to empty his rifle into the side of the stagecoach.

Charlie Parks, the veteran driver, attempted to drive through the brush around the boulders, but Brockie Jack shot the lead horses, stopping the stage. Parks, though wounded, ran for the woods. Williams followed close behind, as did James B. Brown, a Virginia City saloonkeeper who was also a passenger.

Brockie Jack managed to secure Whittmore's rifle, approach

the now silent stage, and shout, "Come out of there with your hands up!" When he opened the door, he exclaimed, "My God, they're all dead."

He had discovered the bodies of Sam Martin, the gambler who had shot Whittmore; Mr. and Mrs. Andy Ditmar, a Mormon couple who had been visiting relatives in Bannock, Montana; Jess Harper, an ex-Confederate soldier who was on his way to visit his parents; and a man named L. F. Carpenter, who was headed for San Francisco to catch a steamship to New Orleans.

As it turns out, Carpenter was injured but faked his death. Later, he was able to supply some of the details of the robbery.

As the robbers looted the stage, Fred Williams staggered out of the woods. He had been shot during Whittmore's angry response to losing his finger.

> *Big Dave Updyke tried to use his reputation as a sheriff and honorable citizen to deny that he had been a part of the affair, but the Payette Vigilance Committee would have none of it.*

When the outlaws broke open the strongboxes, they found 15 gold bars and two pouches filled with gold dust and nuggets. Two more pounds of gold were discovered in the passenger compartment. After packing it all up, they rode off down the canyon.

When they were gone, Parks returned to the stage along with Brown. They managed to save Carpenter, who had covered himself with the dead bodies of the others. Cutting the stage away from the two dead horses, they managed to return to the Miller Ranch Station.

The three surviving witnesses were able to identify the members of the gang, and after paying an $86,000 claim, the insurance company offered a $10,000 reward for information leading to the recovery of the gold and the capture of the robbers.

Meanwhile, the Payette Vigilance Committee issued orders to hang the criminals, including Big Dave Updyke, their newly elected sheriff.

First to be collected was the hot-tempered gunman Willy Whittmore, now missing a finger on one hand. He was found while on a drinking spree in Arizona. When he tried to resist arrest, he was shot and killed.

One week later, Fred Williams was hanged by a local vigilance committee in Colorado. Neither man had any money when he was killed.

Big Dave Updyke tried to use his reputation as a sheriff and honorable citizen to deny that he had been a part of the affair, but the Payette Vigilance Committee would have none of it. They arrested him on September 28, 1865, for fraud and failing to arrest West Jenkins, an outlaw with an equally questionable reputation.

Updyke managed to come up with the bail money, fled the town, and returned to Boise City, where he thought he had more influence. The good citizens there, however, were finished with him. A posse of vigilantes tracked him down and questioned him. They weren't satisfied with his story of innocence and hung him on general principles. He had only $50 on him when he died.

Their explanation for their actions was soon published in the local newspaper: "Dave Updyke was an accessory after the fact to the Portneuf stage robbery, accessory and accomplice to the robbery of the stage near Boise City in 1864, chief conspirator in burning property on the overland stage line, guilty of aiding and assisting the escape of West Jenkins, and the murderer of others while sheriff, and threatening the lives and property of an already outraged and long-suffering community."

Brockie Jack, the leader of the band, disappeared and was never heard from again.

Did he manage to escape with the gold the others did not possess when they died? Well, no record exists of any of the gold bars ever being sold. They were all well marked. The weight of it all prevented one man from carrying it very far, so speculations began to surface. Did the gang bury the gold, planning to come back for it when the coast was clear?

This, coupled with the weight of the bars and the destitute state of the three men who were killed, has led to speculation that the gold was buried near the robbery site. It would now be worth about $1.6 million.

Is it any wonder that gold diggers prowl the canyons around the Portneuf River? If anyone finds it, the insurance company, having paid the claim, would certainly claim a healthy share. Depending on whether it might be on federal lands, state-owned lands, or private property, different laws will come into play. The U.S. government tax office would also want its due.

All told, maybe the treasure, if it's there at all, would be better off remaining lost.

Jesse James and the Knights of the Golden Circle

Earlier, we said that when Confederate Jefferson Davis fled Richmond ahead of Union armies at the close of the Civil War, he split the Confederate treasury into at least two parts.

We've already tried to trace the part that might have been transported north to Michigan. What about the rest?

This story is even more convoluted than the one we just looked at.

It involves Jefferson Davis, Nathan Bedford Forrest, John Wilkes Booth, the outlaw Jesse James, and a mysterious, underground, secret society called the Knights of the Golden Circle.

This story comes with a caveat or two, just as the previous one did. Some historians think the KGC (Knights of the Golden Circle) never existed, or if it did, it was a small, ineffective organization that never rose to the fame surrounding the movement it inspired that espoused similar goals, the KKK (Ku Klux Klan).

We must note as well, though, that secret societies exist in … well … secrecy. Many historians accept the many facts and historical explanations that continue to surface about this group. For example, the 2007 movie *National Treasure: Book of Secrets,* starring Nicholas Cage, thrust the organization into the spotlight in a big way.

These are the facts.

In the years preceding the Civil War, antislavery sentiment began to rise rapidly in the northern United States. In response, white Southerners became increasingly militant about preserving and expanding their system of slavery. With the new country rapidly expanding to the West across the Mississippi, the fears in the South were that new states would be antislavery as well. To those in the South who considered themselves American patriots, this was anathema. Their identity was closely aligned with the institution of slavery and white supremacy. Many influential

Members of the Knights of the Golden Circle imagined an expansive confederacy of connected, proslavery states that included the American South, Central America, the Caribbean, and parts of northern South America.

people considered the states north of the Mason-Dixon Line, a boundary line that follows the borders between Pennsylvania, Delaware, and Maryland, then west to the Ohio River and on to the Mississippi, to be a tyrannical power from whom they needed to defend themselves by force of arms, if necessary.

These proslavery Southerners soon became the base of what was to be called the Knights of the Golden Circle.

The name is derived from the fact that since the North was expanding so rapidly and could soon threaten the institution of slavery in the Americas, proslavery sympathizers wanted to expand as well. They envisioned a confederacy of proslavery nations that would begin in the American South, continue west through Texas and Mexico, then south through Central America and parts of South America and back east to Cuba and the Caribbean, in effect forming a great circle, a "golden circle," that would surround the Gulf of Mexico. Their goal was to build a slave empire that would rival that of Rome.

Some say they formed in 1854. Others insist the year was 1859, when George W. L. Bickley, an adventurer who later became a physician, moved from Virginia to Ohio, launched a fraternal order that proposed the annexation of Mexico to the United States, and proposed the official establishment of American military posts in Mexico. According to Bickley, this move would protect the Southern states and their way of life from being overwhelmed by the industrial and commercial interests of the North. He even went so far as to contact Abraham Lincoln and object to what he felt was happening in the country.

The scheme attracted a lot of publicity, especially in Southern newspapers that favored expansion. Bickley once claimed his organizations numbered 115,000 followers, but this is highly doubtful.

The group's leaders were made up of Southern, influential, proslavery, wealthy, and powerful men, many of whom were

A physician from Virginia, George W. L. Bickley founded the Knights of the Golden Circle as a secret society to promote proslavery states.

also officials of local Masonic lodges. Because of their ties to the Masons, they transferred to their new organization many secret codes, handshakes, passwords, and other means of identification.

A picture of the then governor of Kentucky, for instance, shows him touching the collar of his suit in a particular way that was said to identify him as a fraternal brother to those who knew the group's secrets. Other members included Jefferson Davis, president of the Confederate States of America; John Wilkes Booth, who went on to fulfill one of the organization's stated primary goals of assassinating President Lincoln; Nathan Bedford Forrest, the first leader of the KKK; and the outlaw Jesse James, who would soon figure prominently in the quest for Confederate gold.

In 1860, during the very same month the Republican National Committee held the meeting in which Abraham Lincoln was nominated as their presidential candidate, the KGC held their own convention in Raleigh, North Carolina. Their agenda was quite different. Indeed, in 1861, they plotted to end Lincoln's life by kidnapping him in Baltimore before he could take the oath of office. The plan was discovered and thwarted by Allen Pinkerton and the Pinkerton Detective Agency.

Thus it was that in 1865, when the actor John Wilkes Booth shot Lincoln in the back of the head while the president enjoyed a play at the Ford Theater, shouted, "*Sic semper tyrannis!* (Ever thus to tyrants!) The South is avenged" and jumped onto the

Among the prominent members of the Knights of the Golden Circle was Confederate general Nathan Bedford Forrest, who also was a grand wizard of the Ku Klux Klan.

stage, escaping into the night, he considered his actions to be those of a patriot in good standing with the goals of the KGC. Before his death 12 days later, he was amazed to discover that he was considered a traitorous murderer even in his home state.

"Tell my mother I did it for my country," he was said to have whispered before he spoke his final words, "Futile. Futile!"

As the war slowly wound down to its inevitable conclusion, those with Southern sympathies were understandably let down, and that's an understatement.

Many refused to let go and admit defeat. Although an attempt was made to rewrite the history of the Lost Cause by building statues and monuments across the South dedicated to preserving the myth of great generals and heroes and claiming that the war was really about the rights of states to secede from the Union, the real issue was slavery, and most people knew it. A way of life was over, and white supremacists felt that everything they knew and held dear had been uprooted and destroyed by a tyrannical government who didn't understand them.

To understand what follows about this story of lost Confederate gold and the sentiments that formed the curse surrounding it, we need to take a short detour and set the stage.

In 1976, actor/producer Clint Eastwood released the movie *The Outlaw Josey Wales*. It was loosely based on the book *The Rebel Outlaw: Josey Wales* by Asa Earl "Forrest" Carter, a notorious segregationist who founded and led his local chapter of the Ku Klux Klan. Even 100 years after Lee's surrender of his army at Appomattox, Carter was a staunch white supremacist who never surrendered his Southern sympathies.

In 1958, he quit the Klan after shooting two of its members over a financial dispute and eventually became a speechwriter for presidential candidate George Wallace. He was the one who wrote Wallace's now infamous pro-segregation line in 1963: "Segregation now, segregation tomorrow, segregation forever." Carter went on to run for lieutenant governor of Alabama on a segregationist ticket but finished fifth in a field of five candidates.

After his loss, he disappeared from public view, adopted the pen name Forrest Carter, in honor of Confederate general Bedford Forrest, one of his heroes, and wrote *The Rebel Outlaw: Josey Wales*.

In the 1994 movie *Forrest Gump*, starring Tom Hanks, it was ironic that at one point, it pictured the title character, who was named after Bedford Forrest, listening to George Wallace reciting a speech written by Forrest Carter, who was also named after Bedford Forrest. It would seem that Bedford Forrest and his Southern sympathies had a long shelf life, overlapping many generations.

At any rate, Carter sent a copy of his book to Clint Eastwood, who eventually read it and bought the movie rights. When the book was later re-released, the publisher gave it a new cover and renamed it *Gone to Texas*. That's the title that is used in the movie's credits.

Clint Eastwood didn't know anything about the author's real persona as a rabid segregationist who helped make George Wallace such an infamous politician. If he had, given his political sensibilities, he might never have touched the project, but after the movie was released and became a hit, he was interviewed by Barbara Walters. Several politicians and reporters, seeing the interview, recognized the Carter name. That led the *New York Times* to write an exposé. Carter spent the rest of his life denying his past.

What finally came to light was that although Josey Wales was a completely fictional character, his story was loosely based on a real person named Bill Wilson. In 1938, one of Wilson's descendants, George Clinton Arthur, wrote a biography about him called *Bushwhacker: Missouri's Most Infamous Desperado*.

Like Wilson, the movie character Josey Wales became a wanted man after the Civil War because he refused to surrender. Wilson rode with the notorious group of guerrilla fighters, also known as "bushwhackers," called Quantrill's Raiders, led by William Quantrill. Other members of the group were Jesse James and his brother, Frank.

In the early days of the war, both Missouri and Kansas were, at least in name, under Union government control. But Southern sympathizers were equally vocal and fought for their cause. Widespread violence was the order of the day. Bushwhackers fought antislavery Jayhawkers for control of the area.

Quantrill's Raiders were surreptitiously financed by Jeffer-

Jesse James (left) and his brother Frank were notorious outlaws and bushwhackers after the Civil War, fighting anti-slavery Jayhawkers in Missouri.

son Davis through, according to legend, the Knights of the Golden Circle.

Lawrence, Kansas, was a center for antislavery sentiment. The town had outlawed Quantrill and his men and gone so far as to jail some of them along with a group of women who sympathized with their cause. To put women in jail was strictly against the myth of the Southern gentleman, so in August 1863, Quantrill led an attack, killing more than 180 civilians in retaliation for the casualties caused when the women's jail collapsed.

Under the Partisan Ranger Act of 1862, the Confederate government had granted Quantrill a field commission but was outraged by what was now being called a massacre and withdrew support for Quantrill and his raiders. This led to the breakup of the group. By 1864, Quantrill had lost control. His men split up into smaller bands.

Some of them, including Quantrill, were later killed in various raids. Many rode to Texas to take up residence in what was considered a lynchpin of the golden circle because it connected the Southern slave states with Mexico. That was why Jefferson Davis headed there before he was finally apprehended.

Some brokered pardons with the U.S. government similar to the one portrayed in Eastwood's movie, but just like the fictional outlaw Josey Wales, Bill Wilson never did. He continued to make secret journeys back to Missouri to visit his family. There, the Ozark Mountain people welcomed him as a sort of folk hero. Many years later, remnants of Quantrill's Raiders even held reunions.

William Quantrill was the leader of Quantrill's Raiders, a Confederate guerilla ranger outfit that performed war atrocities against Union soldiers.

This acceptance by local folks helps explains why, when Jesse and Frank James formed their own gang of bank robbers, they were often protected by neighbors. They, too, were seen as heroes because they rode with William Quantrill.

But what happened to all the gold they were said to have robbed during their career as outlaws?

That brings us back to the search for lost Civil War gold and the avowed mission of the Knights of the Golden Circle, of which Jesse James was a prominent member.

During the 1960s and '70s, the name Jesse James rose to prominence following a number of books and TV movies that presented him as a kind of Robin Hood figure. According to these stories, he robbed from the rich to give to the poor, paying off mortgages and settling the debts of grateful neighbors. Before this, he was viewed by historians as a notorious bank robber.

Hollywood recently revived his story with a 2007 revisionist Western starring Brad Pitt as Jesse James and Casey Affleck as Robert Ford called *The Assassination of Jesse James by the Coward Robert Ford*.

Woody Guthrie wrote a song about another outlaw, "Pretty Boy" Floyd, but it could just as well be applied to similar legends surrounding Jesse James:

> *Many a starvin' farmer*
> *The same story told*
> *How the outlaw paid their mortgage*
> *And saved their little homes.*

Others tell you 'bout a stranger
That come to beg a meal,
Underneath his napkin
Left a thousand-dollar bill.

("Pretty Boy Floyd" by Woody Guthrie)

These days, James is the focus of a great debate between those who see him as a simple outlaw and those who believe he was a prominent member of the Knights of the Golden Circle who continued to fight for the group's agenda, stealing lots of money which he then hid away to be resurrected at a future date.

"Save your Confederate money, boys, the South shall rise again" has been a popular expression ever since the war ended. Supposedly, the treasury that once backed Confederate money is still out there somewhere, hidden away in buried deposits that range from Ohio to Utah and New Mexico, thanks to the work of Jesse James and the clandestine members of the KGC.

Some people believe the secret organization still operates, that its members know where the money is and are watching over it, protecting it from seekers and looters.

Many even believe that Jesse faked his own death. As they see it, Robert Ford, "the dirty little coward who shot Mr. Howard (Jesse's alias)" according to the famous song made popular by the likes of Woody Guthrie, Pete Seeger, and Eddy Arnold, was not a traitorous member of the James gang. He was really part of the plot to allow Jesse the freedom to escape into anonymity.

"If Jesse stole so much money," they ask, "where is it? What did he do with it? He wasn't a rich man." The truth is, no one knows, but the theory is that he was adding to the gold shipped out of Richmond by train following Jefferson Davis's flight toward Texas.

According to T. J. Stiles, author of the biography *Jesse James: Last Rebel of the Civil War*, Jesse was more a political figure than an outlaw. He had a cause: namely, what is now called the "Lost Cause" of the South. In this, he was on the same side as the many organizations that erected statues of Southern heroes following the war.

"With Jesse, it was crime plus politics," Stiles believes. "He and his gang weren't modern terrorists, but what distinguishes him from all the other criminals in the 19th century is the way he would use his notoriety to promote a political cause."

An engraving depicts Robert Ford—who was a member of Jesse James' gang—shooting James in the back for the reward money. Some believe that James was hoarding some of his stolen wealth to aid the South in resurrecting the Confederacy.

In other words, James fervently believed in white nationalism. It was a part of his political ideology. He robbed banks and trains that demonstrated Union loyalties. He harassed election officials during the midterms of 1866. He decried the postwar Republican party of Lincoln and advocated against the reelection of Ulysses S. Grant in 1872.

Modern historians tend to consider Jesse a simple outlaw who robbed for personal gain. This, says Stiles, couldn't be further from the truth. In his view, Jesse James considered himself a Southern patriot who never stopped fighting the Civil War.

Jesse "lived his whole life underground, and there's no collection of letters from him." In his book, Stiles wrote:

> All the evidence about him personally has to be delivered with a caveat, so that also means that he's more susceptible to revisions, and sometimes weird revisions. Somebody is going to study, if they haven't already, [the connection] between this kind of conspiracy theory

approach to history in recent decades, and people's willingness to believe that the election (of
2000) was stolen, for example, this belief in the
sensational and conspiracies and hidden hands.

The basis, then, of the theory that says that Jesse James is
connected to the disappearance of the Southern treasury was
laid out by those who were interviewed during the television
series *Beyond Oak Island: Civil War Gold Found in Utah*,
Season 1, Episode 6.

Before, during, and immediately after the Civil War, the
Knights of the Golden Circle were busy stealing and hiding
a war treasury that would support the cause of slavery. This
treasure was hidden all over the South, from Virginia to Arkansas. After the war was over, most of it was retrieved and
taken west to be hidden again, this time to support a future
uprising of states dedicated to the institution of slavery. Jesse
James was the western commander of this effort.

The treasure was hidden in states such as Utah, New
Mexico, and Arizona, guarded by supersecret "sentinels" who
have been watching over it ever since, passing on its location only to others who are part of the clandestine but still active KGC. Their shrouded presence comprises the curse that
guards the treasure to this day.

How can someone find the treasure, supposing they can
avoid the watchful eyes of the sentinels? The answer is found
in the symbolism that has been a part of Masonic ritual ever
since the days of the Knights Templar.

We'll have a lot more to say about them in subsequent
chapters, but for now, it is enough to say that all over the
West are found secret signs and symbols pecked into rock and
carved into trees, mixing with similar signs that go all the way
back to the early indigenous inhabitants of those parts.

One sign that is a dead giveaway of Jesse's presence is the
"JJ" sign, consisting of Jesse's initials, sometimes found one
after the other or else back to back, one facing left and one
facing right. When you find those initials, especially paired
with other Masonic symbols, such as those found on the dollar
bill you carry in your pocket, you can bet you're close to a
spot where treasure either is or once was.

Bob Brewer, for instance, is a veteran treasure hunter from
Arkansas who served with the Navy and experienced combat
in Vietnam. He believes that some of his ancestors have been
guarding caches of KGC gold right into the 20th century. He

talks about being shown, as a boy, a "treasure tree" scarred with strange, carved symbols.

He taught himself how to follow the telltale signs left on trees and rocks in the Arkansas woods. In 1991, in the hills of western Arkansas, he even found a small cache of gold and silver coins minted between 1802 and 1889. Their face value was nearly $460. Today, of course, they would be much more valuable than that.

In 1993, he assisted in another find, this time in Oklahoma, while following a copy of a map with the symbol "JJ" that was thought to be the telltale sign of Jesse James.

Brewer, like many other treasure hunters, is not motivated simply by the thought of personal riches. He's in it for the story and the history behind it. He freely admits that proving the existence of a powerful secret network after the Civil War, one that might still exist, would be the biggest story of his life. It would definitely add a missing chapter to American history.

> *The funny part about it is, all the James descendants would love for the treasure hunters to find the gold, because then we could claim the inheritance!"*

KGC records with examples of the group's coded symbols have been found in the National Archives. The book *Shadow of the Sentinel: One Man's Quest to Find the Hidden Treasure of the Confederacy*, cowritten by Warren Getler and Brewer, is a must-read for anyone interested in this subject. (The paperback edition was renamed *Rebel Gold*.)

Eric James, a direct descendant of Jesse James, feels the burden of such constant treasure hunting. "It's been going on ever since Jesse was assassinated," he said, "and thanks to reality TV, it's not going to stop in the near future or the next 100 years. The funny part about it is, all the James descendants would love for the treasure hunters to find the gold, because then we could claim the inheritance! [Or] if they could prove it came from a bank or a railroad, that money could be claimed by the descendants of those corporations."

Like all good lost treasure stories, definitive proof always seems to elude those who fervently believe in its existence. Someone found a treasure and lost it again. The curse struck and the seeker died or was never seen again. Clues beckon the seeker on but remain forever elusive. Just enough historical evidence suggests the reality of lost treasure but not enough to fully solve the mystery. On and on it goes.

Was a Union treasure shipment lost near Dents Run in Pennsylvania? Definitely! Even the FBI thinks so. Did the Confederate treasury disappear after the fall of Richmond? Undoubtedly! Historical records prove it left by rail before the Yankees captured the city. Has any of it been found? Ah! There's the rub.

As long as the mystery remains, some will follow elusive trails, no matter how much conjecture is needed to connect the missing dots. It's out there, that's for sure. It's probably buried somewhere between Lake Michigan, Pennsylvania, Utah, and Texas. All you have to do is look for it.

The Hidden Loot of Sam Bass

The American West is notorious for attracting just about every type of person one might imagine. Cutthroats and villains running away from a troubled past, politicians such as the honorable Davy Crockett from Tennessee, escaped slaves and free blacks, young teenagers hoping to be cowboys, land speculators, farmers trying to settle down on a little piece of land, and cattle barons hoping to get rich quick all found themselves heading toward the land where the sun set but hope always sprang eternal right over the horizon.

On July 21, 1851, Sam Bass was born near Mitchell, Indiana. He was destined to be one of those to whom the West sang its siren song. His parents died before he was 13 years old, and he found himself living with his uncle, who considered him a cheap source of hard labor. After five years of living a hard farming life, he had enough. In 1869, he ran away from home, just as so many in his position had done before him, and headed south, but less than a year of working at a Mississippi sawmill convinced him that he could do better. He headed west on horseback and eventually wound up in Denton, Texas, wondering what to do next.

As a boy, like so many of his contemporaries, he dreamed of being a cowboy, but it didn't take long for him to learn that his dreams and the reality of cowboy life were not at all com-

Sam Bass was an outlaw and train robber who pulled off an ambitious crime when he looted a Union Pacific train to the tune of $60,000.

patible. It was hard, backbreaking, dawn-to-dusk work with very little pay. He tried a number of jobs, working in stables, looking after livestock, cutting firewood, doing odd jobs, and even working on the railroad. Nothing seemed to fit him.

Finally, he thought he might find a good living racing horses. It worked for a while. Contemporary accounts indicate that he won some races with a horse called the Denton Mare, eventually winding up in San Antonio, but by 1876, he could see it didn't hold much future for him.

When he and a friend named Joe Collins teamed up to trail cattle to Dodge City, they decided the markets looked better farther north. Eventually, he sold the herd and made $8,000 in profits, but, like so many others who were doing the same kinds of things he was doing, he lost most of it to gambling and the many sins that were in business to tempt young cowboys such as himself.

> *He formed a band of losers such as himself and proved to be a talented robber. The gang held up seven stagecoaches without getting caught.*

Stranded in places such as Ogallala, Nebraska, and Deadwood, South Dakota, which were two of the many western towns growing from a gold mine boom, he finally hit upon what he considered to be a good source of income requiring less work than he had been forced to do so far. He decided to rob stagecoaches.

He formed a band of losers such as himself and proved to be a talented robber. The gang held up seven stagecoaches without getting caught. But dividing the money seven ways didn't earn him back the money he had already lost; he had to find a better way.

His chance came in Big Springs, Nebraska, where the gang held up an eastbound Union Pacific passenger train, netting $60,000 in newly minted $20 gold pieces from the express car and $1,300 from the passengers. They also stole four gold watches. This venture was finally profitable and historical as well. It was the first hold-up of a Union Pacific train.

Probably because he didn't fully trust his rather disreputable companions, they split the loot and rode off in different directions.

Sure enough, half the gang was hunted down and shot while resisting arrest, but Bass managed to get all the way back to Texas. On his way, he came across a group of soldiers who were looking for him. He and Jack Davis managed to convince the detectives with the group that the two of them were looking for outlaws, too, so they could claim the reward money. It was a perfect place to hide.

Once he got to Denton, Texas, he concocted a story that his newfound wealth was due to mining in the Black Hills. His devil-may-care, nonchalant attitude about having a good time and sharing it with friends eventually allowed him to form a new outlaw band, which came to be known as the Sam Bass Gang. He started to build a reputation as "Robin Hood on a fast horse" and became known as "the beloved bandit." Songs were later written about him.

Questions remained, however. It was true that he appeared wealthy when he got back to Denton. He flashed gold coins and passed them around to his friends. But how did he manage to spend $10,000 in less than four months? In today's economy, the total bag would have been worth over $1 million, divided between the gang members.

And then he went right back to robbing trains. Why? He didn't need the money or, at least, couldn't spend it that fast. What was he doing with it?

People began to think he was robbing trains just because he liked the work and was stashing away his stolen treasure. This marked the beginning of what came to be known as "The Bass War." It lasted for four months, during which Bass led his pursuers on a merry chase full of derring-do and narrow escapes. His knowledge of the country, gained during his experience punching cattle and hauling freight, really paid off.

Like most western legends, the songs and stories were often nothing at all like the real life he led, but it is known that he pulled off four train robberies in 1878 and led the Dallas posse on a merry chase each time. Eventually, even the famous Texas Rangers got in on the pursuit.

On February 22, 1878, the gang held up Texas Central train at Allen Station, making off with $1,300. They hit the same train at Hutchins on March 18. On April 4, they took on the Texas and Pacific Railroad at Eagle Ford and again on April 10 at Mesquite.

Where was all the money?

People began to go treasure hunting. Some swore he hid it in a cave at East Mountain near Mineral Wells. Others searched near the town of Prairie Dell near Big Blue Spring. Shortly after his death, maps began to appear showing the treasure hidden in an old tree. It was said to be located on what is now Sam Bass Road, two miles west of Round Rock.

Searchers thought they spotted the tree and chopped it down but didn't find anything, but treasure seekers are optimistic, if nothing else. They began to wonder, was that the right tree?

No one has ever found any of the money. It's believed to be buried somewhere, and people still look despite rumors that the ghost of Sam Bass haunts treasure seekers wherever they look.

The secret of his stolen treasure went to the grave with him. He was eventually cornered at the town of Round Rock because one of his ever-shrinking gang turned traitor and betrayed him.

Jim Murphy, member of the Bass Gang, was picked up in a sweep of many residents in the area of Tyler, Texas, and accused of mail robbery. He was offered immunity and a portion of the reward money if he "escaped" from captivity and rejoined the Bass Gang.

Murphy did just that and managed to get word out to the Texas Rangers that the gang was headed for Round Rock to rob its bank. Henceforth, he was called Jim "Judas" Murphy for the rest of his life.

After a fierce gun battle, Sam Bass was shot. A dispute has been ongoing about who fired it. No one wanted to take credit; because Bass was so popular, his killer might not have escaped alive. Although Bass managed to get out of town, his wound was mortal. Somewhere along the present-day Chisholm Trail Road, he gave his money, guns, ammunition, and horse to a gang member and lay down to die.

The next day, the Texas Rangers found him, still hanging on to life. They took him to a shack and tried to question him about

Tombstone marking the gravesite of Sam Bass at Round Rock Cemetery in Texas.

the rest of the gang's whereabouts, but Bass only answered, "It is ag'in' my profession to blow on my pals. If a man knows anything he ought to die with it in him."

He soon did, and the location of his buried money, if it ever existed, died with him.

Perhaps his last dying words, if he really said them, were prophetic: "This world is a bubble. Trouble wherever you go."

Jim "Judas" Murphy lived for only a year after that. He was so afraid that Bass's supporters would kill him that he took his own life by ingesting poison.

John Benton of Gainesville, Texas, eventually wrote the cowboy song that would bring long-lasting fame to the outlaw. He called it "The Ballad of Sam Bass":

> *Sam Bass was born in Indiana, it was his native home*
> *And at the age of seventeen, Sam began to roam*
> *Sam first came out to Texas a cowboy for to be*
> *A kinder-hearted fellow you seldom ever see*
> *Sam used to deal in race stock, one called the Denton mare;*
> *He matched her in scrub races and took her to the fair*
> *I used to coin the money and spent it just as free*
> *He always drank good whiskey wherever he might be*
> *Sam left the Collins ranch in the merry month of May*
> *With a herd of Texas cattle the Black Hills for to see*
> *Sold out in Custer City and then got on a spree—*
> *A harder set of cowboys you seldom ever see*
> *On their way back to Texas they robbed the U.P. train*
> *And then split up in couples and started out again*
> *Joe Collins and his partner were overtaken soon*
> *With all their hard-earned money they had to meet their doom*
> *Sam had four companions—four bold and daring lads—*
> *They were Richardson, Jackson, Joe Collins, and Old Dad;*
> *Four more bold and daring cowboys the rangers never knew*
> *They whipped the Texas Rangers and ran the boys in blue*

Jim Murphy was arrested and then released on bail
He jumped his bond at Tyler and then took the train
    for Terrell;
But Mayor Jones had posted Jim and that was all a
    stall
'Twas was only a plan to capture Sam before the com-
    ing fall
Sam met his fate at Round Rock, July the twenty-first
They pierced poor Sam with rifle balls and emptied
    out his purse
Poor Sam he is a corpse and six foot under clay
And Jackson's in the bushes trying to get away
Jim had borrowed Sam's good gold and didn't want
    to pay
The only shot he saw was to give poor Sam away
He sold out Sam and Barnes and left their friends
    to mourn
Oh, what a scorching Jim will get when Gabriel blows
    his horn
And so he sold out Sam and Barnes and left their
    friends to mourn
Oh, what a scorching Jim will get when Gabriel blows
    his horn
Perhaps he's got to heaven, there's none of us can say
But if I'm right in my surmise he's gone the other way

(John Benton, as recorded by Michael Martin Murphey on
his album *Cowboy Songs III: Rhymes of the Renegades*)

    Sam now lives on in legend and folklore. As for his buried loot, if it really exists, people will continue to search as long as he is remembered. But if you go looking for it, watch out for the ghosts that are said to protect it!

Dutch Schultz's Dough

Anyone who has read the book or seen the movie *The Godfather* is familiar with the story about how the nationwide ban on the sale and import of alcoholic beverages that lasted from 1919 to 1933 in the United States led, for all practical purposes, to the creation of what is now called the Mafia and organized crime.

Conservative Protestants and Progressives, led mostly by women's organizations, spearheaded the drive to institute Prohibition. They no doubt had good intentions, but the result proved catastrophic in terms of putting the word "organized" in organized crime and would cripple America for years to come. People wanted to drink, and the wealth created by selling bootlegged whiskey at greatly inflated prices led directly to the establishment of the notorious Five Families: the mobsters who ran New York. The Lucchese family, Bonanno family, Colombo family, Gambino family, and Genovese family all rose to prominence during this time.

Gangsters such as Al "Scarface" Capone, head of the Chicago outfit, and Benjamin "Bugsy" Siegel, in California, certainly operated with impunity within their spheres of influence, but the New York crime families, led by such luminaries as "Lucky" Luciano and Dutch Schultz, were considered the top echelon of mobsters for many years. They made millions within a relatively short time, eventually forming what they called The Commission and, later, the National Crime Syndicate.

In the midst of this organizing effort, Dutch Schultz might be considered a criminal prodigy of sorts.

His birth name was Arthur Flegenheimer. He was born in 1902 and by 1927 was already a successful and widespread bootlegger who owned a number of speakeasies before expanding his activities to include the numbers racket, protection, and narcotics. He even became the first mobster to extort New York's labor unions.

His reputation for ferocity made him an extremely dangerous mobster, who was believed to have had 136 people killed

Born Arthur Simon Flegenheimer, Dutch Schultz became a mobster as a very young man, specializing in bootlegging and the "numbers racket" (gambling).

---

over a 10-year period. By the time the Roaring Twenties wound down, he ran a criminal empire that was rumored to be raking in more than $20 million a year. When he was just getting started, he led the Frog Hollow Gang in the Bronx and ran his territory with an iron hand. This is when he was given the name "Dutch Schultz." The name stuck.

Eventually, when he saw what happened to Al Capone in Chicago, he began to make plans to protect his wealth. Authorities couldn't convict Capone for racketeering; too many witnesses either disappeared or changed their testimonies under oath to convince juries of guilt, so the government followed the money and arrested him for tax evasion.

Schultz knew he was vulnerable to the newly enacted federal income tax laws the government had employed specifically for the prosecution of mafiosi, so when a grand jury indicted him for income tax evasion, he took steps to hide his wealth in a place that no one but him could find. With the possibility of a long prison sentence ahead of him, he wanted a nest egg waiting for him when he was released.

With the help of two loyal members of his gang, Bernard "Lulu" Rosencrantz and Marty Krompier, he stowed wrapped bundles of $1,000 bills, negotiable Liberty Bonds, gold coins, diamonds, and other gems in a specially made steel-plated strongbox. Schultz had the only key.

Now, where to hide it?

One of the advantages of being a bootlegger and brewing liquor is knowing the countryside at least as well as the locals and maybe even better than the police. For Schultz, this meant the remote areas of the Catskill Mountains, specifically around

Schultz—shown here exiting Malone County jail in upstate New York—evaded efforts to put him in prison for tax evasion, a strategy that had worked in the case of mobster Al Capone.

the locality of Phoenicia, New York, where he had operated stills with impunity for years, so that's where he headed.

With Lulu sworn to secrecy, the two made their way there, along with their loot. After burying the stash in the woods outside of town, Schultz supposedly carved an "X" into the trunk of a nearby tree.

Lulu, however, couldn't keep quiet. Apparently, he shared the secret with Marty Krompier. Some say he even drew him a map.

Meanwhile, Manhattan district attorney Thomas E. Dewey, who would later become governor of New York, was trying to further his political career. He decided that the best way to do it would be to bring down a famous mobster such as Schultz in a high-profile, public trial. Following the downfall of Al Capone, Schultz had been declared public enemy number one by J. Edgar Hoover, head of the FBI. He seemed to be the perfect foil.

After Schultz surrendered to authorities in Albany, New York, his first trial ended with a hung jury. At his second trial, he was acquitted of all charges because of lack of evidence. Some suspected jury tampering, but Schultz seemed to have pulled it off. He was a free man.

The legal problems, however, had loosened his tight control over his criminal empire. Determined to assert his authority, he began a systematic killing spree to eliminate his rivals, including a plot to murder Thomas E. Dewey, his greatest legal adversary.

That worried the rest of the New York Crime Syndicate, which was a sort of loose confederation of New York City mobsters who controlled virtually all the crime in the Manhattan area. They began to fear that Schultz was bringing them all under the renewed scrutiny of the authorities.

Thus, it was that on the night of October 23, 1935, as

Thomas E. Dewey was the U.S. district attorney of the Southern District of New York (and later a mayor of New York City) who butted heads with Schultz, who later put out a hit on Dewey.

Schultz held court from his headquarters in a tavern he owned in Newark, New Jersey, called the Palace Chop House, he was met by two hitmen ordered by "The Commission" to murder him. When Dutch got up from a table to go to the men's room, they were waiting for him, opening fire on Dutch and his gang.

He didn't die immediately, but the next 22 hours would prove crucial to his legend. Lulu Rosencrantz, his trusted friend and bodyguard, had died in the massacre. That left only one man who knew where Dutch and Lulu had buried the treasure.

Marty Krompier, however, was never able to retrieve it. On the night of the Palace Chop House shooting, he was attacked at a New York City barber shop and shot by Jacob "Gurrah" Shapiro. Though he was wounded, he eventually pulled through, but his attacker had managed to steal the map Lulu had drawn. Without that map, Krompier couldn't find the location of the treasure and the tree marked with an "X."

Meanwhile, the legend of Dutch Schultz was about to begin. After he was shot, he survived in critical condition for 22 hours. Before he died, he was heard to mutter seemingly incoherent words from his deathbed. Police officers carefully wrote down everything he said, but it didn't seem to make any sense to them.

Ever since, however, treasure seekers have parsed every word, trying to locate a buried treasure that could exceed $50 million. Those words inspired books, a screenplay, some documentaries, and a PBS special.

These are a few of the phrases, in case you're ever in the area and want to try your hand at treasure seeking: "A boy has never wept ... nor dashed a thousand kin ... don't let Satan draw you too fast."

Many hunters presume this last phrase is a coded reference to a specific landmark. Outside of Phoenicia, west of town, is a geological oddity containing a large boulder called Devil's Tombstone and a rock outcropping called the Devil's Face.

Do the words refer to this landmark? No one knows for sure.

John Conway, author of *Dutch Schultz and His Lost Catskills' Treasure*, doubts that buried treasure exists. It might be hidden, he says, but not somewhere where two city boys would have to hike in the dark of night and do extensive work with a pick and shovel. They might not even own an adequate pair of hiking shoes.

Gary Bennett, a retired detective from Holyoke, Massachusetts, disagrees. He goes so far as to say the treasure is buried somewhere near Route 28 in Boiceville, near the Ashokan Reservoir. He formed this opinion after piecing together all available data and drawing a map he believes is similar to the one Lulu supposedly gave Krompier.

He even pinpointed the exact location, but when he arrived, he found only a hole next to a tree with the year "1934" carved into it.

Bruce Alterman, author of the book *Fear in Phoenicia: The Deadly Hunt for Dutch Schultz's Treasure,* believes the stash is buried somewhere along Notch Inn Road.

Other treasure hunters have different ideas, each based on a bit of information that seems, to them at least, to offer a reasonable explanation.

When an unnamed man spent years walking up and down the nearby tracks of the Ulster & Delaware Railroad with a shovel, railroad officials had to ask him to stop. He was becoming a nuisance.

The owner of a campground near where the supposed treasure is thought to be buried reports that people with metal detectors and shovels continually ask permission to search her

The Devil's Tombstone is located in a park by that name in New York's Catskill Mountains. Some believe that Schultz might have buried over $50 million dollars in cash and savings bonds here.

property. She had gone so far as to draw up an agreement for people to sign, stipulating that she would get a portion of the treasure if they found it, but she had to stop allowing those activities when someone dug up her entire yard.

A Virginia psychic claimed he had visions in which he channeled Otto Berman, a prominent member of Schultz's gang. He was bound and determined to uncover the treasure and donate it to charity so that Berman could rest in peace.

Meanwhile, the local economy of Phoenicia benefits from the riddle, and the Phoenicia Library reports that visitors often arrive asking for maps of the area to inform their search.

Other theories exist, of course. No treasure story worth its salt doesn't grow with each succeeding generation. Some say the treasure is somewhere near Lake George. Others put it somewhere in Yonkers. A few believe the whole thing is a figment of someone's imagination.

One thing is worth remembering, however. Part of the treasure hidden away by Schultz consisted of a number of U.S. savings bonds. These are designed to be redeemed after their fulfillment date for more money than it cost to purchase them. They are guaranteed by the U.S. government. To date, none of them have been cashed in by anybody. Does that mean they are hidden somewhere, along with, perhaps, the rest of the treasure?

That's what makes treasure hunting exciting. In the end, the fun lies as much in the hunt itself as the discovery at the end of the quest, but we can't help wondering if the flamboyant Dutch Schultz is laughing somewhere, enjoying the celebrity that he has found in death even more than he ever did in life.

John Dillinger's Suitcase

From June 1933 to July 1934, much of America was transfixed by the most notorious bank robber in modern U.S. history: John Dillinger and his gang, the most famous member being "Baby Face" Nelson, went on a crime spree that was followed by people who normally bought newspapers and listened to the radio only to keep track of their favorite baseball team.

The FBI placed him on their new "most wanted" list and set traps for him in Minnesota and Wisconsin, but he managed to escape, often in a hail of bullets. In September, he was finally captured and incarcerated in an Ohio jail to await trial, but he was soon sprung by a gang of five former convicts who were led by a man whose own escape from an Indiana state prison had earlier been financed and planned by Dillinger. A sheriff was killed during the prison break.

The gang robbed banks in Indiana and Wisconsin before fleeing south to Florida and then west to Tucson, Arizona. There, Dillinger was captured, jailed, and extradited to Indiana's notorious Point Jail, which was said to be escape proof.

On March 3, 1934, Dillinger proved the experts wrong, staging what was probably the most famous jailbreak in history. Using a razor and a piece of wood, he carved a fake pistol, painted it with shoe polish to make it look realistic, forced his

A wanted poster from 1934 showing John Dillinger, including his signature, fingerprints, photos, and full description and criminal history.

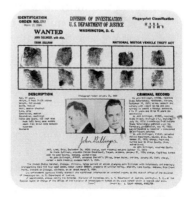

Dillinger hid out at the Little Bohemia Lodge in Wisconsin, and it is said that he hid $200,000 in cash somewhere on its grounds.

way past a dozen guards, and made it to freedom while shouting, "I'm heading for the last roundup."

He then stole the sheriff's car and drove to Chicago. This turned out to be a mistake. Because he drove a stolen car across state lines, he brought down the full attention of the FBI.

In Chicago, he was said to have had plastic surgery to alter his appearance so that he no longer looked like the photos on wanted posters, which were by now tacked to bulletin boards in every post office in the country.

How did he manage to make the transition from a Midwest kid to the most famous wanted outlaw in the country? Most psychologists would say the process began with a difficult child-hood because of a strained relationship with his stepmother. He was almost constantly in trouble and eventually dropped out of school.

He joined the Navy in 1923, serving on the USS *Utah* for a few months before he found that the life didn't agree with him and deserted. Returning to his Midwest roots in Indiana, he was arrested during a grocery store robbery and spent most of the next nine years behind bars. This turned out to be the place where he received his real education. He was taught how to rob banks by the local inmates, who saw great potential in his abilities.

When he was paroled in May 1933, he began to put his new education to good use. He robbed five banks in Ohio and Indiana over the course of the next four months. This is when he earned the reputation of being one of the best-dressed bank robbers in American history.

During the spring of 1934, he hid out at the Little Bohemia Lodge near Manitowish Waters, Wisconsin, but it's hard to remain anonymous when every FBI agent and policeman in the country is looking for you. Sure enough, someone eventually tipped off the authorities, and the FBI planned an ambush.

During the raid, a shootout ensued. Dillinger apparently escaped with a suitcase containing $200,000 in small bills. According to local legend, he apparently buried the suitcase behind the lodge so it wouldn't slow him down as he ran from the scene. It was probably a good idea because he managed to escape from the authorities.

He never had a chance to retrieve it, however. A few months later, on the night of July 22, 1934, his life came crashing down.

Anna Sage, whose alias was Ana Cumpanas, was a madam in a local house of ill repute. She was also pals with Dillinger's girlfriend. Forever after, she became known as "the woman in red," earning the nickname through her actions that night.

Dillinger was shot down by three FBI agents at Chicago's Biograph Theater on Lincon Avenue on July 22, 1934.

She informed the FBI and the local Indiana police that she was accompanying Dillinger and his girlfriend to a movie. The show was appropriate to the occasion. It was a showing in the Biograph Theater of a recently released movie called *Manhattan Melodrama*. Sage was told to wear a red dress so that agents could identify her. She actually wound up wearing an orange skirt, but "the woman in red" had better sex appeal to newspaper reporters, so the name stuck.

The ambush happened as the Dillinger party exited the building. Three FBI agents fired five shots. Three of them connected with the bank robber. He was pronounced dead in the Alexian Brothers Hospital at 10:50 P.M. on July 22, 1934. His last words were said to have been, "You got me," but witnesses at the scene testified that he was probably dead before he hit the ground.

Conspiracies still float to the surface from time to time that it was another man who died that night. Dillinger's allies supposedly accomplished a switch to throw off the FBI, leaving him free to escape once again and go underground for the rest of his life. But because of his many arrests, his fingerprints were on file, and they apparently matched the body in the hospital room.

The death of John Dillinger is often seen as the beginning of the end of the Gangster Era. His name dominated the headlines for a while before fading away into history, but what about that suitcase full of $200,000 in small bills?

It was never found. As far as anyone knows, it remains hidden away to this day, buried somewhere behind the Little Bohemia Lodge in Mercer, Wisconsin. If you go looking, you can't stay overnight at the lodge anymore, but it still offers excellent food in the restaurant and is steeped in gangster lore.

Lots of people have searched. No one has ever found it.

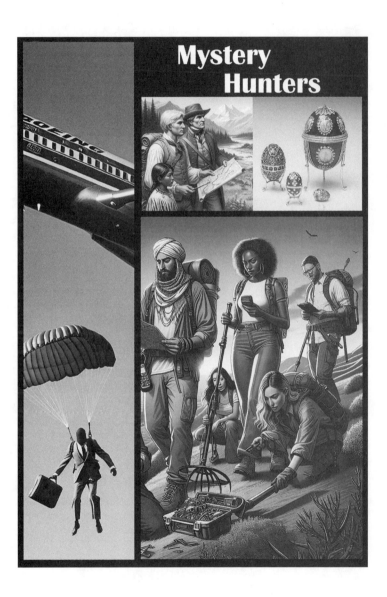

Meriwether Lewis and the Missing Documents

Some lost treasures do not consist of gold, silver, or precious gems. Their value exceeds monetary reckoning. Some are even considered priceless. And a few seem to be cursed, at least if you consider the experience of those who figured in their story to begin with.

I'm talking about lost documents.

Roman leaders, for instance, consulted the Sibylline Books for 900 years before they disappeared. And then, Rome fell.

Many Maya texts, including the famous Codices, were burned by conquistadors and Catholic monks in the 16th century. A precious few were copied and hidden; otherwise, we never would have even known about them. And the once mighty Maya empire collapsed into the mists of time, leaving only magnificent, crumbling ruins in their wake, where once gold sparkled in the morning sunrise.

The Hebrew Bible, called the Old Testament by Christians, cites about 20 "Chronicles" that no longer exist. How can anyone put a price tag on the Dead Sea Scrolls or the Nag Hammadi texts?

These are all considered beyond price for scholars.

Perhaps not in quite the same category but still considered priceless are the missing pages from the journals of Meriwether Lewis, hero of the Lewis and Clark Corps of Discovery expedition.

Lewis's friend, President Thomas Jefferson, had given the expedition some key goals. They were to explore the Missouri River to find "the most direct & practicable water communication across this continent for the purposes of commerce ... and render a knowledge of those people who inhabited the route."

To that end, either Jefferson or Lewis, it's not clear which, created a gridded sheet that listed common English words in the left-hand column and blank columns to the right. The idea was to fill in equivalent Native words to see if common roots existed in any European languages.

Jefferson was obsessed with the idea that Europeans made it to the Americas way before Columbus. He firmly believed, for instance, that the Ten Lost Tribes of Israel, after their defeat by the Assyrians in 721 B.C.E., eventually migrated to the Americas. This was the theory that became the basis of the theology of the Latter-day Saints just a few decades later.

It is still in vogue in parts of the Southeast. Some members of Cherokee tribes to this day find similarities between their language and that of ancient Hebrew. Artifacts still show up from time to time that seem to bear Hebrew inscriptions as well as Phoenician, Greek, and other Mediterranean languages.

When the expedition returned from their explorations, Lewis had collected 14 Native vocabulary sheets for President Jefferson. By September 1806, he had completed nine more. Jefferson's plan was to take Lewis's records and combine them with 40 or so he had already personally documented. He wanted to publish a text that would prove his thesis.

That never happened. When Lewis died, his records were lost to history. No one knows what became of them. After his death, they became a central piece of a conspiracy surrounding Meriwether Lewis and his missing documents. Books have been written about what happened next. Here is a brief summary.

Meriwether Lewis is a bona fide American hero. His close friendship and fruitful partnership with William Clark, their work in opening the new western frontier that America bought in the Louisiana Purchase, and their subsequent journey all the way to the Pacific Ocean is legendary. On the dangerous trip, they lost only one man, and that was to a disease that no amount of planning could have prevented. The work of the Corps of Discovery went a long way toward fueling the fires of Manifest Destiny that would soon grip the country. Jefferson believed it would take 100 generations before the new territory Lewis and Clark had explored would be fully occupied. Americans did it in five.

Statues dedicated to the explorers Meriwether Lewis and William Clark adorn many a city square and park. This one is located in Seaside, Oregon.

But Lewis came to a sad end, and that's where the mystery of the lost documents begins.

Lewis was appointed governor of Louisiana Territory in February 1807. By 1809, his world was falling apart. Massive debt, alcoholism, a genetic predisposition to depression, malaria, and a disappointing love life all took their toll.

Rumors began to circulate that Governor Lewis would be recalled, or at least not reappointed, and that James Madison, who had replaced Jefferson in the White House, had lost confidence in him. The complicated War of 1812 was building on the horizon, and much of the territory Lewis and Clark had explored was threatened by previous claims of other countries.

In August 1809, Lewis decided to make the long journey to Washington, D.C. He wanted a face-to-face meeting with the bureaucrats of the Madison administration but thought it would be good to visit his mother and his friend Thomas Jefferson, who had moved back to Virginia. Then, he would go to Philadelphia to meet with the publisher of his yet unfinished book. After a brief time spent with William Clark putting his affairs in order before an extended trip, he left on September 4, 1809.

His plan was to book passage on a flatboat all the way down the Mississippi River to New Orleans, where he would then secure passage on a ship around the southern tip of Florida and up the east coast to Chesapeake Bay. There, he would go by water up the Potomac River to the capital.

But those plans never materialized. Just 250 miles downstream from St. Louis, he decided to leave the river and travel overland to Virginia. He also seems to have been troubled enough to write a will, leaving everything to his mother, Lucy Marks.

The reasons for his change of mind are often debated. Some say he had come down with a fever that was raging through the lower country of the southern Mississippi region. But others suspect that he was afraid the papers he was carrying might fall into the hands of the British, who were patrolling the Gulf of Mexico and boarding American vessels.

This begs the question: What was contained in those papers that he was afraid might fall into enemy hands?

Reports also existed that during his river journey, he had attempted suicide but was restrained by fellow travelers. A deposition later quoted Gilbert Russell, who captained the vessel: "On the morning of the 15th of September, the boat in which he was a passenger landed him at Fort Pickering in a state of mental derangement, which appeared to have been produced as much by indisposition as by other causes." This certainly speaks to his mental health. Clearly, something was wrong.

Despite a successful career in government and exploration—and being considered an American hero—Meriwether Lewis suffered from depression and alcoholism.

Whatever his mental state, Lewis decided to travel north on the Natchez Trace toward Nashville, Tennessee. From there, he would head east toward Washington.

Along the way, he stopped at a wayside tavern named Grinder's Inn. As it turns out, that's as far as he would go. The mystery that still involves historians was about to play out to its conclusion.

When I recently traveled the historic Natchez Trace, now a scenic highway, I couldn't help but find myself driving in Lewis's shadow.

Its trail was blazed in ancient times by Indians. Only a few years after Lewis used it heading north, Andrew Jackson traveled south with his troops to fight the Battle of New Orleans. It was frequented not only by travelers but by desperados and robbers, who preyed on parties that were not sufficiently protected.

These days, it's a beautiful drive, full of historical significance. One of the most important places to stop is Grinder's Inn, the final resting place of Meriwether Lewis. I couldn't help but pause to visit his grave and relive his final moments.

No one knows for sure what happened that night. Two camps still argue about details, sometimes in very learned, scholarly papers.

One side believes what is probably the opinion of most historians. It was there, they say, that Lewis committed suicide.

Their evidence is based on solid, if circumstantial, facts and the testimony of the one witness to the event. Lewis seemed ready to have taken his own life due to his pressing problems, his state of mind, the fact that he attempted suicide while on the boat, and that he had made out his will. Without going into a lot of detail that has been covered in book after book and pa-

The gravesite of Meriwether Lewis, known as the Meriwether Lewis National Monument, is located at milepost 385.9 on the Natchez Trace Parkway.

per after paper, those who subscribe to this theory have a good argument.

But others believe that Lewis was murdered. They base their case on a few primary and highly significant facts that have continued to buttress a whole conspiracy theory. An article published in 1845 by the *New York Dispatch* outlined the essential facts of the story.

- Lewis died of two gunshot wounds. He was carrying a brace of .69 caliber pistols. They fire a big ball of lead. The first shot was to his head, carrying away part of his forehead. The second was right below his breastbone. According to later testimony, "They found him lying on the bed; he uncovered his side and showed them where the bullet had entered; a piece of the forehead was blown off, and had exposed the brains, without having bled much." Would it have been conceivable for a man to shoot himself in the head and then, when that failed to finish the deed, shoot himself again in the chest and still survive for a few hours? To most laymen, it certainly seems like an impossibility.

- Priscilla Grinder, the innkeeper, heard the shots but waited until morning to check on her guest despite, according to her later testimony, hearing Lewis say, "O madam! Give me some water, and heal my wounds." Her testimony, however, might not be very reliable. It was subject to change over time. Thirty years later, in 1839, she swore that two unknown men had arrived at the inn the same night Lewis was there. Supposedly, he challenged them to a duel before they rode off into the night. Why did she change her story? Was she bought off the night the death transpired and then told the true story years later?

🜚 Her establishment consisted of two cabins linked by what today would be called a breezeway. Then, it was commonly called a dogtrot. Supposedly, she heard Lewis talking either to someone during the night or to himself. In her first testimony, she swore that Lewis was agitated, pacing back and forth. This has convinced quite a few historians that he was of a mind to commit suicide. But what if she was paid to say that or was even part of a murder plot? In the words of historian John Bakeless, "It takes a lot of credulity to believe that a frontier woman, used to hardship and living in a dangerous wilderness, on a trail infested with bandits, would wait until morning before going herself to the barn, or sending children to summon the servants, when a mortally wounded man was crawling around and begging for help."

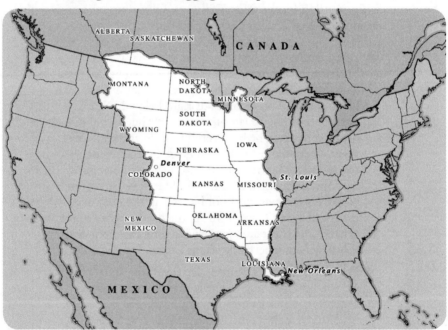

After the U.S. government concluded the Louisiana Purchase with the French in 1903, the Lewis and Clark Expedition of 1804 to 1806 helped solidify America's claim to the vast tract of land. What if the missing papers Lewis carried proved the claim was not legitimate?

§ Finally, in the morning, the papers Lewis had been carrying to Washington, the ones he was so afraid would fall into the hands of the British that he abandoned his original plan and decided to carry them overland instead, were gone, and they have never reappeared. Where are they?

These points are enough to ignite a conspiracy theory that rages to this very day. Was Lewis murdered so his killers could steal the papers he was carrying? If so, what was in them? Was it simply an Indian lexicon? Or was it something else?

When Lewis's friend William Clark, who shared the expedition with him and knew what Lewis was carrying, and, indeed, even helped him pack, heard about the death, his first thought was, "What will be the consequence? What will become of (our) papers?"

That certainly seems a strange reaction to have upon hearing of the death of one of your best friends.

Theories about the contents of the papers form a list that grows almost every year. Some say Lewis and Clark discovered proof that Britain, or another nation, might have a prior claim to the vast area known as the Louisiana Purchase, rendering Jefferson's expensive project obsolete. The papers, they say, carried the secret proof.

Others believe the expedition discovered that Indians such as the Mandan tribe might be descended from other European claimants, such as the Welsh or the Vikings.

The truth is, no one knows for sure.

The passing years produced many theories about who the killer or killers might have been, but they are all based on sheer speculation.

Possibilities include:

§ Lewis's servant, perhaps to recover money that he was owed

§ James Neelly, agent to the Chickasaw nation, who reported the death to Jefferson and seems to have stolen Lewis's rifle, horse, pistols, dagger, and pipe-tomahawk

§ Neelly's servant, who was either bribed or terrified into silence

§ The Grinders, either Priscilla or her husband, who might have been hiding nearby

§ Common robbers who worked the Natchez Trace

❺ Whoever left the moccasin tracks and the impression of the butt of a rifle that were found in the dirt near Lewis's cabin

Why, we might ask, doesn't someone petition to exhume the body and submit it for modern forensic examination?

It is said that the National Park Service won't permit it, but are they just a convenient scapegoat?

Whatever the case, two things are known for sure. Lewis died, and his papers are missing. Unless they resurface, perhaps after being hidden away in some government warehouse or someone's basement vault, we'll never know what happened that fateful night on the Natchez Trace, and the valuable documents will continue to confound scholars into the foreseeable future.

The Mystery of the Beale Treasure

When it comes to the story of the Beale treasure, the original story is a simple one. It's in trying to figure out the map where complications arise. As a matter of fact, it might be said that this treasure is protected by a curse of insanity that strikes people after too many hours of being mesmerized by staring at a string of numbers, trying to make sense of them.

What do you make of this, for instance?

Assuming you haven't cracked the cypher code yet, here's the story, according to the book *The Beale Papers: Containing Authentic Statements Regarding the Treasure Buried 1819 and 1821, Bufords, in Bedford County, Virginia, Which Has Never Been Recovered* by James B. Ward.

But first, a warning: Everything you are about to read sounds perfectly plausible. The facts are straightforward. Aside from the tale of a lost Dutchman's mine and the curse of Oak Island, it is probably the most famous buried treasure story in America, judging by the thousands of people who still show up to follow clues and search for it. But aside from the name of Robert Morriss, who can be found in historical records, not one other single name or fact, including the identity of the author of the book upon which it is based, and the hero of the story, Thomas Beale, can be authentically substantiated. Yet the legend forged from the Beale Cyphers lives on and grows with each passing year.

With that caveat, we begin.

The first Beale cryptogram.

194, 38, 1701, 89, 76, 11, 83, 1629, 48, 94, 63, 132, 16, 111, 95, 84, 341,
975, 14, 40, 64, 27, 81, 139, 213, 63, 90, 1120, 8, 15, 3, 126, 2018, 40, 74,
758, 485, 604, 230, 436, 664, 582, 150, 251, 284, 308, 231, 124, 211, 486, 225,
401, 370, 11, 101, 305, 139, 189, 17, 33, 88, 208, 193, 145, 1, 94, 73, 416,
918, 263, 28, 500, 538, 356, 117, 136, 219, 27, 176, 130, 10, 460, 25, 485, 18,
436, 65, 84, 200, 283, 118, 320, 138, 36, 416, 280, 15, 71, 224, 961, 44, 16, 401,
39, 88, 61, 304, 12, 21, 24, 283, 134, 92, 63, 246, 486, 682, 7, 219, 184, 360, 780,
18, 64, 463, 474, 131, 160, 79, 73, 440, 95, 18, 64, 581, 34, 69, 128, 367, 460, 17,
81, 12, 103, 820, 62, 116, 97, 103, 862, 70, 60, 1317, 471, 540, 208, 121, 890,
346, 36, 150, 59, 568, 614, 13, 120, 63, 219, 812, 2160, 1780, 99, 35, 18, 21, 136,
872, 15, 28, 170, 88, 4, 30, 44, 112, 18, 147, 436, 195, 320, 37, 122, 113, 6, 140,
8, 120, 305, 42, 58, 461, 44, 106, 301, 13, 408, 680, 93, 86, 116, 530, 82, 568, 9,
102, 38, 416, 89, 71, 216, 728, 965, 818, 2, 38, 121, 195, 14, 326, 148, 234, 18,
55, 131, 234, 361, 824, 5, 81, 623, 48, 961, 19, 26, 33, 10, 1101, 365, 92, 88, 181
275, 346, 201, 206, 86, 36, 219, 324, 829, 840, 64, 326, 19, 48, 122, 85, 216, 284,
919, 861, 326, 985, 233, 64, 68, 232, 431, 960, 50, 29, 81, 216, 321, 603, 14, 612,
81, 360, 36, 51, 62, 194, 78, 60, 200, 314, 676, 112, 4, 28, 18, 61, 136, 247, 819,
921, 1060, 464, 895, 10, 6, 66, 119, 38, 41, 49, 602, 423, 962, 302, 294, 875, 78,
14, 23, 111, 109, 62, 31, 501, 823, 216, 280, 34, 24, 150, 1000, 162, 286, 19, 21,
17, 340, 19, 242, 31, 86, 234, 140, 607, 115, 33, 191, 67, 104, 86, 52, 88, 16, 80,
121, 67, 95, 122, 216, 548, 96, 11, 201, 77, 364, 218, 65, 667, 890, 236, 154, 211,
10, 98, 34, 119, 56, 216, 119, 71, 218, 1164, 1496, 1817, 51, 39, 210, 36, 3, 19,
540, 232, 22, 141, 617, 84, 290, 80, 46, 207, 411, 150, 29, 38, 46, 172, 85, 194,
39, 261, 543, 897, 624, 18, 212, 416, 127, 931, 19, 4, 63, 96, 12, 101, 418, 16, 140,
230, 460, 538, 19, 27, 88, 612, 1431, 90, 716, 275, 74, 83, 11, 426, 89, 72, 84,
1300, 1706, 814, 221, 132, 40, 102, 34, 868, 975, 1101, 84, 16, 79, 23, 16, 81, 122,
324, 403, 912, 227, 936, 447, 55, 86, 34, 43, 212, 107, 96, 314, 264, 1065, 323,
728, 601, 203, 124, 95, 216, 814, 2906, 654, 820, 2, 301, 112, 176, 213, 71, 87, 96,
331, 35, 10, 2, 41, 17, 84, 221, 736, 820, 214, 11, 60, 760.

In January 1820, a man by the name of Thomas J. Beale rode into Lynchburg, Virginia, and checked into the Washington Hotel. The proprietor was Robert Morriss.

Morriss later wrote, "In person, (Beale) was about six feet in height, with jet black eyes and hair of the same color, worn longer than was the style at the time. His form was symmetrical, and gave evidence of unusual strength and activity; but his distinguishing feature was a dark and swarthy complexion, as if much exposure to the sun and weather had thoroughly tanned and discolored him; this, however, did not detract from his appearance, and I thought him the handsomest man I had ever seen."

Right away, we encounter the first problem with the story. Morriss was, indeed, a citizen of Lynchburg, and he did rent out rooms. But he wasn't yet the owner of the Washington Hotel. He didn't acquire that establishment until 1823.

It's a small discrepancy, however. Since he did rent rooms in another row of houses, we might give him the benefit of the doubt.

At any rate, Morriss later wrote that Beale spent the rest of the winter in Lynchburg. He was "extremely popular with every one, particularly the ladies," but his earlier life remained a mystery, and he never told Morriss, or anybody else, why he came to Lynchburg in the first place. He was a mystery man.

Then, with the coming of spring, he left town as mysteriously as he had arrived.

Two years later, he returned to spend another winter in Lynchburg. Where had he been?

The details didn't come out until later, but during that visit, he gave Morriss a locked iron box, which he said contained important papers. Morriss was not to open the box under any circumstances for the next 10 years unless he determined that Beale was never going to return.

It soon became apparent why Morriss had garnered Beale's trust. He didn't open the box. Instead, he guarded it, waiting for Beale to return to take possession. It was a full 23 years later, in 1845, that Morriss finally decided that Beale must have died. Perhaps he was correct in this assessment. At this point, Beale disappears from history.

When Morriss opened the box, he found a note written by Beale, plus three sheets of paper filled with numbers.

These were the famous documents now known as the Beale Cyphers. The first dealt with the contents of the treasure. The second gave the exact location. The third told who the treasure belonged to and revealed the identity of its heirs.

The second cypher, which provides the exact location of the treasure, was eventually deciphered by Robert Morriss.

73, 24, 807, 37, 52, 49, 17, 31, 62, 647, 22, 7, 15, 140, 47, 29, 107, 79, 84, 2, 239, 10, 26, 811, 5, 196, 308, 85, 52, 160, 136, 59, 211, 36, 9, 46, 316, 554, 122, 106, 95, 53, 58, 2, 42, 7, 35, 122, 53, 31, 82, 77, 250, 196, 56, 96, 118, 71, 140, 287, 28, 353, 37, 1005, 65, 147, 807, 24, 3, 8, 12, 47, 43, 59, 807, 45, 316, 101, 41, 78, 154, 1005, 122, 138, 191, 16, 77, 49, 102, 57, 72, 34, 73, 85, 35, 371, 59, 196, 81, 92, 191, 106, 273, 60, 394, 620, 270, 220, 106, 388, 287, 63, 3, 6, 191, 122, 43, 234, 400, 106, 290, 314, 47, 48, 81, 96, 26, 115, 92, 158, 191, 110, 77, 85, 197, 46, 10, 113, 140, 353, 48, 120, 106, 2, 607, 61, 420, 811, 29, 125, 14, 20, 37, 105, 28, 248, 16, 159, 7, 35, 19, 301, 125, 110, 486, 287, 98, 117, 511, 62, 51, 220, 37, 113, 140, 807, 138, 540, 8, 44, 287, 388, 117, 18, 79, 344, 34, 20, 59, 511, 548, 107, 603, 220, 7, 66, 154, 41, 20, 50, 6, 575, 122, 154, 248, 110, 61, 52, 33, 30, 5, 38, 8, 14, 84, 57, 540, 217, 115, 71, 29, 84, 63, 43, 131, 29, 138, 47, 73, 239, 540, 52, 53, 79, 118, 51, 44, 63, 196, 12, 239, 112, 3, 49, 79, 353, 105, 56, 371, 557, 211, 505, 125, 360, 133, 143, 101, 15, 284, 540, 252, 14, 205, 140, 344, 26, 811, 138, 115, 48, 73, 34, 205, 316, 607, 63, 220, 7, 52, 150, 44, 52, 16, 40, 37, 158, 807, 37, 121, 12, 95, 10, 15, 35, 12, 131, 62, 115, 102, 807, 49, 53, 195, 138, 30, 31, 62, 67, 41, 85, 63, 10, 106, 807, 138, 8, 113, 20, 32, 33, 37, 353, 287, 140, 47, 85, 50, 37, 49, 47, 64, 6, 7, 71, 33, 4, 43, 47, 63, 1, 27, 600, 208, 230, 15, 191, 246, 85, 94, 511, 2, 270, 20, 39, 7, 33, 44, 22, 40, 7, 10, 3, 811, 106, 44, 486, 230, 353, 211, 200, 31, 10, 38, 140, 297, 61, 603, 320, 302, 666, 287, 2, 44, 33, 32, 511, 548, 10, 6, 250, 557, 246, 53, 37, 52, 83, 47, 320, 38, 33, 607, 7, 44, 30, 31, 250, 10, 15, 35, 106, 160, 113, 31, 102, 406, 230, 540, 320, 29, 66, 33, 101, 807, 138, 301, 316, 353, 320, 220, 37, 52, 28, 540, 320, 33, 8, 48, 107, 50, 811, 7, 2, 113, 73, 16, 125, 11, 110, 67, 102, 807, 33, 59, 81, 158, 38, 43, 581, 138, 16, 65, 400, 38, 43, 77, 14, 27, 8, 47, 138, 63, 140, 44, 35, 22, 177, 106, 250, 314, 217, 2, 10, 7, 1005, 4, 20, 25, 44, 48, 7, 26, 46, 110, 230, 807, 191, 34, 112, 147, 44, 110, 121, 125, 96, 41, 51, 50, 140, 56, 47, 152, 540, 63, 807, 26, 42, 250, 138, 582, 98, 643, 32, 107, 140, 112, 26, 85, 138, 540, 53, 20, 125, 371, 98, 96, 10, 52, 118, 136, 102, 420, 150, 112, 71, 14, 20, 7, 24, 18, 12, 807, 37, 67, 110, 62, 33, 21, 95, 220, 511, 102, 811, 30, 83, 84, 305, 620, 15, 2, 108, 220, 106, 353, 105, 105, 60, 275, 72, 8, 50, 205, 185, 112, 125, 540, 65, 106, 807, 138, 96, 110, 16, 73, 33, 807, 150, 409, 400, 50, 154, 285, 96, 106, 316, 270, 205, 101, 811, 400, 8, 44, 37, 52, 40, 241, 34, 205, 38, 16, 46, 47, 85, 24, 44, 15, 64, 73, 138, 807, 85, 78, 110, 33, 420, 505, 53, 37, 36, 22, 31, 10, 110, 106, 101, 140, 15, 38, 3, 5, 44, 7, 98, 287, 135, 150, 96, 33, 84, 125, 807, 191, 96, 511, 118, 440, 370, 643, 466, 106, 41, 107, 603, 220, 275, 30, 150, 105, 49, 53, 287, 250, 208, 134, 7, 53, 12, 47, 85, 63, 138, 110, 21, 112, 140, 485, 486, 505, 14, 73, 84, 575, 1005, 150, 200, 16, 42, 5, 4, 25, 42, 8, 16, 811, 125, 160, 32, 205, 603, 807, 81, 96, 405, 41, 600, 136, 14, 20, 28, 26, 353, 302, 246, 8, 131, 160, 140, 84, 440, 42, 16, 811, 40, 57, 101, 102, 194, 138, 51, 63, 241, 540, 122, 8, 10, 63, 140, 47, 48, 140, 288

The contents of the note seemed to answer the mystery of where Beale had been and what he had been up to.

In April 1817, three years before he arrived in Lynchburg and met Morriss for the first time, Beale had formed a 30-member party to journey across America, hunting as they went. They traveled through the rich hunting grounds of the Western plains, arriving in Santa Fe before heading north in search of buffalo. Then, according to Beale's note, "The party, encamped in a small ravine, were preparing their evening meal, when one of the men discovered in a cleft of the rocks something that had the appearance of gold. Upon showing it to the others it was pronounced to be gold, and much excitement was the natural consequence."

Here, we encounter another discrepancy, small enough to overlook but large enough to raise eyebrows. At this time, Santa Fe was under the hands of New Spain, and these years saw a number of American parties similar to Beale's arrested, detained, robbed of their possessions, and sent back to the States. "Gringos" from the North were avoiding the place. A group such as Beale's might well have encountered such parties, or at least heard about the dangers. Why would they deliberately go to such a trouble spot?

Apparently, Beale and his men mined the site for the next year and a half, accumulating a large quantity of gold and silver.

Not knowing what to do with their sudden wealth, a few members of the party decided to return to Virginia and cache it somewhere. To cut down on weight, they first went to St. Louis to trade some of the gold and silver for jewels.

In 1820, Beale and a few men returned east and found a place to bury the stash. Beale visited nearby Lynchburg, met Morriss for the first time, and spent the winter.

When he mysteriously left town with the coming of spring, he traveled west and met up with the rest of his company, who had continued to work the mine while he was gone.

Almost two years later, he returned to bury more loot with his original stash, but this time, he wanted to take extra precautions. In case anything happened to Beale or his men, they had agreed that Beale should find a trustworthy local man and give him directions to the treasure so it could find its way back to the party's families.

Considering Morriss to be such a trusted friend, Beale gave him the box containing the note and the cyphers and instructed him to wait at least 10 years to give Beale time to return.

No one knows what happened next to either Beale or the mining party. Their fate became one of history's mysteries.

Morriss, upon finally reading the note in 1845, spent the next 20 years trying to find the treasure and locate any of Beale's relatives. The location of the stash and the identity of Beale's relatives had all been encoded, and Morriss couldn't figure it out.

> *Unfortunately, the identity of the person he chose to share the secret with has never been revealed even though the pamphlet the man wrote was eventually published.*

The key to the code was supposed to have been delivered to Morriss by a third party, said to be a "friend" of Beale's from his time in St. Louis. We'll have more to say about this "friend," but bear with me for now.

Morriss celebrated his 84th birthday in 1862 and knew that he was fast approaching the end of his life. He figured that he had to share the secret cyphers with somebody, or the treasure would be lost for good, and he would die without fulfilling the promise he had made to Beale.

Unfortunately, the identity of the person he chose to share the secret with has never been revealed even though the pamphlet the man wrote was eventually published. But along with the publication, it appears that the writer made the first breakthrough in deciphering one of Beale's cryptic cyphers.

First, we'll deal with the message. How did the anonymous author arrive at his breakthrough?

Well, it's complicated.

Each of the three cyphers contains lists of about 800 numbers, arranged in a square. It was common in those days to key code numbers to a well-known book of some kind that would be readily available to anyone who received the code. The unknown author seems to have correctly deduced that the key document for at least the second cypher was the Declaration of Independence. It was a document that would be readily available to most educated Americans of that time.

If we number each word of the Declaration, we discover that "When" = 1, "in" = 2, "the" = 3, "course" = 4, "of" = 5, "human" = 6, "events" = 7, etc.

The second Beale Cypher starts with the sequence, 115, 73, 24, 807, 37. In other words, if we figure that each number corresponds to a word in the Declaration of Independence, we get the following message:

> I have deposited in the county of Bedford, about four miles from Buford's, ("Buford's" refers to Buford's Tavern, which is now the town of Montvale, Virginia) in an excavation or vault, six feet below the surface of the ground, the following articles: ... The deposit consists of two thousand nine hundred and twenty-one pounds of gold and five thousand one hundred pounds of silver; also jewels, obtained in St. Louis in exchange for silver to save transportation.... The above is securely packed in iron pots, with iron covers. The vault is roughly lined with stone, and the vessels rest on solid stone, and are covered with others....

The author had deciphered the second cypher. Unfortunately, the other two cyphers don't seem to be keyed to the Declaration of Independence. They remain a mystery. We are left with the fact that we know a treasure is buried somewhere, but we don't know exactly where. All we have is a general area.

The unknown author spent a lot of time trying to figure out the rest, but to no avail. In 1885, he decided to unburden himself by publishing everything he knew, choosing to remain anonymous so as not to be pestered by eager treasure hunters.

His efforts were picked up by James Ward, who published them in pamphlet form and gave them the pretentious title *The Beale Papers: Containing Authentic Statements Regarding the Treasure Buried 1819 and 1821, Bufords, in Bedford County, Virginia, Which Has Never Been Recovered.*

To complicate matters, a warehouse fire destroyed most of his published pamphlets.

THE

BEALE PAPERS,

CONTAINING

AUTHENTIC STATEMENTS

REGARDING THE

TREASURE BURIED

IN

1819 AND 1821,

NEAR

BUFORDS, IN BEDFORD COUNTY, VIRGINIA,

AND

WHICH HAS NEVER BEEN RECOVERED.

PRICE FIFTY CENTS.

LYNCHBURG:
VIRGINIAN BOOK AND JOB PRINT,
1885.

The Beale Papers, published in 1885, contains the cyphers and other information about the treasure buried by Thomas J. Beale somewhere in Bedford County, Virginia.

(Note: this fact was disputed in 2011. The new argument was that the pamphlets were, indeed, destroyed in fires. But those fires were located in the fireplaces of those who bought them and later felt cheated. Enough survived, however, to create a story that spread faster than the fire, or fires, that supposedly burned them.)

Before we get into the complicated modern search for the treasure, we must first pause to consider the anonymous "friend" who supposedly wrote the pamphlet, which was the basis for the whole treasure hunt. Was it really James Ward? If so, who was he and how did he get to be Beale's confidant?

This gets complicated. Stick with me.

The "friend" Beale trusted with his story, the one who was supposed to deliver the key to unlocking the secret of the cyphers, was in St. Louis in 1822, the same time as the brief trip Beale made there. How did it happen that Beale was there for such a short time but still managed to meet and form a trusting friendship with someone?

Remember that *The Beale Papers* is credited to a supposed "friend" of Thomas Beale's named James Ward. It just so happens that Ward's father, Giles, worked in St. Louis for a short time in 1822 and returned to Lynchburg in 1923. He was related through marriage to Robert Morriss.

Could this be the man who either wrote the pamphlet containing the key to Beale's cypher or, at the very least, conveyed the secret of the cypher to his son, James?

Peter Viemeister, in his book *The Beale Treasure, New History of a Mystery*, doesn't think so. He believes the pamphlet was published by Ferdinand C. Hutter. According to Viemeister, this was the "friend" who Morriss entrusted with the legend. Hutter died on February 21, 1885, just before the pamphlet was published.

On February 22, 1885, the *Lynchburg News* published his obituary, announcing only typical life-and-death details: *DEATH OF MAJOR FERDINAND C. HUTTER—the surprising announcement was made late yesterday evening that Major Ferdinand C. Hutter had died very suddenly in his home at the southern suburb of this city.... The cause of Major Hutter's death was heart disease.*

But Hutter's "surprising" death just two months before Ward's pamphlet was announced in the *Lynchburg Virginian* could explain why the original *Beale Papers* were never made public. Viemeister believes that Hutter may have had a plan to coordinate the release of the original papers simultaneously with the publication of the pamphlet by his cousin, James Ward. But that plan, if they'd had one, was understandably never realized due to Hutter's sudden death.

Whatever happened, the story lost steam over the years until it was revived in 1897. At that time, Newton H. Hazelwood of Roanoke, Virginia, was asked to copy the supposed Beale Cyphers. This caught the attention of George and Clayton Hart, who studied the cyphers for years. But something unexpected showed up in this newer copy that had not been a part of the original text. Now, the treasure was said to be buried at the foot of "The Peaks of Otter." This information wasn't a part of the pamphlet.

Where did it come from?

No one knows.

Clayton grew tired of the project by 1912. George gave up in 1952. The curse had struck them both. Constant study was ruining their lives.

Hiram Herbert Jr. took up the chase in 1923 and lasted until the 1970s. He, too, had produced nothing for all his efforts.

Herbert O. Yardley, the founder of the U.S. Cipher Bureau, also known at the end of World War I as the American Black Chamber, studied the cyphers to no avail, as did Colonel William Friedman, the dominant figure in American codebreaking during the first half of the 20th century. He even made the Beale Cyphers part of the training program for the Signal Intelligence Service. But still nothing.

He did, however, inadvertently refer to the curse attached to them. He believed them to be of "diabolical ingenuity, specifically designed to lure the unwary reader."

That they have done, to say the least.

Even William Fried-
man, the cryptographer
who ran the U.S. Army
Signal Intelligence
Service in the 1930s,
was unable to crack
the code, even with the
help of the other code
breakers in the SIS.

Maybe the curse is best described in the words of the original pamphlet:

> Before giving the papers to the public, I would give them a little advice, acquired by bitter experience. It is, to devote only such time as can be spared from your legitimate business to the task, and if you can spare no time, let the matter alone.... Never, as I have done, sacrifice your own and your family's interests to what may prove an illusion; but, as I have already said, when your day's work is done, and you are comfortably seated by your good fire, a short time devoted to the subject can injure no one, and may bring its reward.

Carl Hammer is the retired director of computer science at Sperry Univac and one of the pioneers of computerized code-breaking. He writes that the Beale Cyphers have occupied "at least 10% of the best cryptanalytic minds in the country. And not a dime of this effort should be begrudged. The work—even the lines that have led into blind alleys—has more than paid for itself in advancing and refining computer research."

The stories surrounding this legend never end. A popular video published on YouTube asserts that when Beale went west with his supposed hunting party, he was really tracking his ancestors, who at least 15 years earlier had discovered a rich gold and silver mine in Indian country.

As usual, just enough fact exists behind this story to create a conspiracy theory. Jacob Fowler, an American explorer of the American Southwest between 1821 and 1822, noted in his journal that the Pawnee and Crow tribes "speake on the most friendly terms of the White men and Say they are about 35 in number." And a Cheyenne legend dating from around 1820 tells of gold and silver being taken from the West and buried "in Eastern Mountains."

Can any of this be substantiated? No.

Does the story have inherent problems? Yes. For instance, the note Morriss received in Beale's box used the word "stampede." Linguists point out that that word was not used in print until 1844.

Of course, the word could have been used as slang in the West before that date, and Beale might have encountered it then.

On the other hand, although critics who say that no historical record of Thomas Beale exists except the one from the legend are met by counterarguments that claim the census of 1790 and other historical documents include several Thomas Beales born in Virginia whose backgrounds fit the descriptions of the one we encounter in the legend.

What about the logistics involved? Carrying that much treasure would have involved multiple wagons, which would have to cross an international border, the Mississippi River, and several state boundaries, to say nothing of the Appalachian Mountains. Then, it would have to be buried with no witnesses accidentally discovering the act. That would have required a large group of men, all who kept their mouths shut until they died. It sounds like a pretty big endeavor.

Is Beale's treasure still hidden in the hills of Bedford County?

Most say it's an elaborate hoax, but it's hard to figure out who benefited from all the work required to bring it into play.

Still, people keep looking all the same. Let's face it. Mystery is fun.

Long Tom's Treasure

This story is short and depressing, but it's typical of the many stories of lost gold in the Grand Canyon.

Generally speaking, sluicing for gold in the desert is done with what is called a "long tom" or sometimes a "broad tom." Maybe the term comes from a type of cannon used in the Civil War, but no one knows for sure.

It's a sluice box consisting of two sections, which may sometimes be as long as 30 to 40 feet. The upper section is called a "tom." It's a long trough in which dirt suspected of containing gold flakes is placed. A grating of fine screen is placed at the bottom, through which water flows into the lower section, called a riffle box. This section receives any dirt that passes through the screen. Supposedly, organic material is liquified as it passes down the device, and gold nuggets or flakes are trapped in the screen.

In 1910, a man known as Tom Watson found a cache of papers in a remote cabin. His subsequent search for the stash of gold they described forever after earned him the nickname "Long Tom."

Supposedly, the papers were written by outlaws and gave the location of a cache of stolen gold. According to the papers, it was hidden behind a seasonal waterfall in the Grand Canyon, some four miles west of the Tanner Trail, near a Havasupai village.

Some modern gold prospectors—like this man searching for wealth in an Alaskan stream—still use sluice boxes to sift for precious, sparkly flakes and nuggets of the valuable metal.

Two years later, he began to search the area. Two years after that, he had about decided to give up. He returned home on the Horse Thief Trail from Moran Point. While en route, he found a waterfall. Deciding it was worth a look, he checked it out. Behind the waterfall, he found a cave. Sure enough, he was said to have found a bag of gold nuggets inside. As luck would have it, however, as he left the cave, he tripped, fell, and broke his leg.

He had to leave the gold behind but eventually managed to crawl out to the nearby Buggein Ranch.

When his leg healed enough to travel, he went back to retrieve his stash. Unfortunately, he never found it. In the midst of his emotional depression that followed, he committed suicide.

Supposedly, the gold is still out there somewhere.

The Story of Frank from Pennsylvania

One of the strangest stories to come out of the legendary Klondike Gold Rush involves a man from the small Pennsylvania town of Welsh Hill. All that is known about him is that his name was Frank and that in July 1897, he was somewhat down on his luck when he heard about gold being discovered in Alaska and decided that it was a chance to turn his life around. Like many thousands of other gold diggers from what was to become known as "the States," he went north to seek his fortune. Apparently, he found it in a claim he staked out near Dawson City, Canada, about 50 miles east of the Alaskan border.

Klondike City (foreground) and Dawson City (in the background, top right) served as a kind of center of operations for many gold seekers during the Klondike Gold Rush of the late 1890s.

In order to join the rush, the Alaskan government had ruled that fortune seekers had to supply themselves with what amounted to about 1,000 pounds of supplies, much of it in the form of food. Like all the others, Frank transported it preserved in glass canning jars.

Local history has it that he disappeared into the mountains, occasionally coming out to visit the nearby town to resupply. He bought his things with gold dust and nuggets that he carried in empty jars. Attempts to follow him back to his claim proved unfruitful. Few knew quite where he was finding his newfound wealth.

After a few years, he returned to a hero's welcome in Pennsylvania, coming home with a dozen fruit jars filled with gold. His family and friends were proud of him, especially when he told them that what he had brought home was only a small portion of what he had stashed back at his claim.

Eventually, he returned to the Klondike to recover the rest of his money, but he was never seen or heard from again. After a while, his family received a mysterious letter that said he had died of an illness and had been buried in Alaska.

Frank's sister was suspicious. Using some of the money her brother had brought home, she managed to make her own way back to the town near where Frank's claim had been located. After hiring a local guide, she even found his cabin but was shocked to find his body inside, frozen stiff. The cabin itself had been ransacked. Because literally everything in it had been trashed and broken, she deduced that whoever had done the deed had not found what they were looking for. If they had found something, she thought, they would have stolen whatever was there and left the rest untouched. That was not the case, however. Whoever had done the deed must have left frustrated because they destroyed everything in the cabin.

His sister figured that Frank had hidden the gold somewhere nearby, but even after an exhaustive search, no evidence showed up of it ever being found. Everyone in town appeared to be mystified but, small towns being what they are, Frank's sister never quite believed that someone didn't know the story.

She could do nothing, however, and presumably, the treasure is still there.

The Treasure of Cahuenga Pass

Of all the lost treasure curses we have considered so far, by far the most notorious is the lost treasure that might be buried beneath the asphalt in the parking lot of the Hollywood Bowl in Los Angeles, California.

That's right. Hollywood! Tinseltown. The home of the American film industry.

For all those "stars that never were" knew, they might have been within easy walking distance of a fortune in gold, diamonds, and pearls that were hidden away within sight of the famous HOLLYWOOD sign that graces Beverly Hills.

But maybe that's for the best because the curse attached to that fortune has claimed the lives of at least nine men.

The lost treasure of Cahuenga Pass is one of the biggest mysteries of North America. It is sometimes called the most cursed, unsolved treasure story in American folklore. Here's the history behind it.

Beginning in San Diego and extending over 600 miles (965 kilometers) north to Sonoma, the old Spanish trail called El Camino Real ("The King's Highway" or "Royal Road to the Interior Land") was originally built to connect 21 Franciscan missions, four presidios, and three pueblos.

Now recognized as California's first highway, it is the oldest historical trail in the Western Hemisphere. It crosses deserts, rivers, and mountains, but the section that concerns us right now snakes through Cahuenga Pass in the mountains above Los Angeles.

In 1864, four soldiers, representatives of Mexico's Benito Juarez, traveled north toward San Francisco, carrying more than $200,000 in gold, diamonds, pearls, and jewelry they sought to exchange for guns needed to fight the democratic struggle going on in Mexico.

Before they reached their destination, however, one of the agents suddenly died an unexplained death. Some historians believe this was the first death of many to come and marked the beginning of the legend of the curse.

An 1850 map of El Camino Real shows the route that passed north and south through California, connecting numerous Spanish missions.

The remaining three travelers suspected French secret agents, who were following them. They kept alert for the rest of their journey to the Bay Area, but when they arrived, they found the place crawling with French spies. They decided they needed to hide their treasure before getting the lay of the political landscape, so they climbed into the hills of San Mateo. There they divided their loot into six buckskin-wrapped bags and buried them in separate locations.

Little did they realize they were being watched, but not by French agents. A Mexican shepherd named Diego Moreno was quietly observing their every move. He could not believe his good fortune as he dug up the buried hoards and quickly headed south toward his home in Mexico.

When the Mexican couriers returned to where they had stashed their loot, they discovered that it was gone.

Suspecting one another, they began to argue, and two of them killed each other. That made three deaths.

The third participant survived the scuffle but later died while trying to break up a fight in a bar he owned near Tombstone, Arizona.

Now the death total was four.

Meanwhile, Diego Moreno traveled south, following the traditional path that wound its way through Cahuenga Pass. There he stopped for the night at a local tavern in the place called La Nopalera ("Cactus Patch").

Moreno was superstitious. That night, he experienced a nightmare in which he dreamed that he would die if he entered

Los Angeles with his stolen treasure. He thought it best to bury it beneath a large ash tree up in the hills outside of town. Then he continued his journey, intending to return with help.

Unfortunately, when he arrived in Los Angeles, he began to feel terribly ill. A friend called Jesus Martinez cared for him as best he could, but Moreno felt death knocking at his door. To repay Martinez for his kindness, Moreno revealed the secret of the buried treasure, telling him about the ash tree "on the side of the pass about halfway from the tavern to the summit on the hillside opposite the main road."

Soon after, Moreno suffered violent convulsions and died. His death became number five.

Martinez and his son, Jose Gumisindo Correa, buried him and then lost no time heading north toward Cahuenga Pass. There, they located the ash tree and began to dig. But while doing so, Martinez suffered a heart attack and died.

That made six.

His son, Correa, was terrified. Convinced the treasure was cursed, he ran away.

Now, fast forward to 1885. A Basque shepherd was grazing his flock in the pass when he noticed that his dog became excited about something near an old ash tree.

When he checked out what the dog was worrying about, he found a tattered leather bag full of jewels and coins. He didn't realize that five more were hidden in the vicinity. He felt himself fortunate to find just one. It made him rich enough to return to Spain.

To hide his fortune from others, he sewed almost 20 pounds of gold coins into the lining of his coat and booked passage home.

When his ship approached port, he leaned over the rail to wave to those who were there to welcome him, but as he did

Highway 101 (the Hollywood Freeway) slices through the Cahuenga Pass in Los Angeles, California.

In 1939, treasure hunters Walter and Ennis Combes used a metal detector to search for the gold behind the Hollywood Bowl, which is near the Cahuenga Pass.

so, he lost his balance, probably due to the weight of the gold sewed into his coat. He sank like a stone, dragged under by the treasure he had tried to conceal.

The death toll stood at seven.

Now move forward another 10 years. Remember the sixth fatality, Jesus Martinez, and his son, Jose Gumisindo Correa, who fled the scene when his father died of a heart attack? Correa had by now decided that the curse was worth the risk of recovering the gold his father had died trying to find. He was by now a grown man and served as an officer of the law in Los Angeles. He told himself it was time to seek out the treasure again, but before he could put together the courage to do so, he was killed by his brother-in-law in a shoot-out in East Los Angeles.

No one knows why exactly, but the death toll now stood at eight.

By now the legend of the cursed treasure of Cahuenga Pass had spread. In 1939, a San Francisco mining expert named Henry Jones partnered with a mechanic from Bakersfield named Walter Combes and his uncle, an inventor named Ennis Combes, in an attempt to locate the stash. They decided they would simply challenge the curse that followed its legend. It's easy to be brave when you're in the safety of your own living room, planning an adventure.

Ennis Combes had built a newfangled invention called a metal detector. With it, they decided that the lost treasure lay some 14 feet below the surface of the parking lot behind the Hollywood Bowl. They purchased a $200 lease from the Los Angeles County Board of Supervisors to dig in the area, provided they agreed to give half of whatever they found to the local government.

Suddenly, the threat of the curse kicked in. They got scared and terminated their plans, but the publicity bolstered Jones's courage. According to newspapers of the time, Henry assembled another team that included Ray Johnson, a former Hollywood vaudevillian, and Highland Park inventor Frank Hoekstra. "Curse or no curse," he said, they would try again.

Thus it was that on November 27, 1939, three film crews, reporters from CBS radio, and a crowd of onlookers assembled to watch as the team began to drill through the asphalt of the Hollywood Bowl parking lot.

Vendors sold popcorn. A security fence was put up around the site. Guards were hired to keep order. Every time an animated needle on Hoekstra's "electrochemical recorder" registered a hit, the crowd cheered them on.

Twenty-four days later, after they had dug a pit 9 feet wide and 43 feet deep, they hit a boulder and could go no farther.

A few weeks later, filled with remorse after his wife divorced him and no longer willing or able to stand the strain, Henry Jones committed suicide.

That made nine.

After that, treasure hunters were denied permission to dig. The story gradually faded away, as such things often do, but the question remains: Is the treasure still there?

Next time you attend a concert by the Hollywood Bowl orchestra, an ensemble that consists of some 80 highly trained musicians drawn from the pool of talented studio artists who you've heard whenever you watch an Indiana Jones film, it might be a good idea to pause and ask yourself whether you are standing on a vast treasure that might, by this time and at today's economic value, go a long way toward reducing our national debt. It's there, somewhere. All you have to do is find it.

The Missing Fabergé Eggs

How would you like to find a lost treasure without having to pick up a shovel or follow a faded map into the mountains? Surprisingly, you might be able to do just that.

In 2015, a man visited a Midwestern antique store and spent a whopping $13,000 for a trinket that he thought he might be able to make a profit on if he disassembled it, smelted it down, and sold the rest for scrap. He figured he could clear about $1,000 on the project but was bitterly disappointed. No one was interested. All his potential buyers told him he had overvalued the item by many thousands of dollars.

Just about the time he decided he wasn't going to break even, he went online and googled "gold egg." Only then did he realize what he had: it was an Imperial Fabergé egg, lost since 1922 and worth about $33 million. It is now thought to be one of the most valuable works of art in the world.

That's not to say that all Fabergé eggs are worth that much. Another sold in 2007 for a paltry $8.9 million.

So, what's in your attic? Are you interested? Here's the story.

For more than 30 years, from 1885 until 1916, Peter Carl Fabergé was one of the most famous jewelers in the world. He was catapulted into fame because Czar Alexander III of Russia began an Easter tradition. Every year, he commissioned Fabergé to make a jeweled Easter egg for his wife. They were built with

The House of Fabergé in St. Petersburg, Russia, created about 60 bejeweled and gold-encrusted ornamental eggs between 1885 and 1917. Valued for their intricate beauty (and rarity), each one is worth millions of dollars.

the finest gold, silver, diamonds, rubies, other precious gems, and expensive lacquers. Each took a whole year to create, and they all contained hidden surprises when opened. Over a period of three decades, many of them were made for a variety of costumers, but the most famous were known as the Imperial Easter eggs. They came to symbolize Russian royalty and the splendor of an age.

Then came the Bolshevik Revolution of 1917. First, the revolutionaries assassinated the royal Romanov family, including the czar, his wife, and all of their children. Then, they came for the House of Fabergé. That's where the money was. The Bolsheviks confiscated every egg they could find, a total of 50 of them (it is estimated a total of 69 were made in total, but not all were available to be stolen).

Fabergé managed to escape to Switzerland but died only a few years later. Most say that what killed him was a long depression that began when he had to flee his beloved homeland.

The Fabergé company of today, although not nearly as splendid and opulent as it once was, describes the Imperial eggs as "deeply imbued with the spirit of their age." They were "the swan song of a dying civilization." The modern company has no direct connections with the old one. They have no Russian roots and had to buy the rights to the name. But they did hire Peter Carl Fabergé's great-granddaughter in 2007 to maintain the ties.

Meanwhile, what did the communists do with their stolen Fabergé eggs? The answer is right out of *Indiana Jones and the Lost Ark*. Their new owners considered them a decadent reminder of an opulent era, stored them in a crate in the basement of the Kremlin, and forgot about them.

That brings us to the story of Armand Hammer and his close ties with the Soviet Union. Hammer was an American businessman who ran Occidental Petroleum from 1957 until he

Peter Carl Fabergé fled Russia when the Bolshevik Revolution targeted him and his family for execution in 1917, traveling to Switzerland, where he died three years later.

Oil magnate Armand Hammer was called "Lenin's chosen capitalist" because he formed ties with the Soviet Union's leadership, which gave him the opportunity to make lucrative business deals where other American businessmen feared to tread.

died in 1990. Besides being a multimillionaire in business, he was also a philanthropist and an art collector.

Newspaper reporters, however, labeled him "Lenin's chosen capitalist." His father was one of the founders of the American Communist Labor Party, and he made much of his fortune through deals he negotiated with nations who were sometimes open enemies of the United States. He maintained such close ties with the Soviet Union that Leonid Brezhnev provided Hammer with a luxurious Moscow apartment as a home away from home and lobbied then President Ronald Reagan to appoint him ambassador to the Soviet Union.

The nomination never came because, as one unidentified U.S. official put it, "We simply don't know which side of the fence Hammer is on."

After Hammer successfully negotiated deals with Muammar el-Qaddafi that led to the growth of OPEC, Qaddafi made Hammer a major beneficiary of Libya's oil wealth.

Thus it was that when the 50 Imperial Fabergé eggs were finally discovered in the basement vaults of the Kremlin, Hammer was in a unique position to buy 10 of them and bring them home for his personal collection. He then began to sell some of them.

In the process, although no one knows how, eight of them disappeared. One, as we already related, was found in a Midwest antique store. But the eggs made for the Easter seasons of 1886, 1888, 1889, 1897, 1902, 1903, and 1909 are still missing. Presumably, they are either hiding in plain sight, their owners unaware of how much they are worth, or they reside in someone's private collection. No one knows.

They could be anywhere in the United States by now, worth untold millions of dollars, unclaimed and probably unacknowledged as some of the most valuable pieces of art in the world.

Sometimes, treasure isn't purposefully hidden away in the earth. Sometimes, it is just ignored. In this case, thanks to the ineptness of Bolshevik armies, a shady American entrepreneur with ties to the Soviet Union, and an art public who didn't know enough to be curious, a fortune can be found without having to get dirty or lift a shovel.

Who will find it? Maybe you.

The Great D. B. Cooper Highjack

On a cold Thanksgiving eve in 1971, passengers boarded Northwest Orient Airlines Flight 305 in Portland, Oregon, and strapped in for the brief, 37-minute flight to Seattle, Washington. Little did they know they were about to be participants in the only unsolved plane hijacking in public aviation history.

Despite the many thoroughly researched books that have since been written, FBI records which have been made public, a popular, four-part Netflix documentary entitled *D. B. Cooper: Where Are You?!*, an episode of the riveting TV series *Brad Meltzer's Decoded*, Leonard Nimoy's *In Search of . . .*, a National Geographic movie, and the 35 passengers on that flight who must have glimpsed the hijacker without knowing what was about to happen, a mysterious, audacious thief managed to pull off what amounts to the greatest heist of all time and, for all anyone knows, remains at large to this day. Of course, if he were still alive, he would be somewhere between 85 and 95 years old today.

As for the money he stole, except for $5,800 in cash that a young boy found on the banks of the Columbia River in Vancouver, Washington, in 1980, money that was confirmed to have been stamped with the same serial numbers as the money given the hijacker, none of the $200,000 he demanded and received has ever been found. In today's economy, it would be worth some $1.3 million, and it forms one of the most interesting tales of lost treasure found in modern times.

Airline representatives insist he was "the most clever and certainly the most audacious airplane hijacker" in recent history.

Darren Schaefer, who hosts *The Cooper Vortex* podcast, is quoted in the Netflix series: "What he accomplished was totally amazing. He got away with it, he stuck it to 'the man,' and he didn't hurt any civilians doing it. That is why he is the legend he is today."

Tom Colbert and Tom Szollosi call him "the last master outlaw" in their book by the same name.

Urban legends equate him with famous antiheroes such as

Sketch of Dan Cooper
drawn by an FBI artist.

Jesse James, "Baby Face" Nelson, Bonnie and Clyde, and John Dillinger.

An annual CooperCon bills itself as the "world's only annual event focused on the legendary 1971 skyjacking," where fans come to share and debate their own theories, the more outlandish the better.

To make things even more exciting, his legend has inspired what is called the "Cooper Curse." The curse is not on the *treasure* as much as the *story*, which has snared any number of searchers who devote their lives, fortunes, and professional reputations to latching on to suspects and refusing to let go, even when evidence suggests they might be on a false trail. In one case, it even led to a suicide.

Perhaps the curse is best summed up by one searcher who said, "You want to believe so much (in your chosen suspect) that your belief system takes over your logic."

Who was D. B. Cooper, and why has his story caused such a stir?

Well, to start with, his name wasn't D. B. Cooper. The name listed on the passenger manifest, used by the man who bought the ticket, was Dan Cooper. A reporter simply made a mistake when, in an early newspaper article, he wrote about "D. B." instead of "Dan." The name stuck. As another reporter expressed it, "'D. B.' sounds more bad-ass than 'Dan.'"

This may have influenced the whole legend beyond simple journalistic flair. As we'll see in a minute, "Dan Cooper" may have been a carefully chosen alias that never made the intended headlines, thus misdirecting the search in its infancy and perhaps even centering it in the wrong country.

Here's a condensed version of what happened on the fateful night of November 24, 1971, when the man known as D. B. Cooper parachuted into history.

Younger readers probably don't understand what it was like flying back then. To say it was different from today is, at best, an understatement. Those of us who were college students in those days would often simply show up at an airport, ready to fly "standby." That meant we would wait until the flight had boarded, and if any empty seats from no-shows were left (and, almost always, some were), we would get to fly half rate. No one inspected us. We didn't have to take off our shoes. Checking bags didn't incur an extra charge.

Those were good times. I used to joke that when I went to my local airport and asked when the next flight to New York was scheduled, the pilot would reply, "How soon can you be ready to go?"

All that is to say that on that Thanksgiving eve, one of the busiest days of the year for the airline industry, Flight 305 from Portland to Seattle was just a routine, 37-minute jump. Home for the holidays, with visions of turkey and stuffing in your head.

Flight attendants in those days were called stewardesses. Having talked to more than a few women (and they were almost always women) who had those jobs back then, it was a rough gig. Sexual harassment was rampant and, if reported, almost always went unacknowledged. It was common for stewardesses to be given a folded piece of paper that contained nothing but a first name and a telephone number. They were just supposed to grin and bear it.

So, when a stewardess named Florence Shafter was given a note by one of the passengers, she thought nothing of it until he urged her to read it right away. That's when her world was shaken. She immediately passed it on to Tina Mucklow, the other stewardess on the flight.

The note said that the passenger had a bomb in his briefcase and would blow up the plane and everyone on it unless, when they landed in Seattle, he was given $200,000, specifically in "American" currency (remember that fact), and four parachutes.

The airplane highjacked by Cooper, a Boeing 727, carried 36 passengers and a crew of six.

Mucklow asked to see the bomb, hoping it was just a bluff, but when the passenger opened his case and showed her eight red cylinders in two rows of four, she was assured that she was looking at dynamite. He held two exposed wires and explained that all he had to do was touch them together and the whole thing would go off.

She was told to contact the pilot, who, in turn, notified air traffic control that his plane was being hijacked.

In those days, hijacking was a growing concern. People even told jokes about hijacking a plane and flying to Cuba. It was that common of an occurrence back when radicals had come of age in the 1960s and was what made necessary all the rules and regulations we experience today.

The other passengers were not notified. Most didn't have any idea that their Thanksgiving plans were about to be challenged. Some didn't even find out until they reached their destination and, on Thanksgiving Day, heard Walter Cronkite report it on the evening news.

Officials at Northwest Orient agreed to the demands, prepared four parachutes, and authorized the payment of money.

Officials at Northwest Orient agreed to the demands, prepared four parachutes, and authorized the payment of money.

At this point, we might ask, why *four* parachutes?

Airport officials considered two possible answers.

First, if the hijacker had ordered just one, it might have been possible to sabotage it, thereby sending the terrorist to his death. Two might mean he simply wanted a backup. But the more likely reason was that he intended to take hostages and was thus sending a message to ensure cooperation.

Whatever the case, four parachutes were prepared, and the money, in small bills, was provided. The serial numbers were secretly recorded for future help in identifying the hijacker.

This might have caused an unintended problem for the hijacker. He didn't specify the denomination of bills he wanted. Two hundred thousand dollars in $20 bills, which they prepared, weighed about 26 pounds. If they had chosen $100 bills, it would have been only a few pounds. If you parachute with an extra 26 pounds strapped to your chest, it can cause trouble in the first few moments of disorientation while in free fall.

When the plane reached the Seattle-Tacoma Airport, it circled for two hours to give police and FBI agents time to pull together the ransom demand. The passengers were, of course, disgruntled, but they were mollified with typical airline-speak about presumed problems.

When they finally reached the ground, the plane was directed to a spot on the runway that was almost a mile from the terminal. A bus was provided for transportation, the ransom delivered, and the passengers deplaned.

When all was ready, the plane took off again with a minimal crew, this time headed for Mexico City.

The hijacker demanded that the landing gear of the plane was to be kept down and the flaps at a specified angle. The aircraft was to be flown at a speed slower than that which the crew thought was possible and, at 10,000 feet, a lower altitude than they were used to flying. When they questioned the orders, the hijacker assured them it could be done. He had obviously done his homework and understood more about this particular craft than some of the crew. When told that a Boeing 727-51 couldn't make it that far without refueling, given his conditions, it was agreed that they would land in Reno, Nevada, to top off the tanks.

Two fighter jets shadowed the plane, but they couldn't fly that slow and had to continually circle, so they constantly lost touch for brief periods of time.

Twenty minutes into the flight, the cockpit crew experienced a popping sensation in their ears. The air pressure had changed.

This was the only type of commercial airplane that had an exit ramp in the rear, which could be deployed while the plane was in flight. The pilot reported that their "guest" seemed to have departed the airplane, either with or without his bomb, by lowering the rear exit door and parachuting down into the dark night, a gathering storm, and miles of nothing but dense forest near what is now presumed to be Ariel, Washington. The bomb was never found, so he probably either threw it out into the night or took it with him.

Although rumors continued to proliferate, he was never seen or heard from again.

Did he survive the jump? Maybe. An extensive FBI-led search involving planes, helicopters, soldiers on the ground, and plenty of publicity never turned up a sign of a parachute, let alone a body.

The FBI explored thousands of leads, suspects, and confessions. Amateur searchers considered even more. Analysis conducted on a tie clip he left behind showed traces of a type of titanium used, at that time, only in the aviation industry. This suggests that he might have been a disgruntled Boeing employ-

In 1980, eight-year-old Brian Ingram discovered bags along the Columbia River containing cash that was confirmed—via serial numbers—as part of the loot stolen by D. B. Cooper.

ee, but that's only conjecture. Pollen found embedded in the tie itself proved inconclusive.

As of this date, Cooper's identity remains a mystery.

Only one substantial clue has been discovered.

In 1980, eight-year-old Brian Ingram was camping with his father along the banks of the Columbia River on a beach called Tena Bar. In his words, "We are out here making a campfire, my father and I, and that's when we discovered the three packets of $20 bills, later to be proven as ransom money of D. B. Cooper."

He had found $5,800 in $20 bills, which still had intact rubber bands, although they fragmented when touched. They were later identified by their serial numbers, which matched some of the ransom paid to Cooper.

According to an article in the *Los Angeles Times* on May 22, 1986:

> The boy who found $5,800 of hijacker D. B. Cooper's loot six years ago would get to keep almost half of the cash under an agreement submitted to a judge Wednesday by the four parties claiming shares of the find.

Tuesday was the deadline for submitting claims on the $5,800 in decaying $20 bills found by Brian Ingram, now 14, on a Columbia River beach in Vancouver, Wash., six years ago.

During a family vacation nine years later, Ingram was scrounging for firewood in the sands along the Columbia River when he uncovered three bundles of deteriorated $20 bills. He said the rubber bands around the money "turned to powder" when touched.

The parties that filed claims on the money were Ingram and his parents, Northwest Orient Airlines, the FBI, and the airline's insurance company, Globe Indemnity Co.

Under the proposed judgment, which must be approved by U.S. District Judge Helen Frye, the federal government would keep $280 for use as evidence should anyone be prosecuted in the unsolved 1971 hijacking in which $200,000 was paid as ransom. Ingram and Globe Indemnity would split the remaining $5,520 equally.

Aside from that one discovery, no evidence could stand up in court as to the identity or whereabouts of Cooper, but that hasn't stopped conspiracy theorists.

- 💰 Lynn Doyle Cooper, for instance, was an army veteran who, on the day before the hijacking, supposedly told his niece he was planning something "very mischievous."
- 💰 One of the most entertaining suspects, just because it's such a novel theory, is Barbara Dayton, a transgender woman who had held a grudge against airline companies that had refused her application to receive pilot training because of her sexual identity.
- 💰 Both Duane L. Weber and Walter R. Reca allegedly made deathbed confessions.
- 💰 Brad Meltzer's team of researchers ultimately decided that chances were good that Kenny Christiansen, a

former purser for the hijacked airline, was the culprit. He had the experience, the skills, the means, and the motive. In one of the places where he lived, the team even found a recessed hiding spot that might have once contained the money.

Netflix, in the four episodes of its series *D. B. Cooper: Where Are You?!*, offers probably the most in-depth and balanced account of the theories involving Robert Rackstraw, a likely candidate according to Tom Colbert and his research team. Rackstraw's profile seems to fit the hijacker perfectly.

Rackstraw had served in Vietnam and seemed to have close ties with the CIA. This makes Colbert wonder if the CIA influenced the FBI to cover up his identity because he was really an undercover agent who was worth more outside prison, keeping CIA secrets, than inside, spilling the beans on covert activities.

The team confronted Rackstraw personally while he was still alive and living in California.

He was the owner of a pleasure yacht called *Poverty Sucks*, and Colbert met with him face-to-face, offered him $20,000 if he admitted to being Cooper, and further enticed him with a chance to make millions on a tell-all book and the possibility of a Hollywood movie.

Although seeming to enjoy the attention, Rackstraw denied the accusation.

Tina Mucklow, a stewardess on the fateful flight, later declared that he didn't look like the man who had hijacked the plane, but that didn't stop Colbert. He was a man who had caught the Cooper Curse and continued his obsession even after his team endured a split because of differing opinions.

Another promising suspect surfaced when, less than a year after the hijacking, a man by the name of Richard McCoy was heard bragging to a friend that he could have pulled off the heist, but he would have demanded half a million dollars. On April 7, 1972, someone did just that. This time, it was a United Airlines flight, but the type of aircraft was the same. The demands were the same as well: four parachutes and half a million dollars. This time, the hijacker bailed out over Utah.

Acting on a tip, the FBI raided McCoy's house and found a satchel containing half a million dollars. He was arrested for both hijackings, and for a few days, officials thought they had solved the case, but it turned out that McCoy was a copycat. He had committed the second crime, but not the first.

In a 2009 TV movie called *The Skyjacker That Got Away*, National Geographic concluded that D. B. Cooper never survived the jump. They based their findings on circumstantial evidence, such as the fact that an experienced parachutist never would have attempted the jump while wearing only a business suit and loafers; no signs existed that he changed into a jumpsuit.

Also, aside from the money that was discovered along the Columbia River, none of the rest of the cash has ever surfaced. Someone would have spent some of it by now. Their theory is that Cooper landed in water, probably the Lewis River, the money satchel was torn from his body, most of it was destroyed, and his body was eventually washed out to sea.

They acknowledged that their theory had some holes in it, mostly trying to figure out how $5,800 could have somehow made it upstream to the banks of the Columbia River, but they came up with ideas that might explain it. Some of them sounded pretty far-fetched, involving the money satchel getting caught up in the prop of an upstream barge, but they are no more outlandish than many other theories.

> *Their theory is that Cooper landed in water, probably the Lewis River, the money satchel was torn from his body, most of it was destroyed, and his body was eventually washed out to sea.*

One of the most entertaining treatments of the story can be found in the television series *Leverage*, starring Timothy Hutton, Gina Bellman, Christian Kane, Beth Riesgraf, and Aldis Hodge. "The D. B. Cooper Job," which aired in August 2012 during the show's fifth season, took the novel approach that D. B. Cooper hid in plain sight for his whole life. After making his daring escape, he married the stewardess of the flight, who faked the famous artist's sketch to cover for him. He then joined the FBI and spent his career investigating the highjack that he himself had perpetrated.

Their depiction of the case is very accurate, right up until the part where Cooper jumps from the plane. From then on, the completely fabricated plot is justified by a moral imperative. "When you spend most of your time getting inside the minds of bad people, looking for their flaws and their weaknesses, it's pretty much all you see ... in everyone," says Timothy Hutton's character.

In this version, Cooper spends his life atoning for his crime by doing good. It's a refreshing take on the story.

Earlier, we pointed out that "Dan Cooper" might have been an alias and that getting the name wrong might have concentrated the early search in the wrong country.

Here's the background.

"Dan Cooper" is a comic book hero who regularly jumps out of planes. His stories are called *Les Aventures de Dan Cooper* and feature, in vivid, comic-book glory, the adventures of a fictional Canadian military flying ace and rocket ship pilot.

Does this suggest that D. B. Cooper was really a Canadian military veteran who used a familiar alias when buying his ticket? It might explain the curious request for $200,000 in "American" currency. Would an American have insisted on that stipulation? If I, an American citizen, go to a bank to take out a withdrawal, I don't insist on "American" currency. It's just understood. But a foreigner from Canada might make this demand without thinking about it.

In other words, Cooper might have slipped up by choosing this alias, but because the newspapers preferred "D. B." to "Dan," the connection was not made until weeks, maybe even years, had passed and Cooper's trail had gone cold. Authorities had been looking in the United States. Maybe they should have been looking in Canada. Would it have made any difference? We'll never know.

In 2016, the FBI announced that it would no longer actively investigate the hijacking, calling its probe "one of the longest and most exhaustive investigations in our history."

What can we say about D. B. Cooper and "Cooper's Curse"? The two are joined forever. Just as many people have fallen under its spell now as were following it in 1971. It might even deserve to be called the first real internet treasure story. Without social media, it never would have attained the status it now affords.

> *What can we say about D. B. Cooper and "Cooper's Curse"? The two are joined forever. Just as many people have fallen under its spell now as were following it in 1971.*

But the internet is a two-edged sword. It can connect people in wonderful ways and offer a sense of good-hearted community to people who would never otherwise have met. But it is also a home for bullies, liars, and cheats. Quite a few instances of mean-spirited, sometimes even ugly, threats have been placed on social media sites aimed at people who disagree with a particular point of view or an opinion of the case that is less than serious. Instances of people publishing facts that agree with their opinions, while hiding those that don't, abound. More misinformation on this case exists than even the resources of the FBI can effectively deal with, although they have certainly tried.

Does any evidence exist, for instance, beyond conspiracy theory that says that the FBI was pressured by the CIA to hide evidence?

Not one shred, but that doesn't keep some people from believing it anyway just because they want to.

This story is probably a portent of things to come in the internet age. It may have been the first of such cases, but it certainly won't be the last.

In the absence of new factual evidence, which now might very well be impossible to unearth, it looks like the mystery of D. B. Cooper is here to stay.

Forrest Fenn and the Thrill of the Chase

As I have gone alone in there
And with my treasures bold,
I can keep my secret where,
And hint of riches new and old.
Begin it where warm waters halt
And take it in the canyon down,
Not far, but too far to walk.
Put in below the home of Brown.
From there it's no place for the meek,
The end is drawing ever nigh;
There'll be no paddle up your creek,
Just heavy loads and water high.
If you've been wise and found the blaze,
Look quickly down, your quest to cease,
But tarry scant with marvel gaze,
Just take the chest and go in peace.
So why is it that I must go
And leave my trove for all to seek?
The answer I already know
I've done it tired, and now I'm weak.
So hear me all and listen good,
Your effort will be worth the cold.
If you are brave and in the wood
I give you title to the gold.

(From "The Thrill of the Chase" by Forrest Fenn)

Since so far, we have ended so many stories on inconclusive notes, it's only fitting to finally get to a tale with a satisfying conclusion. On Saturday, June 6, 2020, this treasure was found!

But the curse still might be working. Five people died, and another was sentenced to jail after authorities caught him digging up graves in Yellowstone National Park. Plus, it unleashed a raft of lawsuits.

Here's the story.

By the year 2010, Forrest Fenn, during his 80 years on Earth, had accumulated what most of us would call a small fortune by dealing in antique art. Because of this profession, he had, over the years, quite naturally acquired an active interest in treasure hunting of all kinds, but in 1988, he had been diagnosed with kidney cancer; nothing like a glimpse of mortality to turn someone's mind toward leaving a legacy. That's when he came up with the idea of creating a hunt for hidden buried treasure.

"My desire was to hide the treasure and let my body stay there and go back to the soil," he later reminisced.

While fighting the cancer, his idea was put on hold for 20 years, but he finally took advantage of opportunities and carried out his dream.

"This country was going into a recession," he thought. "People were losing their jobs, and despair was the headline in every paper. I want to give some hope to those who were willing to go into the mountains looking for a treasure."

From his personal collection, he filled a small chest full of gold coins, jewels, and other precious valuables, worth between $1 million and $5 million, and hid it somewhere in the Rocky Mountains north of Santa Fe and south of Canada. Then, he wrote a poem that served as a sort of treasure map. The poem contained nine different clues as to the whereabouts of the cache.

"Please don't say I buried it," he told interviewers. "Just say I hid it."

For two years, nothing much happened. Then, he published a memoir titled *The Thrill of the Chase*. It talked about his interesting life as an Air Force pilot. He described selling moccasins to members of the Rockefeller family and amassing a collection

Forest Fenn filled a box with somewhere between $1 and $5 million worth of gold coins, jewelry, and other valuables, and then he hid it somewhere in the Rocky Mountains.

of artifacts that ranged from Sitting Bull's original peace pipe to a mummified falcon from King Tut's tomb.

At first, nobody really took notice. As is often the case, self-published books tend to languish with only local sales. Take my word for it. I've been there. In Fenn's case, his book was sold only in a local New Mexico bookstore.

Slowly, however, word began to spread. Less than a year later, a small community of determined hunters had coalesced around it. Then, the national media got hold of it, and the hunt was on. It wasn't long before, by some estimates, 350,000 people, many from foreign countries, were out searching for it. Some even quit their jobs to devote full time to the chase. Websites were created so seekers could exchange information.

The popular TV series *NCIS* used the stunt as a plot device in their Season 18, Episode 3, show entitled "Blood and Treasure." They also threw in a veiled reference to the three Beale Cyphers, which has nothing at all to do with Forrest Fenn, but it made for great entertainment.

Make no mistake, Fenn wanted the treasure to be found. That was his whole point. But his object was always the same as the title of his book. He wanted people to revel in the thrill of the chase, not just the discovery of riches, but after a while, things started to get out of hand.

In January 2016, Randy Bilyeu and his dog, Leo, set off to search for the treasure in the Rio Grande, northwest of Santa Fe. Bilyeu was gone for 10 days before he was reported missing. A helicopter crew found his raft and rescued Leo. But Bilyeu's body wasn't recovered until six months later.

Three people died during the summer of 2017. Jeff Murphy fell 500 feet while hiking in Yellowstone National Park. Eric Ashby drowned while ratting the Arkansas River in Colorado. Paris Wallace's body was discovered seven miles from his car in the New Mexico mountains. All had been searching for the treasure.

In 2020, Mike Sexson and Steven Inlow were searching near Dinosaur National Monument. They ran out of supplies and had no cell service to call for help. Inlow survived by drinking his own urine, but Sexson died of hypothermia. His body was airlifted off the mountain.

Dal Neitzel runs a cable TV station in Bellingham, Washington. He has taken as many as 70 road trips in search of the treasure, and he writes a blog named *The Thrill of the Chase* that, over the years, has reported several offbeat characters who have risen from the ranks of his thousands of daily visitors.

"Tim Nobody," for instance, collects pinball machines. A

one-legged motorcycle rider named Michael Hendrickson and a woman from Connecticut named "Grandma" are regular contributors. "Diggin' Gypsy" from Georgia gathers her family together a few times every year, along with a pet rooster she calls John Wayne, to travel to the mountains of Montana.

Some seekers have been obviously troubled individuals as well. A man from Nevada was convicted of stalking after he became convinced that the treasure was not a box of precious coins and jewelry but actually Fenn's granddaughter. A man from Pennsylvania was arrested after using an axe to break into Fenn's home.

Bill Sullivan is a 60-year-old homeless man from Seattle. He says chasing Fenn's treasure is all he has. Living out of his car, he sees himself as following a path his ancestors blazed. "My grandfather prospected gold in Alaska a hundred years ago," he recalls. "He had a sled dog team and trapped beaver. So that's in my blood."

Nevertheless, crazies to the contrary, an annual gathering in New Mexico called Fennboree grew from a dozen people to hundreds.

Fenn himself constantly urged people to be careful. "Remember that I was about 80 when I made two trips from my vehicle to where I hid the treasure. Please be cautious and don't take risks."

He told people to stay out of old mine shafts because they were too dangerous. "The treasure isn't in a mine," he said. "I mean, they have snakes in 'em." It's not in a tunnel. "It's between 5,000 feet and 10,200 feet above sea level. It's not in Canada or Idaho or Utah or a graveyard."

When authorities in New Mexico asked him to call off the hunt because of the dangers, Fenn refused. In 2017, responding to Jonah Engel Bromwich of the *New York Times*, Fenn said, "Life is too short to wear both a belt and suspenders. If someone drowns in the swimming pool we shouldn't drain the pool, we should teach people to swim."

Some people were certain the whole thing was some kind of publicity hoax. One even called for Fenn's arrest.

Then, just when people began to doubt the most, the treasure was found on Saturday, June 6, 2020, by a 32-year-old medical student named Jack Stuef. The location remained undisclosed to protect the local environment from tourists, but the treasure hunt was over. Three months later, at the age of 90, his life's great dream completed, Forrest Fenn died.

Was the treasure actually found, or was it a hoax that provided a way out?

As promised, the small treasure box with millions of dollars in gold and jewels was not buried, nor was it in a mine or tunnel. It was found lying on the ground, surrounded by trees, in a lush Rocky Mountains forest.

It seems to be a bona fide discovery. Fenn met with Stuef on June 11, 2020, to confirm its authenticity. On September 19, 2022, Stuef sold the treasure to Tesouro Sagrado Holdings, LLC, which put most of the items up for auction.

Stuef had this to say: "After my identity was revealed almost two years ago, some fans of the treasure hunt reached out to tell me they hoped they could purchase an item from the treasure to commemorate their own adventures searching for it. I'm happy that today those people finally have the opportunity to do so, with a large number of items from which to choose."

Where had it been all those years? Fenn says it best, employing his typical lyricism: "It was under a canopy of stars in the lush, forested vegetation of the Rocky Mountains, and had not moved from the spot where I hid it more than 10 years ago."

The question remains: Why? Why did he do it? Why do people give up so much to engage in the pursuit? What is it about hidden, lost, or buried treasure that excites us so?

In numerous interviews, Fenn recalled an email from a law student who thanked him "for reminding me of a part of who I am that has waned greatly during the last years of my legal studies."

Fenn's reply was classic: "Don't you dare work as a lawyer! If you do, you will wear a coat and tie and sit at a desk all day. You will not have time to smell the sky or experience the soft breeze ripe with sun. Go looking for my chest full of gold and all of the other treasures that lurk once you leave the fluorescent lights behind."

Other seekers speculate that if they had found the gold, they might have just buried it again somewhere else to keep the thrill of the chase going for future generations. One of them said, "Somewhere deep inside, I hope that I never find your treasure. The journey will be treasure enough."

Fenn's book was called *The Thrill of the Chase*, not *The Thrill of the Find*. Maybe that's the secret. In modern lives, which are steeped in practicalities, maybe we need to recapture an element of possibilities.

The elusive pot of gold at the end of the rainbow might be more than a dream. It might be a necessity.

Oak Island's Lost Relics

"Seven Must Die": The Mysteries of Oak Island

We've saved the most popular, and maybe the biggest, lost treasure for last. Due to the History Channel's blockbuster series *The Curse of Oak Island*, very few people who have read this far are not familiar with the mystery of what transpired on a small island off the coast of Nova Scotia in the shrouded mists of long ago. Since 2014, a growing audience of viewers has tuned in to see what the Lagina brothers Rick and Marty, along with metal-detection specialist Gary Drayton, Oak Island historian Charles Barkhouse, heavy equipment operator Billy Gerhardt, and a host of fan favorites such as Jack Begley, Craig Tester, Alex Lagina, and many, many others, will dig up next. The island has been the subject of a mysterious treasure hunt since 1795, and the Lagina brothers, along with the team they call "The Fellowship of the Dig," in honor of J. R. R. Tolkien's famous phrase, are determined to be the ones who finally hit pay dirt.

Marty (left) and Rick Lagina head up a team of treasure hunters on the History Channel series *The Curse of Oak Island.*

Never have so many spent so much and found so little but generated such excitement. Historical figures such as Sir Francis Drake, William Shakespeare, Sir Francis Bacon, Captain Kidd, Blackbeard, and Marie Antoinette are all associated with the treasure. President Franklin Roosevelt and famous actors Errol Flynn and John Wayne have contributed to the search. Anyone from ancient Aztecs to the Knights Templar might have originally buried it.

No one even knows for sure what it consists of. Is it the lost Templar hoard, the crown jewels of Marie Antoinette, the works of William Shakespeare, or the Ark of the Covenant? What is coconut fiber in large quantities doing all the way up there?

The treasure hunt has consumed millions of searcher's dollars. So far, all that has been found are some fascinating artifacts and enigmatic bones, some gold and copper coins, buttons, a few links of gold chain, a lead cross, a garnet brooch, lots of tools and ox shoes, and other mysteries. But the search continues, and it's just as exciting as ever.

The reason for this ongoing fascination is tied to the optimistic intentions of Marty and Rick Lagina. Many detractors write in every week and fill internet chat rooms, complaining that years have gone by with no treasure found. They accuse the TV network of dishonest marketing. But those viewers completely miss the point. Something huge happened on Oak Island. The complex required vast amounts of resources in manpower, money, time, and effort. No one goes to that much trouble to engage in a hoax. They were hiding something very, very expensive and important, and the whole undertaking, until relatively recently, has gone unrecorded in the historical record.

The search began in 1795. On a fishing trip, a 16-year-old boy named Daniel McGinnis, accompanied by two friends, Anthony Vaughan and John Smith, found themselves unknowing pioneers in a project that would soon consume hundreds, and then thousands, of people.

Fueled by mysterious folklore about pirate treasure buried beneath a sunken pit on Oak Island off the coast of Nova Scotia, the boys began digging with picks and shovels in a depression beneath an old oak tree that had appeared to have been scarred by a rope and pulley system. With tales of pirate treasure filling their imaginations, little did they know what they had begun.

It took almost 10 years and some financial backing from Simeon Lynds, a local businessman, but after uncovering layers of logs every 10 feet or so, they eventually uncovered coconut fibers, clay, and finally, some 40 feet down, a stone not native to

Nova Scotia that bore an inscription: "Forty Feet Below Two Million Pounds Are Buried."

Then, they encountered the curse of Oak Island. Booby-trapped tunnels siphoned water from the ocean into the dig. Collapsed walls proved dangerous. And that was only the beginning. The curse continues to cast its spell as all sorts of equipment failures and dead ends add to the suspense and danger. The mystery continues to grow.

We might not know what was buried in that labyrinth of booby-trapped tunnels, deep pits, and enigmatic stone roads. We might never determine why an ocean was deliberately turned into a swamp. History is silent concerning people such as Samuel Ball, a slave who fought for the British in the Revolutionary War, moved to Oak Island, and somehow became the richest man in the district, but the fact that all this happened behind the scenes of recorded history is a great mystery. If the Lagina brothers and their team never discover another single gold coin or silver bar, they have already discovered the true treasure that lies in the hidden past of Nova Scotia and, indeed, the whole world.

Something happened there. It was an immense undertaking, implying an important objective. It deserves to be written up in the history books, but it isn't. Without the Lagina brothers, few would ever have known about it. That is treasure, indeed. It's not just the loot. It's the *story* that is the real treasure.

Six men have lost their lives on the quest. Legend has it that one more must die before the mystery is solved.

Twenty-seven-year-old Franklin Delano Roosevelt, future president of the United States, was once a financial backer of the Old Gold Salvage Company. In 1909, Captain Henry Bowdin used the resources of that company to attempt to solve the mystery of the money pit.

Franklin Roosevelt with his family in 1908, around the time he helped financially back the Old Gold Salvage Company, which sought treasure on Oak Island.

Actor John Wayne bought drilling equipment used on the island, and William Vincent Astor, heir to the Astor family fortune after his father died on the *Titanic*, was an investor as well.

It's safe to say that some important figures have been involved in the quest, but what exactly have they been looking for?

That's part of the mystery.

My interest in the project was generated by something that has nothing to do with hidden treasure or, on the surface at least, very little. What made me tune in every week was something called Nolan's Cross. I've come to believe that it carries on a very ancient tradition.

Nolan's Cross

Fred Nolan worked on the island as a land surveyor in the 1970s. In the course of his work, he uncovered a series of what he called "marker stones." Six of them seemed to be of special significance. When he plotted them on a map, they appeared to be in the shape of a cross. Nolan had come under the spell of Oak Island.

I completely understand. The very same thing happened to me in the course of work on the property I call home in South Carolina. Way before I discovered the TV series about Oak Island, I, too, found a series of six stone piles surrounding my house and spilling over into the woods around me. When I spent the day with a surveyor, who brought along all his tech gizmos so he could accurately plot them on a map, we discovered that they formed the shape of a cross that exactly coincided with the shape of Nolan's Cross.

The scale is different. Nolan's Cross measures 360 feet (109.728 meters) at the cross pieces and 867 feet (264.2616 meters) long. Mine is considerably larger than that and composed of rock piles, not single boulders, but all the significant structures are located on ridge tops that, were it not for the surrounding forest, would be visible from a central point.

The "headstone," which marks the point of intersection of Nolan's Cross, appears to be sculpted in the shape of a human face. That might be attributed to the habit of humans to see forms and shapes where they don't exist, but it certainly is interesting.

What fascinated me about the Oak Island cross was that way before I had seen even the first episode of the TV show, I had followed the same lines of questions and dealt with the same speculations.

Before we continue the Oak Island story, let me share mine with you. When it comes to any connections that might exist, you'll have to be the judge. If they exist, we might be dealing with a worldwide phenomenon because in the course of my research, I've discovered other places around the world that raise the same mystery.

Throughout just about every state in the American Southeast exist enigmatic stone piles. Some people don't consider

The workers on the team found marker stones—six of them—
that, when mapped out in an aerial view of Oak Island, clearly
form the points of a cross.

them mysterious at all. They attribute them to early farmers
who wanted to clear their land. No doubt that explains many,
if not most, of them, but the facts simply don't lead to that
assumption when you try to explain a few of them, especially in
terms of written historical records. One archaeologist, Thomas
H. Gresham, has even referred to them as the "problem" of
rock piles.

Following an archaeological dig in Georgia, Gresham wrote
an article for a 1990 issue of *Early Georgia* (Volume 18). He
called it "Historic Patterns of Rock Piling and the Rock Pile
Problems."

His excavations had produced some curious results. Some
of the rock piles he studied were modern. Others appeared to
be much older. Some even contained artifacts that went back
much further in time than was expected. That's why he used the
term rock pile "problem." They refuse to be pigeonholed and
neatly filed away.

When the European people first came to this part of the
country, many of their journals record the fact that they found
rock piles all over the place. This predates European agricultural
practices.

When they asked the Native Americans about them, they
got some curious replies. In some cases, the piles were said to

have been built by the "old ones" long before people then alive came along. Sometimes, it had become a tribal tradition to pick up a small rock and toss it on a pile whenever they came across one as a way of saying something that was beyond the ability of words to express. It might mean, "I was here." It could be seen as an offering to some god or spirit who might be entreated to grant traveling mercies. Some Native American traditions speak of honoring warriors who died in battle by burying them beneath piles of stone and continuing the honor by throwing a new rock on a pile every time they passed one. Maybe it was just a superstitious habit. No one knew exactly why it was done. It was just a tradition. Modern hikers sometimes do the same thing.

When I decided to try my hand at amateur archaeology and excavate one of my stone piles, I discovered that the first layer consisted of large rocks, piled on top of one another roughly in the shape of a circle. Much of it was aboveground, signifying a recent origin, perhaps attributable to farmers who cleared their land for grazing or growing tobacco and cotton.

Further research taught me that I had to consider the fact that World War II German prisoners were brought into parts of the South and made to work for the U.S. Forest Service. They would clear rocks from fields and woods, piling them up for later use in construction projects or simply to get them out of the way.

When I talked to a few neighbors who were old-timers, however, they assured me that that had never happened around here. My surveyor friend had lived here all his life, and he remembers seeing old rock piles that predated the war by a long time.

In the second layer, things start to get interesting. The deep-

Rock piles like this Scottish cairn have been discovered all over the planet. Some are ancient, and some are relatively modern. There may be many reasons for such rock piles, ranging from boundary and location markers to places that honor the dead or gods.

er I went, the smaller the rocks I found. It seemed to me that if they were piled up for agricultural reasons, I would have found just the opposite. I've piled plenty of rocks in my time. My custom was to start with big ones and gradually add smaller stones as the pile grew taller. As a matter of fact, the location of the biggest rocks in the field would tend to mark where the piles would be in the first place. Why move the biggest rocks when you can just build around them?

I then turned my attention to location. Many of my rock piles are found near the top of a hill, usually facing east toward the rising sun. Perhaps this might be because it doesn't make a lot of sense to roll rocks all the way down a hill if you're planning to use them later. You would probably want to just clear the part you might later be plowing. I couldn't help but notice, though, that it was very pleasant to just sit and admire the view. It was a very nice place to work.

When I got to the bottom of the rock pile, things started to make some sense. The stones got smaller and smaller until I eventually found a floor of rock chips that had obviously been worked by human crafters. "Lithic debitage" is what they are called. Stone debris. The chips are the result of crafters who made stone tools.

From this, I developed my admittedly unproven theory of rock piles.

It begins thousands of years ago, when the ancient ones found a source of good stone from which to quarry blanks for making the tools they depended on. It just seems to make sense that a crafter would sit at a place with a nice view as his apprentices brought him raw material to work up. After many years and lots of trips back to the quarry, he would have built up quite a pile of rock chips. Later on, when one of his descendants, removed by perhaps thousands of years, came back to this traditional place, he might have developed the habit of throwing another rock on the growing pile, perhaps saying to himself something like "same time next season," or the metaphorical equivalent of "next year in Jerusalem," or something to that effect. After a while, it would become tradition and, later, maybe even superstition. Layers of history would have been piled on, similar to customs carried out every Sunday in every church in America.

Then along came Europeans, completely ignorant of native traditions. All they saw was a pile of rocks. They wanted to clear this land to make it easier to work, but it was covered with stones.

"Let's clean them up."

Might it be possible that the Northern Cross constellation (also known as the Christmas Cross or the Swan or Cygnus constellation) inspired Native peoples to arrange marker stones in a similar pattern? For what reason?

Cygnus

"Sure, but where do you want to pile them?"

"How about over on this pile that someone's already started?"

And so it went. Thousands of years later, we are faced with the "problem" of rock piles.

It was good theory, and I was happy with it, until I plotted on a map the GPS coordinates of the six rock piles I had found.

They formed a familiar icon. When I first saw Nolan's Cross on Oak Island, I almost jumped out of my chair. They were identical.

Although I've been an ordained minister all my life, I did not associate a cross just with the Christian faith. Every December morning before sunup, I step outside to look at another cross, the Northern Cross, sometimes called the Christmas Cross, that stands high in the northwest sky before, and just after, the winter solstice. I overlaid the rock pile pattern I marked with GPS coordinates on top of a constellation map, and it fit perfectly.

The cross is an ancient symbol, predating the Roman/Christian connection. Its roots go back to the beginning of symbolic thought, picturing the marriage of heaven/Earth and male/female, all coming together at the heart. Could the old ones who used to live here have had this same thought and replicated the great mystery here in my front yard? If so, they predated in stone the meaning of the familiar prayer: "Thy will be done on earth as it is in heaven." They also were in complete harmony with the ancient doctrine found from Egypt to Mesoamerica in the west and Anatolia in the east: "As above, so below."

The Northern Cross forms the basis of the constellation Cygnus, marking what is often referred to as the "great rift" or the "backbone" of our Milky Way.

The ruins of Göbekli Tepe in southeastern Turkey are over 8,000 years old, and, like some other archaeological sites around the world, include animal symbology such as snakes and birds.

Right across the Savannah River, only 100 miles away from where I live, is evidence of what once was a bird cult. The famous Eagle and Hawk Effigy Mounds in Ohio attract hundreds of tourists every year. In some cultures, the constellation Cygnus is pictured as a swan. In others, it is a hawk, eagle, or condor. The three "belt stars" of Orion, which are echoed on the ground by the Giza Pyramids of Egypt, form the same configuration as the crosspiece of the Northern Cross. They might be found at Turkey's Göbekli Tepe as well. And now, here they show up again on Oak Island.

All this evidence is circumstantial. But when I gaze at the sky and ponder people who once lived in what is now my backyard, it makes me think.

Nolan's Cross is not composed of rock piles. It is formed by six large, deliberately placed boulders. No one knows for sure what they mean or what they might point to. Some dismiss them as boundary demarcation lines. Others see complex geometry that points from the Knights Templar directly to the Oak Island money pit. Still others speculate about their possible connection to the Kabbalah's Tree of Life.

Mystical or mundane? That's the question.

If they are, indeed, a code that points to a great treasure, what might that treasure consist of? It must be important. No one would go to the effort, expense, and danger of building such a vast, underground, booby-trapped edifice unless they wanted to protect something that was really important. This is far too big to be a simple pirate stash.

Here are just a few of the ideas which have been put forth. All of them are based on evidence that has been dug out of the earth at Oak Island.

Hang on to your hats. We're about to go for quite a ride!

The Knights Templar and Jacques de Molay

O f all the mysteries unearthed at Oak Island so far, one of the most intriguing stories revolves around the Templar Order or the Poor Fellow-Soldiers of Christ and of the Temple of Solomon, commonly known as the Knights Templar. Evidence pointing to them creating the Nova Scotia treasure mystery, first found in Europe and then uncannily echoed on Oak Island, is, at least in the TV series, approaching the stage where it might even be called overwhelming.

Who were the Templars? What was the nature of their treasure? And how could it have been buried on Oak Island?

In 1129, the Crusades had been raging for 33 years, ever since the first Christian knights heeded the call of Pope Urban II at the Council of Clermont to unite and recapture the city of Jerusalem from Muslims. Skilled fighters were needed to protect travelers along the dangerous routes from Europe to Jerusalem, and the Templars filled the bill. The Order grew quickly as new recruits were drawn to the colorful, white uniform mantels that bore the distinctive red cross which, much later, would grace the three famous ships of Christopher Columbus. When school-

The Poor Fellow-Soldiers of Christ and of the Temple of Solomon—or Knights Templar—were a military order of the Catholic Church in France that played a dominant role protecting Christian pilgrims to the Holy Land from 1119 to 1312.

A recreation of what Solomon's Temple probably looked like. Built in the 10ᵗʰ century B.C.E., it was destroyed by the Babylonians in 587 B.C.E. The Babylonians took many treasures, too, likely including the Ark of the Covenant.

children see pictures of his 1492 voyage, they are looking at Templar crosses.

The knights were great builders, establishing strong fortifications from Europe to the Holy Land, but mostly, they were known for inventing the process that would later form the basis for modern banking.

It was dangerous to carry money or any other kind of wealth overland. Robbers were drawn to travelers because they were easy prey. The Templars would safeguard the riches of such travelers by storing it in strong locations and issuing writs of credit that could be cashed in and redeemed at journey's end. In other words, those traveling west would be paid when they reached the "banks" of those who had headed east and vice versa. Like bankers everywhere, the Templars soon amassed fortunes that belonged to others.

When the Templars first arrived in Jerusalem, however, they did a strange thing. They housed themselves in the catacombs under what is now called the Temple Mount. They used the old Temple of Solomon as a horse stable and apparently began digging. From 1119 until 1128, they excavated in tunnels they discovered beneath the temple. Some believe they found the Holy Grail, the long-lost Ark of the Covenant, the Shroud of Turin, the head of John the Baptist, the Spear of Destiny that pierced the side of Jesus on the cross, or a host of other sacred artifacts.

The Temple of Solomon had been destroyed in 587 B.C.E., when the armies of King Nebuchadnezzar II besieged the city of Jerusalem, eventually burning it to the ground. It is thought by many that, with no hope of surviving the siege, Jewish priests had carefully hidden that which was most important to them. They dug elaborate tunnels and caves, disguising their entrances in the hope of someday returning to reclaim them. The Ark of the Covenant, whose history we will look at next, disappeared at this time and was not seen again for nearly 500 years, if at all.

The priests couldn't bury all their treasure. Much of it was captured and taken back to Babylon. There, in the famous biblical incident known as Belshazzar's feast, the king of Babylon hosted a great banquet in which guests were served on dinnerware stolen from the Temple of Solomon.

This was the occasion that gave birth to the expression "the writing on the wall." A hand appeared, writing the words *mene, mene, tekel, upharsin*. The prophet Daniel interpreted them to mean that Belshazzar had been tried in the balance and found wanting. That night, the Persians captured Babylon.

Obviously, whatever treasure the priests of Jerusalem had buried beneath the Temple Mount consisted of something far more precious than the gold and silver taken by the Babylonians. Whatever it was, they thought it much more valuable than gold dinnerware.

In 516 B.C.E., a group of Jewish patriots led by a man named Nehemiah was given permission by Cyrus the Great to rebuild a temple on the same spot of ground as the first so that pious Jews would again have a place to conduct sacrifices and practice their religion.

Later, just before the birth of Christ, Herod the Great would greatly expand the building to the point where it was called Herod's Temple. According to the Bible, he was the one

The Holyland Model of Jerusalem, which was conceived by Michael Avi-Yonah and can be viewed in Jerusalem, includes a detailed model of the Second Temple (Herod's Temple) that was destroyed by Roman legions in 70 C.E.

Constructed in the late 7th century, the Dome of the Rock was built on the Foundation Stone that is a Muslim holy site. When Jerusalem was captured by Crusaders in 1099, the Dome of the Rock was turned into a church. Today, it is part of the Al-Aqsa mosque and is recognized as the oldest Islamic structure in existence.

who, when notified by three Magi from the East that a Messiah had been born, ordered the "Slaughter of the Innocents" in a vain attempt to destroy the child who could one day replace him.

This temple was not destined to stand, either. In 70 C.E., it was burned to the ground as an example for anyone who might have thought they could stand against the rule of Rome. For the next 600 years, it remained only a conspicuous rubbish dump.

The site was cleared in 691 C.E. by Muslim leader Caliph Abd al-Malik so that he could build a structure dedicated to Allah. It would become known as the Dome of the Rock and, in 705 C.E., was joined by the Al-Aqsa Mosque.

The Dome of the Rock was built over what was known as the "Foundation Stone." That was a huge slab of bedrock on which the Jews believe Abraham attempted to sacrifice his son Isaac. Later, it would become the place from which the Prophet Muhammad departed Earth on his famous night journey from Mecca to Jerusalem and then up to the seventh heaven and the presence of God.

In 1099, Jerusalem was retaken by the Crusaders. Rather than destroying the structures that by now had stood on the Temple Mount for 400 years, they instead chose to repurpose the site.

The Dome of the Rock was given to monks of the Augustinian order and converted into a church. The Al-Aqsa Mosque was given to the newly formed Templars in 1120.

This was when the Templars' full name was given to them. They were called the Poor Fellow-Soldiers of Christ and of the Temple of Solomon. The Temple Mount would be their Jerusalem headquarters for the next 67 years until Jerusalem was captured by the Muslim war leader Saladin in 1187.

It was when they were here that they were said to have carried out the excavations that supposedly made them fabulously rich and fueled conspiracy theories that are still in vogue. It was also where a young Templar named Jacques de Molay, who was born around 1243 C.E., served for a while. On April 20, 1292, he would become the 23rd and final grand master of the Order of the Knights Templar after having been one of its greatest reformers.

Let's assume for a minute that the Templars discovered great wealth hidden by the priests of Solomon during the siege of 587 B.C.E. and by the priests of the second Temple during the time of the Romans. What might they have done with it?

No one knows for sure, but it seems a historical fact that by the early 1300s, Philip IV, king of France, began to borrow money from the Templars. They were obviously wealthy, having virtually invented the banking system, and were good at exacting even more wealth through their investments. In other words, they expected their money to be repaid with interest.

By 1307, Philip decided he didn't want to pay his vig to an

Grand Master Jacques de Molay was the last person to lead the Knights Templar before the order was dissolved in 1312 by Pope Clement V, who was intimidated by the Templars' power and influence, and King Philip IV of France, who saw this as an opportunity to expunge his financial debts to the order.

order he considered to be loan sharks. With the aid of Pope Clement V, who had begun to worry about the influence the Templars were wielding within the church, they concocted a plan to bring an end to the Order.

Secret commands were issued throughout the land that on Friday, October 13, hundreds of Knights Templar would be arrested and charged by the Inquisition with trumped-up accusations of heresy. Many were executed after horrible tortures as the Inquisition tried to extract from them where their rumored treasure was hidden.

(Although many people trace the superstitions surrounding Friday the 13th to this time, it is probable that by then, the date was already firmly ensconced in the popular mindset. Maybe that's why Philip and Clement chose the date. It was their idea of irony.)

On March 18, 1314, Jacques de Molay, after enduring torture for seven long years, was executed in public in a horrible manner. He was by then an old man, tired of his life but proud of his achievements. He knew he was innocent. He knew his

The Knights Templar were falsely accused of crimes, tortured, burned, or otherwise killed in order to rid the pope and the king of what they saw as a threat to their power.

brothers who were executed were also innocent, so as he was dying, he cursed both the king and the pope to die within a year and a day and that Philip's bloodline would never again rule in France.

Pope Clement died first, wasting away with a terrible disease before breathing his last on April 20, 1314.

Philip was next. Before the year ended, he died of a stroke while hunting. Between the years 1314 and 1328, his three sons and grandsons died as well. Within the next 14 years, Philip's line, which had lasted for 300 years, no longer existed.

To say Europe was shocked is to put it mildly. Politics were put into turmoil because even foreign royalty didn't want to risk the curse falling on them if they collaborated with France.

The question then became this: Did de Molay's curse extend to the treasure as well as the political/clerical debacle?

In June 2011, Pope Benedict XVI apologized for the killing of de Molay and acknowledged that he was a victim of false accusations.

Barbara Frale is an Italian paleographer who works in the Secret Vatican Archives. In September 2001, she discovered a previously unknown document called the Chinon Parchment. It states that in 1308, Pope Clement V had absolved Jacques de Molay, along with the rest of the leadership of the Knights Templar, from all charges brought against the Inquisition. Six years later, the Vatican published 800 copies of the document, but by then, it was too late. De Molay was dead, and the curse had already begun its work.

In June 2011, Pope Benedict XVI apologized for the killing of de Molay and acknowledged that he was a victim of false accusations. It took centuries, but the Vatican finally admitted that they were wrong and that the Templars were innocent.

Meanwhile, what became of the treasure? Now, we return to the Oak Island saga.

Although rumors and conspiracies abound, the one that most concerns us in this context is that the Templars' treasure eventually made its way across the western ocean to Nova Scotia following the path explored by Vikings 300 years earlier, where it was to serve as a basis for a resurgence of the Order in a new land, free from religious persecution.

The most popular story is that the Templars, through their underground system of secret spies, had been alerted to the Friday the 13th purge. During the Inquisition trials, a member of the Order named Jean de Chalon testified that the preceptor

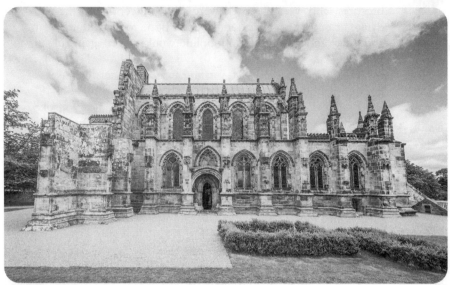

Some of the Templars escaped the persecution in France and sailed to Scotland, where they aided Robert the Bruce in 1314 and also built Rosslyn Chapel, which bears the evidence of Templar codes all over the building.

of the French Templars, Gérard de Villiers, had been alerted to the coming arrests and managed to lead over 50 pack horses and carts out of Paris, where they had stockpiled their wealth and then, according to the trial records, "set out to sea with 18 galleys."

The port city of La Rochelle, France, seems to be the place from where they set sail. Other conjectures exist, of course, but all that is known for sure is that by the time the Inquisition authorities rushed the docks, the ships were far out to sea. Wherever they went, the Templar fleet vanished from history.

The best guess is that they probably were welcomed in Scotland, where they helped Robert the Bruce gain victory against English forces at the Battle of Bannockburn in 1314. As a reward for their efforts, they were given land upon which to build Rosslyn Chapel, inscribing secret Templar codes all over it. The chapel was built by the grandson of Henry Sinclair, who we're going to look at in a minute. Sinclair was associated with the Templar Order, as anyone who is familiar with Dan Brown's book and movie *The Da Vinci Code* knows.

Some legends claim that the treasure is still beneath the chapel behind a stone wall, set back from the detailed wall carvings and beneath a stone crypt, but other stories are even more interesting.

In his book *The Westford Knight and Henry Sinclair: Evidence of a 14th Century Scottish Voyage to North America*, David Goudsward probes the long-standing belief by some historians that Henry I Sinclair, the Earl of Orkney and Lord of Roslin, made a visit to North America in the 14th century. One of the pillars of that argument concerns a mysterious, controversial carving on a stone in Westford, Massachusetts. Some see a figure of a knight and possibly a crest that stem from the Sinclair expedition. Supposedly, the expedition made it all the way to what is now the eastern United States, and while climbing a hill in full armor, one of the men suffered a heart attack and died. The stone is thought to be his memorial.

I've visited this stone a few times and really tried to see the image without success. But the weathering on the rock makes it very difficult. I suppose I just didn't want to see it badly enough even though I love the story. It's a mixture of Templar lore, history, archaeology, sociology, and fantasy, but it has recently become much more believable due to openness among the archaeological community to give serious consideration to evidence such as the Westford Knight and other mysterious carvings and

A monument in Guysborough, Nova Scotia, marks the spot where Henry I Sinclair supposedly landed with an expedition in 1398.

structures found all over New England. If the stories continue to be considered possible rather than speculative, then we might have to conclude that the Knights Templar, led by Henry Sinclair, visited the continent of America, arriving at least 100 years before Columbus landed in the Caribbean.

The story goes that after the treasure fleet regrouped in Scotland, they studied legends and rumors enshrined in Viking literature about a vast land to the west where it might be possible to resurrect their order in freedom. The route followed a path that led from Scotland to Iceland, then Greenland, then Canada, then south at least as far as New England, and possibly down the St. Lawrence to the Great Lakes and inland to Minnesota.

Employing the breathless style and signature phrase of Robert Clotworthy, the narrator of the TV series *The Curse of Oak Island,* "Could it be?"

> *It was her firm conviction that a dozen ships sailed with Prince Henry Sinclair in 1398. Some of them were part of the vanished Templar fleet.*

The late Zena Halpern was a Knights Templar scholar and researcher based in New York. Before her death, she passed along a map that seems to be of the Oak Island area. It was her firm conviction that a dozen ships sailed with Prince Henry Sinclair in 1398. Some of them were part of the vanished Templar fleet. This was a voyage of discovery, not immigration, so upon arriving at Oak Island off the coast of Nova Scotia and before journeying farther south toward New England, they decided to bury the treasure they carried. It would then be available later, when future Templars arrived in sufficient numbers to begin a new chapter in their history.

Such a treasure would demand an extra special hiding place. Thus it was that the elaborate, booby-trapped money pit was created. It was to be, in effect, a Templar bank, just as they had used during the Crusades.

Without going into much more detail, which is explored in many books and articles on the subject, a wealth of information in the forms of artifacts, hidden archaeological clues, new European excavations, and historical documents has been unearthed and reexamined in the last few decades. The old theory has taken on a new life, based on some astute observations:

💰 The Oak Island money pit and its surrounding features would not have been possible for a single pirate crew, such as that of Captain Kidd, to design and build. It is unquestionably the work of numerous expert builders over many years. The Templars were known for their building expertise, and it is almost certain that the Order didn't disappear after the Inquisition's work early in the 14th century. They just went underground.

  ठ The Knights Templar continued their Order in Portugal, now called Ordem Militar de Cristo (Military Order of Christ). Denis I, the Portuguese king, refused the extinction order of the Pope. He simply changed the Order's name. It might be that Columbus was aware of Sinclair's route to the New World. Joao Alvares Fagundes, a Portuguese explorer, supposedly sailed to Nova Scotia in 1521. In 1607, Samuel de Champlain found an old, moss-covered cross near what is now Advocate, Nova Scotia. Some people believe it was first erected by Fagundes on his voyage. Could all of these people have known about the work the Templars were carrying on there?

  ठ If all this is true, the Templars would have had the expertise, the experience, the manpower, the time, and the motivation to construct the various projects that are now being uncovered by the Lagina brothers and the Fellowship of the Dig.

Suppose the Templars were the ones behind the treasure of Oak Island. What might the treasure consist of? Let's examine a few ideas.

The Curse of the Holy Grail

In 1898, a farmer in Minnesota worked hard at the task of clearing trees from his property. Tangled in the roots of one of them, he discovered a large stone covered with mysterious runes. When translated, they seemed to tell the story of a group of explorers who had claimed that land as far back as 1362. The stone itself appeared to be some kind of claim marker.

What happened next set off a firestorm of historical charges and countercharges. When Scott Wolter, a forensic geologist, examined the stone, he discovered a rune that he called the "Hooked X." He began an investigation that has led to three books and many TV episodes that make up his series *America Unearthed*.

In one of his books, *Cryptic Code: The Templars in America and the Origins of the Hooked X*, he produces evidence from both sides of the Atlantic that when it came to New World discoveries, Columbus had arrived late in the game.

The Hooked X seems to be a Templar code that can be found throughout Europe as well as a few mysterious examples discovered on American soil. According to Wolter, it stands for the Holy Grail. His search led him to the Knights Templar and their connections to secret underground associations such as high levels of Freemasonry that are unknown to most Masons.

An enigmatic tower in Rhode Island, Oak Island itself, and clues found in the American Southwest raise the level of public interest in Templar activities. Many of the Founding Fathers of the United States, some of whom were Freemasons who seemed to have known about the Templar treasure on Oak Island, reasoned that if the treasure was found, it could serve to finance the American Revolution.

Indeed, one who fought in the Revolution, a former slave named Samuel Ball, moved to Oak Island after the war and almost overnight became the richest man in the area. The trouble was, he fought for the British, not the Americans. Did he find

Did the Holy Grail end up in Canada after the Knights Templar escaped Europe to travel to North America in the 14th century? An astounding theory, but there are hints it might be true.

the rumored treasure? Is that why a black slave could become so wealthy so fast?

Michael Bradley, in his book *Holy Grail Across the Atlantic*, takes the search even further. He believes that at the heart of the Templar treasure was the mythical Holy Grail, which has been hidden in the Americas for hundreds of years. One of those hiding places, the money pit on Oak Island, contained the Grail before it was moved to higher ground for safekeeping.

His theory is that the mystical Cup of Christ, used at the Last Supper and later employed to catch the shed blood of Jesus on the cross, was discovered by the Knights Templar when they excavated below the Temple of Solomon in Jerusalem during the Crusades.

This might come as a shock to the knights of King Arthur, who sought it in England after it was supposedly brought there by Joseph of Arimathea, a relative of Jesus who traveled to Cornwall as part of his participation in the tin trade. Be that as it may, Bradley believes it was smuggled back to Europe from Jerusalem and kept at the fortress of Château de Montségur until the castle was besieged in 1244. Facing defeat, the inhabitants managed to move it before the end came.

Eventually, it ended up as part of the Templar hoard that sailed away from the port of La Rochelle to Scotland and then to Oak Island in Nova Scotia, where the legends only grew.

If Henry Sinclair of Scotland was responsible for bringing the Grail to Nova Scotia, some interesting corroborating evidence exists. After his initial voyage, which has some documentation, Sinclair disappeared from the historical record. According to legend, after hiding the Holy Grail and Templar treasure for a while on Oak Island, he moved inland to higher ground after establishing relations with the local natives. His destination was New Ross, Nova Scotia, where he built a castle and lived out his days. According to Scott Wolter, evidence exists of something being buried there, but the site has been dug up and back-filled. If it was the Templar treasure, it has since been moved.

Michael Bradley, who, besides the book *Holy Grail Across the Atlantic* that we already mentioned, also wrote *Secrets of the Freemasons* and the *Secret Society Handbook*, thinks that Samuel de Champlain was a secret agent for what came to be called the Grail Dynasty. Champlain's coded maps and journals purposely obscure the Grail's location. He believes it was moved to Montréal, protected there by a secret society. After that, who knows?

Of course, many legends and stories exist about the Holy Grail. Its resting place is sometimes said to be in England, continental Europe, or the American Southwest. Some don't believe it to be a cup at all but rather a bloodline, descending from the child of Jesus and Mary Magdalene. Others believe that the whole Grail saga is a mythical legend. But none of those stories include Oak Island, so we'll have to leave it to others to trace them.

The Grail, however, is only a part of the Templar treasure legend. Assuming Templar artifacts include treasure found underneath the Temple of Solomon, what else might be buried deep in the money pit on an island off the coast of Nova Scotia?

The Ark of the Covenant

Perhaps the greatest lost treasure of all time and, certainly, aside from the Holy Grail, the one most familiar to people is the long-lost Ark of the Covenant. Indiana Jones made it popular in the 1981 movie *Raiders of the Lost Ark*, starring Harrison Ford. It has been sought in places as far removed from each other as America's Grand Canyon and a monastery in Ethiopia.

No one even knows for sure exactly what it was, but that hasn't stopped people from speculating about it. It is said to have been everything from a capacitor of some kind to a communicator with which to converse with ancient aliens to a weapon of mass destruction. Fantastic claims exist about beams coming from it that destroy entire armies.

The Bible doesn't make those claims. It just describes scenes that got expanded and enlarged into full-blown legends. Usually, the Ark is said to have been the place where the Ten Commandments were kept. As we shall see in a moment, that's only partially true.

When Moses received the commandments of the law from God, delivered to the Israelites after their escape from Egypt, he was told to build an ark upon which the glory of God would rest.

"Ark" comes from the Greek word for chest. "Covenant" means contract or agreement. The Ark became a constant reminder of God's contract with his chosen people.

It was a box about 2½ feet high and wide and 4½ feet long. It was made of wood and covered with gold leaf, transported by means of two long poles and placed within the Holy of Holies, or the inner sanctuary, in the Tabernacle or Tent of Meeting during the 40 years the Israelites wandered in the wilderness. After the conquest of Canaan, it was housed in the sanctuary at Shiloh and was later brought by King David to the site of the future Temple in Jerusalem. This was the occasion that so inspired David that he "danced before the Lord," much to the disgust of his wife.

The Ark of the Covenant contained the Ten Commandments and had been stored in Solomon's Temple.

When the Babylonians destroyed the Temple of Solomon in 586 B.C.E., the Ark disappeared. Although many have tried to locate it, its location has remained a mystery ever since. Some doubt it ever existed.

According to accounts found in Exodus and Numbers, three symbolic objects were placed within the Ark. Each recalled stories that, when taken together, represent the very essence of early Judaism.

The first objects were the stone tablets containing the Ten Commandments. They represented God's law. But the people had broken God's law. While Moses was on Sinai receiving instructions that forbade the worship of idols, the people were down below dancing around a golden calf. The tablets, then, would forever symbolize the people's *rejection* of God's law.

The second was a pot of manna. "Manna" literally means "What is it?" When the people needed food in the desert, God told Moses to have them go outside and gather a daily supply of a light bread that formed with the dew each morning. Only one day's supply could be gathered because it quickly spoiled if hoarded. The bread gathered on Friday, however, would keep for an extra day so that people would not have to break the Sabbath commandment of forbidding work on the seventh day.

When the people went outside on the first morning to discover the miracle of God's provision, they saw the manna and said, "What is it?" The idea was to teach the people to trust in God's provision. But after the novelty wore off, the people complained, longing for "the leeks and onions of Egypt." So, manna came to represent their *rejection* of God's provision.

The third item was Aaron's rod that budded. Aaron, Moses's brother, had been selected by God to be High Priest. But the people wanted to elect their own leaders. They complained to Moses, who passed the word on to God, so Moses was told to have each tribe select a candidate for high priest. Each would place his rod, or walking staff, in the ground to be inspected during the next morning's convocation. The rod that budded, or took root, would indicate God's choice. The implication was that God's leaders bear fruit.

Aaron's rod produced a bud, and he went on to become the first high priest of Israel. But the people would always be reminded that they had *rejected* God's leadership.

On the cover of the Ark stood the Mercy Seat. Two carved angels, one on each side, with their arched wings meeting in the middle looked down at the Ark's contents. There they saw *rejection*: rejection of God's law, God's provision, and God's leadership. That doesn't leave a lot more of God left to reject.

But on one day a year, the Day of Atonement, or Yom Kippur, the high priest sprinkled the blood of a sacrificial lamb on the Mercy Seat. On that day, the angels would see not *rejection* but the blood of the innocent substitute, and the sins of the people would thus be atoned.

Much speculation has arisen over the true meaning of the Ark. Because the Bible makes a special point of saying that Moses's face glowed when he came out from the visible presence of God, some have speculated that the Ark contained a radioactive source of light.

It was said that at the Ark, Moses would hear the voice of God. This has sparked tales of it being a transmitter through which Moses was in contact with aliens from outer space, using details supplied from their blueprints to build the Ark to their specifications.

Because of the Ark's supposed ability to inspire armies in war and because at least one man is said to have died after he touched it without proper consecration, speculation arose as to its mystical or military powers.

Popular opinion to the contrary, the Bible does not mention death rays, except for one incident where one man was struck dead, and no secret communications from on high, at least not from anyone other than God. As a matter of fact, a careful reading of the text even casts doubt on Moses's face "glowing." The Bible seems to imply that Moses's face wasn't glowing at all. That caused him embarrassment because he thought it *should* glow. After all, he had just been in the presence of the God of Light, so he covered his face out of shame.

Were the Ark of the Covenant and the Holy Grail buried on Oak Island by the Knights Templar to protect them from their European persecutors?

Unfortunately, so far at least, the whole idea is speculation. Evidence seems to point in that direction, but did that treasure include the sacred relics people hope will be found? It's just too early to tell.

Little of this popular speculation rests on the shoulders of Rick and Marty Lagina. The brothers seem to have been guided in their search by facts and evidence. All indications are that they are open to any theory, but as season after season unfolds, they appear to be extremely levelheaded.

Their lifelong enthusiasm is admirable. It began with an article in *Reader's Digest* that Rick read when he was 11 years old. The article is framed and hangs on the wall of their War Room, where so many episodes are filmed.

His brother, Marty, was able to help finance their project after a very successful career in business, which helped supply not only money but compatible experience. His son, Alex, a fan favorite, became an engineer, and viewers have watched him grow up on television. Throughout the show's tenure, they all have sustained an effort that emphasizes playing by the rules, obtaining the necessary permits, rolling with the punches, and relying on the expertise of professionals.

We can only hope that they are successful in the end, but the fact remains that they have already uncovered a real historical treasure. It lies not in gold, jewels, or precious artifacts but in the fact that the world now knows that something of historic importance occurred on Oak Island—something heretofore unknown in the historical record—and they are doing their best to uncover the story.

That is treasure indeed!

Conclusion: The Quest and Its Real Objective

What gives your life meaning? What have you accomplished that makes it worthwhile? Why is the world different because you were born into it? *Is* the world different because you were born into it?

The vast majority—maybe even *all* the people who read these words—would probably have to admit that none of us makes much of a difference in the great scheme of things. Oh, we are probably important to a few friends and family members. But that's about it. If we make a list of real world-changers, like Newton, Edison, and Einstein, we wouldn't need many pieces of paper.

Let's face it, most of us live our lives one day at a time. We find purpose, maybe we even *manufacture* purpose, in our jobs and activities. We find meaning in a few relationships. We look forward to the weekends and then usually find the results unsatisfying. The time flies by, and then it's Monday again.

Even those who dedicate themselves to becoming successful, famous, or rich come to realize that the result is not nearly as glamorous as they thought it would be. Our possessions begin to possess us. Our fame withers away and eventually fades. Our accomplishments are replaced by the next bright wannabe who follows in our footsteps.

What is the one thing that keeps us moving forward? What is the one dream that gives purpose to each day? What is the one goal that motivates us, sometimes beyond reason?

For some, it is creating a perfect work of art, a memorable song or symphony, a mathematical equation that makes sense out of seeming chaos. For a few, it's finding a lost treasure. It's the search for the Holy Grail. It's the pot of gold at the end of the rainbow.

In other words, searching for lost treasure is more than looking for money. That's what it may seem like on the surface. The seeker is usually not aware of what's going on at the deepest level of their endeavor. They might *think* they are just trying to get rich, but deep down, something is guiding them. A bigger

> Hunting for treasure is more than a quest for money; it is often about seeking adventure in life and even some self-discovery. What are we really made of? What is our place in the world?

motivation than simple greed must be present that makes people devote a whole lifetime to the search. Most of them end up spending more than they ever find.

As soon as we acknowledge such a thing as a quest, which a search for lost treasure is really about, we move into the realms of mythology, archetypes, and spirituality. This is the land of King Arthur, Odysseus, Indiana Jones, and Luke Skywalker. Its bards are Homer, Carl Jung, Joseph Campbell, and George Lucas. Richard Wagner and John Williams compose the soundtrack. John Wayne and Clint Eastwood ride again. Searching for lost treasure feels heroic.

And that might be exactly the answer we are searching for when we ask why people look for lost treasure. Whether they realize it or not, seekers are on a hero's journey. Something bigger than the mundane has taken over. They are *driven* by something spiritual, not *enticed* by something physical. Sure, a material reward might be their immediate goal, but it's a lot bigger than that.

It must be because when you come right down to it, finding a treasure doesn't always mean you get to spend it. Suppose you get lucky and find a pirate's stash in your back yard. It's not like you can go down to the grocery store and pay your bill with a Spanish doubloon. What if you unearthed a gold bar? What would you do with it? Few places will cash in gold or silver bars in exchange for dollars. Even if you found some of D. B. Cooper's $20 bills, as soon as you tried to spend them, a computer somewhere would red-flag the serial numbers and send the FBI to your front door.

Then there is the matter of official interference. Most states will latch onto a share of your profits faster than a bully will steal your lunch money. If you report a significant discovery to the proper authorities, you will soon be embroiled in lawsuits that might take years to resolve. Insurance companies who paid out claims after your discovery was first stolen will be joined by long-dead descendants of those who were the original owners. Not only will those court cases stretch on endlessly into the future, if they ever get resolved, but you will find that a much smaller portion of the treasure belongs to you than you had assumed, and from an emotional standpoint, you will have aged considerably due to all the stress you have undergone.

Even most professional treasure hunters agree that they usually invest much more in a search than they reap from the profits. They gain their income from investors who are willing to play the long game and be a part of a grand adventure, not just cash in on a pot of gold at the end of the rainbow.

No, they have other reasons for the quest. They are much deeper and more spiritually significant than dollars in a bank.

The hero's journey is a story that reaches far, far back into antiquity. Homer's *Odyssey* is a classic quest story. The Arthurian Grail sagas are another example. Frodo's journey into Mordor and Luke Skywalker's confrontation with his spiritually lost father are all threads in an ancient tapestry.

Joseph Campbell calls it a *monomyth*: one myth that is found all over the world and throughout time. Carl Jung sees it as an allegory for each individual's journey through life.

Don't be too quick to dismiss this idea just because it sounds rather philosophically grandiose. Remember that the searcher probably doesn't fully understand his or her reasons, either. They are rooted in the idea that life, especially in today's world, is often bereft of magic or, more meaningfully, spirituality. It wasn't always this way.

Think of the simple act of staying warm and nourished on a winter's day, expressed in a traditional Thanksgiving hymn:

> *Come, ye thankful people, come,*
> *raise the song of harvest home;*
> *all is safely gathered in,*
> *ere the winter storms begin ...*
> *Raise the song of harvest home.*
> *Wheat and tares together sown*
> *are to joy or sorrow grown.*

("Come, Ye Thankful People, Come,"
Henry Alford, 1844)

In former days, knowing what lies ahead, you would have recognized the need to prepare. You would have gone out into the woods, surrounded by nature and the sounds of silence. Each stroke of the axe or rasp of the saw meant you were closer to your goal. You would have heard the birds sing. Without a boss to oversee your efforts, you would have willingly bent your back to the labor of hauling and reveled in the accomplishment of splitting and piling cut logs in neat and strong rows. It was work and not always fun, but the result was worth it. When the winter storms howled outside your snug home, you could put another log on the fire and take pride in the fact that you provided for your family and secured their safety through the coldest season of the year.

Hot food that brings nourishment was supplied by your own hand. The gratitude you felt deep in your soul was the joy of participating in real life.

Nowadays, when you get a little chilly, you push a button on a thermostat. Where's the magic in that? Where's the fulfillment? Where's the sense of being one with the mystery of life? When the snow piles up, all you hope is that the plows will get it cleared from the roads before your morning commute.

Western prairies and mountains no longer beckon in the sense they once did. No new lands to discover are lying just outside the margins of our maps, places where the only directions read, "Here there be dragons."

Even though outer space still beckons, it is a team endeavor, involving millions of dollars and thousands of people. You can't just hitch up your horse, point its nose toward the setting sun, and "adventure" yourself to the moon. It's also true that much of the undersea world remains unexplored, but again, it takes teams of people and huge financial backing to delve into the ocean's dark depths.

It is probably true that many, if not most, people today have never experienced this kind of thing. I have and understand the changes that occurred in a very short time, evolutionarily speaking. The technology of our age has replaced spiritual connections, the sense of oneness, self-sufficiency, and mystery that formed the reality of the past.

When that happens and mystery fades away, only one way exists for some people to scratch the itch they feel. They devote themselves to a quest. They go looking for lost treasure.

The treasure they seek is not just gold and silver, however. The treasure is magic and wonder. It lies in the quest itself.

Perhaps that explains the essence of the curse that accompanies lost treasure. Without danger along the way, the hero's

The danger and won-
der of the quest—the
adventure!—have more
value to many treasure
seekers than any hope
of monetary gain.

journey is an empty saga. A sense of fulfillment cannot be obtained without confronting obstacles.

Curses are more than booby-trapped pits. They consist of
an almost magical force that mysteriously reaches out to assail
the hero.

Today, not many of us believe in curses, so maybe we should
redefine our belief structures and understanding of them to include a sense of real magic, or quantum reality, that goes beyond
simple scientific fact. If the search for lost treasure is a spiritual
journey, we might need to start looking for spiritual realities,
such as curses that affect us. Gold lust is real. Greed is real. It
can reach out and haunt us right to the grave.

When the rock group the Beatles led what is now called the
"British Invasion" of the Sixties, they were looking for a treasure that consisted of fame and fortune.

One of the "Fab Four," however, saw, perhaps better than
the others, that the quest was more important than the treasure. In a 1987 interview for the TV show *Entertainment Tonight*,
George Harrison recognized the nature of the curse that accompanies a search for treasure: "When we became the famous
Fabs it was really all over."

The four young men, admittedly inexperienced with the
kind of popularity few, if any, musicians have enjoyed since,
came to see that the quest—the trying and failing, the creativity
and obstacles, the striving to create—were what made the journey worthwhile. Harrison especially came to see that in the end,
their success became their curse. The treasure they sought, fame
and fortune, signified the beginning of the end for the group.

His experience illustrates what many, if not most, treasure
seekers eventually come to understand if they are true to their
spiritual natures and face their true selves. In the end, they are
not just in it for the gold. The search itself is the treasure they
seek. The *magic* of the quest is the *purpose* of the quest.

Without meaning to preach too much here at the end of our journey together, I will suggest that maybe one thing we have learned is that we all need a lost treasure to seek, a purpose to beckon us forward.

Purpose is treasure because it is valuable. It is lost because somewhere in the press of modern life, we have forgotten where we buried it in the daily grind of growing up.

- "What do you want to be when you grow up?"
- "What do you want to accomplish with your life?"
- "What is important to you?"

These are all questions we were asked as children. They are valuable questions. They set us to thinking. Perhaps back then we knew what was important, but we buried it deep in our psyche because we couldn't achieve it yet. We thought we would return and dig it up someday when we had the time and opportunity.

But most of us never went back, did we? Our treasure, our hopes and dreams, now lie buried in the mud of our past, gone but not quite forgotten. Maybe, if we're lucky, we can find an old map that will lead us back to it. The map contains codes that mean something special only to us. No one else can quite decipher them. The landscape has changed. Things look different from an adult perspective, but the clues can be found if we take the time, commit to the journey, and remain faithful to the quest.

It can be a solitary journey, full of mystery, frustration, joy, sorrow, intrigue, and suspense. The curse of cultural displeasure lies over the whole endeavor. Others will surely seek to dissuade us and even attempt to steal some of the reward. They will not understand the nature of the quest.

Ignore them as best you can. The quest, which is the real treasure, is yours alone. It's never too late.

Let's go treasure hunting!

Further Reading

Alterman, Bruce. *Fear in Phoenicia: The Deadly Hunt for Dutch Schultz's Treasure*. Bloomington, IN: iUniverse, 2014.

Ashton, John, and Tom Whyte. *The Quest for Paradise: Visions of Heaven and Eternity in the World's Myths and Religions*. New York: Harper Collins, 2001.

Barbarisi, Daniel. *Chasing the Thrill: Obsession, Death, and Glory in America's Most Extraordinary Treasure Hunt*. New York: Penguin Random House, 2022.

Bitter, Rand K. *Minty and His Cavalry: A History of the Saber Brigade and its Commander*. Self-published, 2006.

Bradley, Michael. *Holy Grail Across the Atlantic*. Toronto, ON: Dundurn Press, 1988.

Bradley, Michael. *Secret Societies Handbook*. London, UK: Cassel Illustrated, 2004.

Bradley, Michael. *The Secrets of the Freemasons*. New York: Union Square & Company, 2008.

Campbell, Joseph. *Transformations of Myth through Time*. New York: Harper & Row, 1990.

Colbert, Thomas J., and Tom Szollosi. *The Last Master Outlaw: The Award-Winning Conclusion of the D. B. Cooper Mystery*. Jacaranda Roots Publishing, 2021.

Conway, John. *Dutch Schultz and His Lost Catskills' Treasure*. Fleischmanns, NY: Purple Mountain Press, 2000.

Cordingly, David. *Under the Black Flag: The Romance and the Reality of Life Among the Pirates*. New York: Random House, 2013.

Defoe, Daniel. *A General History of the Pyrates: From Their First Rise and Settlement in the Island of Providence to the Present Time*. London, UK: Ch. Rivington, J. Lacy, and J. Stone, 1724.

Dobie, J. Frank. *Coronado's Children: Tales of Lost Mines and Buried Treasures of the Southwest*. Austin, TX: University of Texas Press, 1978.

Felser, Joseph M. *The Way Back to Paradise: Restoring the Balance Between Magic and Reason*. Charlottesville, VA: Hampton Roads Publishing Co., 2005.

Fenn, Forrest. *The Thrill of the Chase*. Santa Fe, NM: One Horse Land & Cattle Ltd. Co., 2010.

Freeman, Gordon R. *Hidden Stonehenge*. London, UK: Watkins Publishing, 2012.

Getler, Warren, and Bob Brewer. *Shadow of the Sentinel: One Man's Quest to Find the Hidden Treasure of the Confederacy.* New York: Simon & Schuster, 2003.

Godwin, Parke. *The Last Rainbow.* New York: Avon Books, 1982.

Goudsward, David. *The Westford Knight and Henry Sinclair: Evidence of a 14th Century Scottish Voyage to North America.* Jefferson, NC: McFarland Publishers, 2010.

Gray, Geoffrey. *Skyjack: The Hunt for D. B. Cooper.* New York: Crown Publishers, 2011.

Keehn, David C. *Knights of the Golden Circle: Secret Empire, Southern Secession, Civil War (Conflicting Worlds: New Dimensions of the American Civil War).* Baton Rouge, LA: Louisianna University State Press, 2013.

Kindar, Gary. *Ship of Gold in the Deep Blue Sea.* New York: Grove Press, 1998.

Lewis, David. *The San Saba Treasure: Legends of Silver Creek.* Denton, TX: University of North Texas Press, 2019.

Martin, Sean. *The Knights Templar: The History and Myths of the Legendary Military Order.* London, UK: Thunder's Mouth Press, 2004.

Oliphant, Ashley, and Beth Yarbrough. *Jean Laffite Revealed: Unraveling One of America's Longest-Running Mysteries.* Lafayette, LA: University of Louisiana at Lafayette, 2021.

Orozco, Cecilio. *The Book of the Sun.* Fresno, CA: California State University Press, 1992.

Stiles, T. J. *Jesse James: Last Rebel of the Civil War.* New York: Vintage Books, 2002.

Turpen, Roger Edwin. *DARK SILVER: Legend of the Lost Southern Indiana Silver Mine* (documentary film). Turpen Pictures, 2017.

Turpen, Roger Edwin. *The Legend of the Ohio River Indian Cave* (documentary film), Turpen Pictures, 2023.

Wagner, Kip. *Pieces of Eight: Recovering the Riches of a Lost Spanish Treasure Fleet.* New York: Dutton, 1966.

Viemeister, Peter. *The Beale Treasure: New History of a Mystery.* Landham, MD: Hamilton Books: 1997.

Ward, James B., with Thomas J Beale (contributor). *The Beale Papers: Containing Authentic Statements Regarding the Treasure Buried 1819 and 1821, Bufords, in Bedford County, Virginia, Which Has Never Been Recovered.* Lynchburg, VA: Self-published, 2019.

Wells, Don and Diane. *Deciphering the Signs: Sacred Indian Trees and Places.* Jasper, GA: Mountain Stewards, 2021.

Wells, Lamar, Don, and Diane; Dr. John Nardo; and Robert Wells. *Mystery of the Trees: Native American Makers of a Cultur-*

al Way of Life That Soon May Be Gone. Jasper, GA: Mountain Stewards, 2011.

Willis, Jim. *The Religion Book: Places, Prophets, Saints and Seers.* Detroit, MI: Visible Ink Press, 2004.

Wolter, Scott F. Cryptic Code: *The Templars in America and the Origins of the Hooked X.* St. Cloud. MN: North Star Press, September 17, 2019.

Index

Note: (ill.) indicates photos and illustrations.

I

J